CALLED FROM ISLAM TO CHRIST

Called From Islam To Christ

Why Muslims become Christians

DR JEAN-MARIE GAUDEUL

MONARCH
B O O K S

First published by Monarch Books 1999

ISBN 1 85424 427 2

Editorial Office: Monarch Books,
Broadway House, The Broadway, Crowborough,
East Sussex TN6 1HQ

British Library Cataloguing Data
A catalogue record for this book is available
from the British Library.

Cover photo by Paul Yates

Designed and produced for the publisher by
Bookprint Creative Services
P.O. Box 827, BN21 3YJ, England.
Printed in Great Britain.

CONTENTS

INTRODUCTION

The title of this book indicates that Muslims who convert to Christianity have been called to do so by God. Muslim readers will not see it in this light. Those whom Christians call 'converts' they will call 'apostates'. The same applies to those who move in the opposite direction. Muslims welcome Christian converts to Islam, regarding them as people who have discovered the true path; Christians on the other hand will often consider such persons as renegades and traitors.

To say that someone has been called by God to change religion might seem to imply that God is found only on one side of the religious divide; that only Christianity, or only Islam, is the true religion, and that the other is in error.

God transcends our thought

The Bible declares: 'God is greater than our hearts, and he knows everything' (1 John 3:20). We should never lose sight of this when we venture to speak of God. Our ideas of the way in which he should govern the world may not correspond at all to the way in which he actually governs it. We have no right to tell God his business.

In particular, neither Christians nor Muslims should reduce God to their thoughts about him. He is beyond, transcendent.

Does God seek the triumph of Islam? Or the triumph of Christianity? The answer to both these questions must be a resounding 'no'.

God is not at the service of our parties and interests; his glory does not consist in the triumph of one community over another. Such a triumph would not be of God, but only of our collective human pride, of our military power, of our techniques of ideological persuasion.

God calls

Both Christians and Muslims believe that God calls every human being to know the truth, and to submit to that truth in adoration and obedience. Muslims say that if we lived in a perfect world, and if people correctly apprehended the call of God, then every human being would realise that he or she was called to join Islam. Christians believe, in a similar way, that if the world was perfect, and if all people were properly attuned to the call of God, then all would know that they were called to embrace Christianity.

The fact is, however, that we do not live in a perfect world, nor are we capable of hearing with total accuracy what God is saying. Even if our Scriptures and traditions were wholly without error, there is still the question of the capacity of the hearer: for whether we are Christians or Muslims, we all inevitably interpret what we hear.

This may be due to the hardness of our hearts. It may simply be due to the fact that we live in different worlds and cultures, and these worlds condition how we hear God's word. It is not possible for any individual totally to grasp God's truth.

The reality of God goes far beyond any human culture. It is literally too much for us. Some people understand one aspect of God's truth, others another. Quite often our cultures simply lack the words to express some particular teaching about God and these words will have to be coined first before we are able to express that teaching.

Each human being has a unique call

As God is unique, so is his call, and so is his teaching. On that point, at least, Muslims and Christians are in agreement.

We all receive God's call in brains and hearts that work differently from those of others. As the same liquid takes a different form when it is poured into a glass or into a bottle, so the call of God is heard by the individual according to his or her own capacity for understanding, according to the particular mixture of subtlety and clumsiness marking his language, his culture and his time . . . and according to the unique qualities of his or her own life-story.

The God of all is also the God of each individual being, whether a blade of grass or a human person. And because he is God, he is careful to guide and call each one in the way best suited for them.

The problem of conscience

A Muslim may be convinced that Islam is the only true revelation. He prays God 'to guide him along the right path',[1] and the more he prays, the more he is confirmed in his faith. No one can doubt that God's call is mediated to the Muslim through Islam, through all the truth conveyed by this religion; and that can only be cause for rejoicing.

In the same way, the Christian believes that Jesus the Christ is the only Saviour of all people. He prays to Christ and feels that he is loved and forgiven by him, led by him to the Father. This is the Christian's call, this is how God's word reaches him.

However, some people, both Christians and Muslims, do not experience such confirmation in their faith. Why is this so?

Sometimes an individual has been so upset by certain elements in his original religion that he experiences only sadness and rejection there.

Others may have so misunderstood their religion's teaching that they believe it really distorts the truth of God. Their consciences compel them to reject such teaching.

It can often happen that a person's temperament is not in tune with the main emphasis of the religion in which she has been brought up. Every religion has its strong and its weak points. There are certain truths which it regards as fundamental and others which it treats as secondary. The emphasis, moreover, may vary according to different times and places.

Thus classical Islam, like medieval Christianity to a considerable extent, emphasises the Law, whereas modern Islam tends to stress social reform. The earliest Christianity invited people to open their hearts to the freedom of the Spirit.

One can understand that a personality in love with freedom cannot endure a religion based on law, and that a legal-minded person has great difficulty with a religion of freedom.

So it comes about that some believers experience a religious uneasiness which they often cannot explain. The more they search and the more they pray, the more they feel blocked in their faith. If, while they are in this state, they encounter another religion, they may feel that God is present there in a more genuine and striking manner than in their religion of origin. They may experience a mysterious correspondence between the central teachings of the new religion and their own deepest yearnings. When they pray for guidance, they really feel that they are being led to the truth by some power deep within themselves. They hear God's call and they respond.

This does not mean that their first religion was nothing but lies. Nor does it prove that their new religion is the only true one. It does however mean that there has been a moment when the new religion has allowed them to hear God's call in a way that they have never heard it before.

We are talking here about consciences, not principles. At the level of principle, neither Islam nor Christianity admits the possibility of a legitimate reason for what both call 'apostasy'. But God reaches beyond principles to the depths of the human heart, and it is there that the individual hears and interprets God's call as nobody else does.

An attempt at a conclusion

As a result, this book is not trying to prove the truth of Christianity. It only seeks to show how a real 'call' has led some Muslims to leave Islam and embrace Christianity.

Evidently there are people who change religion, and join either Islam or Christianity, for reasons which have nothing to do with an interior call of any kind.

Muhammad himself recognised this phenomenon at the very beginning of Islam and warned these 'hypocrites', as he called them, that they could not deceive God. One tradition records him as saying: 'Actions are only worth the intentions behind them. Anyone who has accompanied the Prophet in his emigration for the sake of God and his Messenger will be recognised as having done so for God and his Messenger. But the action of one who follows the Prophet for some worldly advantage, or for the sake of a woman, has only the value of the objective he has in view.'

Christians or Muslims who condone so superficial a way of recruiting members, dishonour their religion and reduce it to the level of a corrupt and worldly association; they are no longer seeking the glory of God but are intent on procuring its own petty growth.

The following pages will show us that many human beings have changed their religion, not out of any worldly motive but because they have been conscious of an imperious call to do so. Can we say that God is calling them, directly and explicitly?

Is it perhaps the case that the creator God has implanted in our human nature (*al-fitrah*) a deep need to search for him, even blindly at times? But can God keep aloof from this quest for him? We hope that answers to these questions will emerge from the stories recounted in this book.

In recent years, Islam has attracted scores of Westerners, such as the American T.B. Irwing, and the Austrian L. Weiss. A recent article in *The Times* talked of as many as ten thousand English women converts, and there have, over the century, been many notable Englishmen such as the explorer Richard Burton, the translator Marmaduke Pickthall, Martin Lings the writer and scholar, and former pop singer Cat Stevens. Some have been drawn to Islam by a new sense of God's majesty as presented by Muslim theology, while others have found in the Muslim community a sense of fellowship, and of a striving for social justice not apparent in the contemporary Western world.

There have been some highly competent recent accounts of conversions from Christianity to Islam.[2] It was right to show as well the existence of an equally dramatic and remarkable traffic in the opposite direction, that is, from Islam to Christianity. This will not be lacking in valuable information about the way human beings thirst for their God.

Whatever our convictions, the movement of conversion has to be respected. It must not be exploited for purposes of propaganda. Nor may it be distorted and degraded in the interests of counter-propaganda. Our task is to try and let go of our prejudices, one way or the other, and let the facts speak for themselves. In this field, 'only the spirit of man knows what is in man' (1 Corinthians 2:10). Let us listen to the witnesses then and hear what they tell us of their search and their discovery.

Notes

1 The Koran, chapter 1.
2 See, for instance, M. Asad, *The Road to Mecca* (M. Reinhardt: London, 1954), *Islam, Our Choice* (Mecca Muslim World League, 1961). L. Hixon, *Coming Home* (Doubleday: New York, 1978), L. Rocher and F. Cherqaoui, *D'une foi l'autre—Les conversions à l'islam en Occident* (Seuil: Paris, 1986), Cat Stevens, *Islam, My Religion* (Ta-Ha Publishers, London, 1981).

CHAPTER 1

YES, CONVERSION IS POSSIBLE

Pray for MM, Father C said to me.
I cannot. Who would I be deceiving? God? It would be a mockery, a
 prayer of the lips with anger in the heart.
Pray for their conversion.
That must be a joke. Conversion of such people is impossible.
For God, all things are possible.
Not that.
'To deny it is almost a blasphemy,' said the priest.
I shook my head obstinately. I could not pray for MM, and even if I did
 it would be a waste of time. There are people who can never change.
'I did not think that you could be so harsh,' said the priest, in a shocked
 tone.

Banine, *J'ai choisi l'opium* (Stock: Paris, 1959), p.216

You must be joking!

This was many people's reaction when they heard the subject of
this book for the first time. The idea that Muslims can become
Christians contradicts everything that the Western media present
to us about contemporary Islam. And the media's message is not
contradicted by the spokespeople of either Islam or Christianity.

The average Christian today takes it for granted that
Muslims do not become Christians. On the contrary, is not our
age witnessing rather the inexorable march of Islam? This

presentation of the situation is false. It takes account only of certain facts and ignores others. In fact there are conversions in both directions.

Barriers are crumbling

People are moving about today more than they have ever done. And they bring with them their ideas. Modern communications mean that ideas are being exchanged at every level. Even the most closed society cannot prevent its members from listening to foreign radio stations. No curtains, whether of iron or bamboo, can totally prevent the movement of people; much less can they halt the movement of ideas.

The twentieth century has been the century of mass movements of people. There were the displaced persons in Europe after 1945. Since then vast numbers of immigrants from the South have come to live in the North. Volunteers and businessmen from the North are working in the South. There are tourists and holidaymakers by the million. Hundreds of thousands of people from the Philippines and India are working in Saudi Arabia, millions of Turks and North Africans have settled in Europe.[1] The world is moving towards an ever-increasing mobility.

This mobility began with the great discoveries of the fifteenth century and increased with colonisation. It now touches human life at every level. Governments have to take it into account, and families may find their children bringing the most unlikely guests into the home. Perhaps more important still, many of our received ideas are being challenged by foreign cultures and ideologies. It cannot be a surprise that religion too is affected and is experiencing the phenomenon of interconversion.

The reality of interconversion

The name may be new, but the thing itself is not. For years we have been talking about de-christianisation and secularisation—that is, about Christians who change faith. Now we are hearing of 'the sects' and of 'a return to religion', of militants disenchanted with their ideology. Those who change their convictions are variously labelled as dissidents, reformers, terrorists, penitents. All these terms express the phenomenon of interconversion. Every day, people move in opposite directions. In reality, the opposition may be only apparent. Those possessed by a thirst for truth and justice may be in conflict with each other at one level and yet be unaware that they are moving towards the same goal at a deeper level.

Christianity and Islam

We often hear today of 'the new vitality of Islam', of 'militant Islam', of 'Islamic terrorism'. Newspapers and television programmes publish declarations from groups or individuals claiming to speak for Islam, condemning the corrupt and decadent West, threatening reprisals, taking hostages, proclaiming a world Islamic revolution.

A few years ago, a group of Islamists[2] spoke of a plan to restore the cathedral of Cordoba as the mosque which it had been.[3] Islamic centres are springing up in the Western world and make no secret of their missionary ambitions. Islamic publications regularly publish lists of Christians who have become Muslims. The Great Mosque of Paris claimed two hundred thousand converts, increased to three hundred thousand by the media.[4] Famous people who become Muslims are celebrated as 'scalps' in faraway Muslim lands.

Several recent books have described the evolution of Westerners converting to Islam.[5] Indeed, these people often come to public conferences and debates to discuss Islam, faith, and the modern world. There is certainly some kind of movement towards Islam, even if observers are still in disagreement about its extent.

What is much less well publicised is the movement from Islam to Christianity.[6] The statistics are uncertain, but the curious fact is that while Christians try to minimise the number of their converts from Islam, Muslims, especially traditionalists, exaggerate them and raise regular cries of alarm at the growing influence of

Christianity among their co-religionists in Europe and throughout the world.[7]

Fifty years ago Christian missionaries were using the same kind of language about the spread of Islam in Africa and elsewhere. It is true that Islam's fastest expansion in sub-Saharan Africa took place during that period when it was able to spread thanks especially to the communications facilities established by the colonial governments.

While precise figures are unobtainable, it seems certain that the number of converts from Islam to Christianity remains very small and certainly does not justify the Muslim outcry. Perhaps religious leaders everywhere, Christian and Muslim alike, are tempted to sound the alarm when there seems to be even a hypothetical threat to their flock.

How big is the move towards Christian conversion?

Most of the statistics about religious conversions are mere guess-work.[8] What is abundantly clear is that there are no tidal waves of conversion in either direction, and that cries either of alarm or triumph are quite out of place.

It is true that there have been some mass movements. It seems certain, from both Christian and Muslim sources,[9] that between 1965 and 1970, after the massacres of communists and their followers,[10] some two or three million Muslims in Indonesia became Christians. In general, however, the number of converts remains modest. In African countries there are a few thousand each year, and a number of Christian clergy, including some bishops, come from Muslim families. In Arab countries there are perhaps a few hundred clandestine converts each year, but it is impossible to know how many.

In France too there are Muslims who become Christians. No information can be obtained from the census, since French law forbids the mention of religious affiliation on official government forms. The Church keeps baptismal registers, but no serious count has ever been made of Muslims who have been baptised in French parishes. Perhaps this is just as well, for statistics can feed an unhealthy and unhelpful triumphalism. It might be tentatively suggested that perhaps two or three hundred Muslims ask for baptism in France every year.

We are not then dealing with a mass movement, but with a few individuals whose personal pilgrimage cannot amount to either a triumph for Christianity or a defeat for Islam. Neither conversions from Christianity nor conversion from Islam should be interpreted as condemnation of the religion of the milieu of origin. On the contrary. Such conversions are signs that this particular milieu has offered to the individual the type of education which promotes human freedom.

Interconversion, a sign of society's health

It is time that we rid ourselves of a number of dangerous clichés. All of us, whether Christians or Muslims, must stop seeing 'the other' as a dangerous rival, or a threat to the nation's identity. Such an attitude can only generate a sense of rejection on the part of individuals and lead to widespread social tension. Some French people resent the presence of Muslims on 'their' soil, afraid that Islam is about to spread like a bush fire. Muslim countries react in the same way to the presence of Christians in their midst: they consider them a danger to their identity which, they say, must remain Arab and Islamic.

There is a popular theory that a society's health depends on the unanimous acceptance of the same values by all its members and, in particular, on a common religious faith. History provides many examples of how societies, both Christian and Muslim, in obedience to this theory, have sought to preserve their homogeneity by every means, including force.[11] The temptation of enforcing unanimity has by no means disappeared in the modern world.

The use of social constraint to preserve uniformity of belief can only be interpreted as a lack of faith, for it implies that the faith itself is not strong enough to satisfy the religious aspirations of its faithful, hence dechristianisation or deislamisation as the case may be. The Tunisian Mohammed Talbi has this to say on the subject:

> The best remedy (against unbelief) is the creation of a tolerant, pluralist and well-informed society, where believers and non-believers can live side-by-side in openness and sincerity, without mutual suspicion, without pretence, in genuine mutual respect. The right to be different, and in particular the right to non-belief, must be affirmed and scrupulously respected, because such a right belongs both to 'natural law' and to the mystery of God, as the Koran clearly states: 'If such had been the Lord's will, everyone on earth without exception would believe in Him' (10:99; cf. 6:149, and 26:9). Hypocrisy, whether by choice or under pressure from outside, is not the homage which vice pays to virtue, but rather the grub which poisons and ruins the fruit. In the interests of authentic Islam itself, the Islam of faith, it is essential to take heed of the legitimate fears of non-believers.[12]

If the symptoms of unbelief are hidden by social constraints or, even worse, by fear of the police, the faith of the whole community is weakened and reduced to simple group conformity. People are then Muslims not because they believe but because they have been born in a certain place. They carry on the pretence of belief, even if they have no personal faith.

Neither early Islam nor early Christianity encouraged the abdication of personal liberty in favour of a totalitarian system which imprisons people within a culture, a nationality or a religion not of their own choosing. On the contrary, both Muhammad and Jesus regarded religious faith as a personal choice, a genuine *metanoia* issuing from the heart and not simply dictated by one's place of origin.[13]

Seen from that angle, the presence of 'dissidents' who choose a religious alternative is a sign of a healthy society, for it shows that those who remain in their original religious community do so by choice and not because of any external constraint. The essential point is that all conversions, in either direction, should take place within the perspective of a personal search for truth.

Popular fallacies

Some theories, which have been commonly accepted for centuries, need to be exploded if we are to understand the modern phenomenon of interconversion. I mention some of them:

1. The expansion of Islam

When we look back on historical events, we are tempted to form them into a consistent pattern, to see them perhaps as stages in some kind of inevitable 'macro-process'. We give them a coherence which was conspicuously lacking when they were taking place. So it is often believed that Islam spread like lightning from the time of its foundation, overwhelming the Christian churches of the Middle East and North Africa in the space of a few years.

It is true that Muslim armies conquered vast areas and had reached Spain within a century of the appearance of the Islamic faith in Arabia. But conquest is one thing, religious conversion quite another. For a very long time Muslims remained a minority in the countries which they had conquered. It has been estimated[14] that it took two or three centuries before Islam won over half of the populations in the conquered countries, about the same time in fact that it took Christianity to win over Europe.

The history of Islam in sub-Saharan Africa is a similar story of very slow progress. Islam first appeared there between the ninth and the eleventh centuries. The beginnings were difficult, but eventually the new faith took root and reached its climax in the fourteenth and fifteenth centuries. There was then a decline and the traditional religions revived. It needed a new period of religious revival at the end of the eighteenth century, followed by a series of 'holy wars' in the nineteenth, to give Islam in West Africa the dynamism it needed to take advantage of the possibilities of expansion offered by European colonisation. The combination of peace and the new communications enabled Islam to expand rapidly in Africa in the 1920s and 1930s, in very much the same way as the facilities provided by the Roman Empire enabled Christianity to spread in its early centuries.[15]

There has been talk of 'galloping Islam' in Africa. In fact in most countries the situation has been stable since the 1930s. But the media still present a picture of the menace of an Islam remorselessly on the march.

We should not be deceived by statistics.

A journalist[16] stated that in fifty years Islam in black Africa had increased by 235%. Thus stated, it looks phenomenal, but a simple calculation shows that in fact it amounts to no more than an annual increase of 2.44%. Between 1939 and 1983, the annual rate of population increase in black Africa was estimated to be 2.27%; in 1985 it was thought to be 3%. In other words, what was presented as an alarming increase in the number of Muslims turns out to correspond almost exactly to the increase in population.

There is, no doubt, demographic increase in the number of Muslims in Africa, and this, combined with petro-dollars, has led to an increase in the number of mosques. There has probably been some revival of popular faith and there has certainly been an increase in fundamentalist activity.[17] But it would be a mistake to see either of these things as proof of successful propaganda or of an absolute increase in the number of adherents.

In the same countries, and over the same period, the missionary vitality of Christianity has not been weaker than that of Islam.[18] Placed in this context, the conversion cases reported here are far from exceptional.

2. Muslims 'never convert'

Even more widely credited is the myth that Muslims never become Christians. We shall see in the succeeding pages that such a belief is simply untrue. Conversions are fairly common, so common in fact, especially in certain countries, that they cannot be regarded as 'abnormal'.

Muslim society is organised on the basis of a unity between the political and the religious life. Furthermore, traditionally non-Muslims in the population were separated from the rest and even governed by different statutes. During the centuries of the Ottoman Empire in particular, governments recognised different 'nations' within the same boundaries: Jewish, Orthodox, Armenian, Melkite, Nestorian. Each of these communities had its leader who was accountable to the Muslim political authority, while the religious (or 'canon') laws of each had also the status of civil laws.

Continual wars between so-called Christian and Muslim states, interrupted by occasional truces and treaties, hardened attitudes on both sides and shut the different communities off from each other.

In this situation, religious conversion implied also political and social conversion. A Muslim lived in a Muslim country and belonged to the Muslim community. To become a Christian amounted to a kind of social suicide, involving a total rupture with one's family and culture. As for Christians living in Christian countries, for them to become Muslims was regarded as an act of treachery. The only people who could safely change religion were emigrants or people prepared to emigrate: prisoners, slaves, travellers, traders, refugees of one kind or another.

In these circumstances one can understand that conversion between Islam and Christianity was very rare. Nevertheless, conversions there have always been, in both directions. The Ottoman Empire benefited greatly from Christian 'renegades' who brought with them the latest results of Western scientific research and received in return the possibility of prosperous careers in a variety of professions. Christian countries in turn welcomed converts from Islam. They included doctors, like Constantine the African (1015-1087), princes like the Jesuit Balthazar Loyola (died in 1667), and comparatively large numbers of prisoners, both actual and freed, artisans, traders, peasants.[19]

Sometimes political change allowed conversions to take place without any forced emigration in their wake. Crusader states in Palestine, border territories changing hands during the reconquista in Spain, and modern colonial systems have all made conversion easier by reducing the risk of reprisals. One can easily understand why conversions have been more numerous in some periods than in others.

3. Fear of Proselytism

Some Christians are disturbed by conversions from Islam, fearing that they may be accused of 'proselytism'. For centuries Christians and Muslims have regarded each other as rivals and, very often, as enemies. Relations between them have been determined, not by friendship, but by force. Two ideological blocks have been formed, each constantly comparing itself with the other and seeking to gain the upper hand in nearly every field: philosophy, military might, numbers, culture, virtue. All actions are judged in the light of this mutual competition: Is the other side arming itself at our expense? Or weakening us by winning converts?

One can understand that in this poisoned atmosphere many Christian thinkers, especially in missionary circles, have felt it important to show Muslims that their friendship is completely disinterested and that they have no thought of 'winning converts'. They seek simply to be present in Muslim communities and to offer humble service for its own sake.

There have been Christian witnesses of this kind in Muslim lands for centuries—Francis of Assisi and Sister Emmanuel of Cairo, the Little Brothers and Sisters of Jesus, and the Sisters of Mother Teresa. Countless Christians, both today and in the past, have given their lives for the ideal of disinterested Christian service, even if they have often been wrongly regarded by their Muslim hosts as agents of Christian propaganda.

No doubt the Church will continue to spend—apparently to waste—the lives of these men and women called by Christ to bear witness to the gratuitous love which God has for all human beings, whatever their race, language or culture. Perhaps only through such lives can the word 'gratuitous' here become meaningful.

It can seem to some of these dedicated Christians that the enormous sacrifices they have made are being compromised by the communal agitation which is always the result when a Muslim becomes a Christian. They fear that people will say that their disinterested love was no more than a façade and that they too are religious imperialists at heart.

On these grounds, there are those who would positively discourage any Muslim from embracing Christianity, advising him to seek God in his own religion.[20] The following story, which we cannot independently confirm, was given to the author as authentic:

Some years ago in Paris a university-educated Muslim was converted to Christianity and received baptism. His decision was not lightly taken. He had made deep friendships with a number of Christians, including priests, over a period of ten years before he finally asked for baptism. The sacrament was administered privately. Some time later the new convert received a visit from a priest-friend of his and informed him of the step he had taken. All that the priest could find to reply was, 'You disappoint me.' This was the end of their friendship.

Surely no reasons of pastoral expediency can justify such condemnation of a conversion undertaken in good faith by any human being. We have no right to suspect the authenticity of conversion or to cast doubt on the convert's motives.

The claim to be witnesses to a totally disinterested love must involve refusing to be deterred by a fear that our actions will be wrongly interpreted. The fear of being accused of proselytism conceals in fact a desire for 'results' which is itself only a subtle form of proselytism and betrays a hidden ambition to gain influence.

We should be clear about the meaning of the term 'proselytism'. It suggests a desire to recruit adherents without enquiry into the presence or absence of a truly personal vocation.[21] The other extreme is a kind of religious apartheid which refuses to welcome any convert, without considering what may be his or her personal religious vocation. It makes it a rule that people have no right to leave their religion of origin.

The proper attitude must be to abandon all preconceptions and help each individual to discover what God is asking him or her to do at this moment, whether it be to remain a Muslim or to become a Christian. It is in view of making this discovery easier that we present in this book the stories of believing Muslims who, apparently, have been called by God to become Christians.

The God of surprises

We should be prepared to be surprised by the paths taken by these converts. Their route cannot be foreseen, and the stories include failures as well as successes. Sometimes the road leads back to the starting-point. Such cases are very painful, both for the person concerned and for the religious community which welcomed him or her. But we should not conclude that this means that conversion is impossible. We are talking about a pilgrimage, a spiritual journey. To accompany a person on such a journey is to take a risk, for there can be no guarantee that, ultimately, the way will be found with our help or will lead to us. If God is in control, we may, at times, get out of our depth!

We may be surprised for another reason. Muslims who become Christians come from a different religious and cultural milieu, and they may ask questions which we find strange and disconcerting. Christian thinkers in the West have responded to the secularist challenge by developing new ways of speaking about God. Instead of the 'tyrant God' of certain schools of medieval theology, modern Christians may speak of the 'humility of God', 'the poverty of God', 'the suffering God'. There has even been a school which spoke of 'the death of God'.[22]

All this falls very strangely on the ears of men and women who come out of a culture which insists above all that 'God is', and that he is all-powerful, rich and sovereign.[23] They have no problem with the existence or transcendence of God, and may find our modern theology so strange as to be superfluous and even inappropriate. Unlike typical modern Europeans, converts from Islam take the existence of God for granted. Their problems lie elsewhere, and it is up to us to discover their real questions.

Sources

We have preferred to use written testimonies and public accounts rather than to record private interviews. This is partly to protect the identity of persons who could be endangered by indiscreet exposure. The danger is real.

One morning in the spring of 1975, in a park in Minneapolis, in the United States, a young member of an Indian family of traders from Uganda was set upon by three men who beat him savagely and then put a knife to his throat, ordering him to pronounce the Muslim profession of faith. He was only saved by the arrival of children from a nearby school. The young man was a recent convert to Christianity whose story had just been published in a mass-circulation review. It had excited the attention of a group of militant Islamists from an Arab country.[24]

Many Muslims will not tolerate a change of religion by a member of their family, even if the social and family links are maintained. Assassination attempts are not uncommon. Moreover, accounts of religious experience call for a certain distance if they are to be properly assessed, and this is difficult to achieve in a simple recording of live interviews.

Variety

We have not attempted a methodical collection but have simply taken what lay to hand. Some accounts were too summary to allow any analysis of the path followed by the convert, but a hundred or so were sufficiently detailed to make possible a deeper understanding.

The converts in these pages are of both sexes and all ages, although the majority are between eighteen and thirty-five.

They also come from everywhere. The more detailed accounts come from the following countries:

Africa

Algeria	9	Morocco	3	Sierra Leone	1
Ivory Coast	1	Niger	18	Sudan	70
Egypt	8	Nigeria	2	Tunisia	1
Gambia	1	Uganda	1	Zanzibar	3

Middle East

Iran	21	Lebanon	1	Syria	1
Turkey	1				

Indian Sub-continent

India	9	Pakistan	12

South-east Asia

Indonesia	1	Philippines	1

Others

France   9   Mauritius   1

They join all possible denominations. As we shall see, they do not tend to join one Christian church rather than another: they may become either Catholics or Protestants. Some do not join any established Christian church at all, but prefer to live out their faith in small Christian communities of their own.

We should avoid placing them into categories. Each case is unique. It is possible however to discern certain common elements which enable us to group these spiritual odysseys into five or six 'typical' families. We have attempted to regroup them by spiritual kinship and have devoted one chapter, or sometimes two, to each 'spiritual way'.

All these converts suffer from exclusion. In nearly every case they have been rejected by their community and family of origin, and sometimes they also feel rejected by Christians. What kind of welcome can they expect among us? Our book ends at this point, but it is precisely this question which Christians need to put to themselves: what kind of reception do we give to the Muslim converts who come to us?

Notes

1 It has been calculated that foreigners form 8% of the population of France, 7.5% of that of Germany, 14% of Switzerland, 25% of Saudi Arabia, 60% of Kuwait, 1.5% of Algeria, 0.5% of Morocco.

2 It is well to be precise about terminology. Here the word 'Muslim' is used for people who live out their faith in God in the community of Islam; 'Islamic' is used to describe the religion of Islam; and 'Islamist' means the militant fundamentalist ideology which the media often, and wrongly, identify with religious Islam.

3 *Le Monde*, 18 May 1980. The mosque of Cordoba was turned into a church after the Christian 'reconquest' of the city in 1236. In the same way, the church of St John the Baptist in Damascus was destroyed in 705 to make way for the Great Mosque; similarly St Sophia's, Constantinople, was turned into a mosque after its capture by the Ottoman Turks in 1453.

4 The Catholic press (*La Croix*, 20 November 1984, p.13) then suggested a more reasonable estimate of thirty thousand. In fact, a recent study of the conversion registers at the Paris mosque showed only 1,628 conversions between 1964 and 1989 (Mohamed Telhine, 'Les convertis de la Grande Mosquée de Paris', *Hérodote*, Nos. 60–61, 1°–2° Trim. 1991, pp.209–234). Of course, this mosque is not the only place where converts can join Islam. For a rough estimate of this movement in France, one should probably multiply that number by three or four and estimate at six to seven thousands the real number of French converts to Islam.

5 Reference has already been made to the excellent book by L. Rocher and F. Cherqaoui: *D'une foi l'autre* (Seuil: Paris, 1986).

6 That there is such a movement is clear from, for example, P. Assouline, *Les Nouveaux Convertis* (Albin Michel: Paris, 1982), which examines examples of movements between the three religions of Judaism, Christianity and Islam.

7 One could consult the publications of the *Muslim World League*, and magazines such as *Impact International* (London).

8 The recent *L'Etat des religions dans le monde* (M. Clévenot, ed., La Découverte-Le Cerf: Paris, 1987), with the World Christian Encyclopaedia, perhaps come as near to the reality as it is possible to get.

9 From Muslim sources, one can quote: Muhammad Rasjidi, 'The role of Christian Missions, the Indonesian experience', *International Review of Mission*, 65, 1976, No. 260, pp.427–438, see p.435 where he speaks of these converts but labels them as converted 'communists'. From Christian sources, read: A.T. Willis, Jr, *Indonesian Revival, why two million came to Christ* (William Carey Library: Pasadena, Ca., 1977).

10 The number of victims, according to various estimates, varies between 300,000 and 500,000. Cf. A.T. Willis, *op.cit.*, p.25, n.1.

11 Christianity had its inquisition, Islam its police, its persecutions of 'dissidents' and its 'martyrs of conscience'. One need only remember the legal status of the 'renegade' or the 'heretic' in Islam. See B. Lewis, 'Some observations on the significance of heresy in the history of Islam', *Studia Islamica*, 1953, pp.43–63; M. Talbi, 'Religious Liberty: A Muslim Perspective', *Islamochristiana*, 11, 1985, pp.99–113.

12 Mohammed Talbi, 'Islam and the West: Beyond confrontations, ambiguities and complexes', *Encounter*, No.108, October 1984 (available at PISAI, Viale Trastevere 89, 00153 Rome).

13 Christ taught that 'Anyone who loves his father or mother more than me is not worthy of me' (Matthew 10:37–42). Similar passages occur in the Koran: 'Take not your fathers and your brothers for friends if they prefer disbelief to faith' (Koran 9:23–24).

14 Cf. R.W. Bulliet, *Conversion to Islam in the Medieval Period* (Harvard University Press, Cambridge, Mass., 1979). In North Africa this evolution took place more rapidly as shown in J. Cuoq, *L'Eglise d'Afrique du Nord du 2° au 12° siècle* (Centurion: Paris, 1984).

15 On this, consult J. Cuoq, *Histoire de l'Islamisation de l'Afrique de l'Ouest* (Geuthner: Paris, 1984), or P.B. Clarke, *West Africa and Islam* (E. Arnold: London, 1982), or J.S. Trimingham, *The Influence of Islam upon Africa* (Longmans: London; Lib. Libanaise: Beirut, 1968).

16 A. Woodrow, 'Dernière étape: le Maroc—Le dialogue avec l'Islam', *Le Monde*, 18–19 August 1985.

17 For a general survey of the situation in recent times, read R. Otayek, *Le Radicalisme Islamique au sud du Sahara—Da`wa, arabisation et critique de l'Occident* (MSHA: Karthala, Talence: Paris, 1993).

18 See, for example, D.B. Barrett, 'AD 2000: 350 million Christians in Africa', *International Review of Mission*, 59, 1970, No.233, pp.39–54; 'Analytical methods of studying religious expansion in Africa', *Journal of Religion in Africa*, 3, 1970, pp.22–44, where the growth rate of Christianity in Africa from 1900 to 1970 is shown to be twice that of the population growth.

19 On Constantine the African, see that name in *Encyclopedia of Islam*. On B.L. Mendez: H. de Castries, 'Trois princes marocains convertis au christianisme', *Mémorial Henri Basset* (Geuthner: Paris, 1928, 2 vols), pp.141–158; J. Henninger, 'Un Marocain converti jésuite au 17° siècle', *Nouv. Rev. de Science Missionnaire,* 1954, p. 207.

20 For an example of this attitude, read *The Tablet*, May 25, 1985, pp.544–545.

21 This is the 'attitude of he who calls on his interlocutor to meet him on his own ground without being concerned about the other's true vocation'. This definition of proselytism was given by the Roman Catholic bishops of North Africa in their pastoral letter of May 1979: 'Christians in the Maghreb—the meaning of our encounters', see *Encounter*, Nos.73–74, March 1981. (*Encounter*, Viale Trastevere, 89, 00153 Rome.)

22 This expression has been used by some to mean that God does not

exist. Others simply meant that a certain way of thinking about God—a human idea of him—had to be abandoned.

23 One could consult the list of the ninety-nine names of God frequently used in Muslim devotions.

24 Hass Hirji-Walji and Jaryl Strong, *Escape from Islam* (Kingsway Publications: Eastbourne, 1981), pp.99–102.

CHAPTER 2

JESUS IS SO ATTRACTIVE

Why should we fear Christian proselytism? I invite you to consider what a Bishop, or any 'evangelising' Catholic, can offer to a believing Muslim. He may ask him to believe in Christ and to respect him. But the Muslim believer already does both of these things, even more than Catholic missionaries. The Koran in fact exalts 'Issa' more than the Gospel does. For the Gospel casts a shadow over Jesus' morality, presenting him not only as a wine-drinker but even as one who multiplied wine at the wedding-feast of Cana.

Salman Ghaffari, Ambassador of the Islamic Republic
of Iran to the Vatican[1]

This statement might sound astonishing to a reader unacquainted with Islamic teaching; but similar comments about Jesus are often heard in Muslim countries.

Jesus in Muslim teaching

Islam knows Jesus, the son of Mary. It calls him Issa. Several passages in the Koran describe the annunciation and the birth of Jesus from a virgin mother. There are also references to the miracles which he performed with the permission of God.

In the Koran Jesus is presented as a simple prophet who would never have allowed Christians to honour himself and his mother as if they were two Gods in place of the one and only God. At the same time the Koran gives him mysterious titles like 'Word of God' and 'Spirit coming from God'. Other passages insist on his 'elevation' to God at the end of his prophetic career, thus apparently casting doubt on the reality of his death on the cross.

These mysterious passages have given rise to Muslim commentaries in every age.[2] Muslim mystics present Jesus as 'the seal of sanctity', describing him as a wandering monk preaching perfect poverty and urging people to search for God.

Theologians, zealous for orthodoxy and anxious to protect the faithful from the influence of Christian neighbours, insist that Jesus was only a prophet and that his mission was restricted to the Jewish people, while Muhammad was sent to the whole world, with the superior message of the Koran.

Muslim controversialists have built up a body of polemical anti-Christian literature, sometimes making fun of Jesus as he is presented by the Gospels, and sometimes giving one-sided explanations of the remarks about him in the Koran. This approach gave rise to the legend that someone else was crucified in Jesus' place: Judas perhaps, or Peter, or Barnabas. All these imaginative fictions are presented as facts aimed at crushing adversaries. There have even been Muslim claims that Jesus' tomb is to be found . . . in Kashmir.

Jesus is still fascinating

The fact remains, however, that many Muslims find Jesus a strangely fascinating figure, and one in four Muslim converts to Christianity speaks of the role which Jesus played in his or her religious development. Jesus has attracted them, fascinated them, spoken to them, even in a very direct way.

The mysterious Jesus of the Koran

At times, where no outside influence has been at work, the Koran texts are the only source presenting Jesus, and that is enough.

The Nigerian Mallam Ibrahim bears witness to this. Throughout the nineteenth century West Africa was ravaged by a series of wars carried out in the name of Islam and intended to stamp out the traditional religions and build authentically Islamic societies. Kano, in what is now Nigeria, was in the centre of one of the new empires established in this way. In the market square of this city, in 1867, a strange person known as the founder of a Muslim sect called 'the Issawas', 'the disciples of Issa' (Jesus), was impaled.

It seems that this Mallam Ibrahim, a religious teacher, had been struck by the personality of Jesus as presented in the Koran. He perceived, in particular, that, according to the Koran itself, Jesus is the only prophet now living with God and the only one whose return will precede the last judgement. From this Mallam concluded that Muhammad was inferior to Jesus, and he was only willing to pronounce the first part of the Muslim profession of faith, 'there is only one God', omitting the second part, 'and Muhammad is his prophet'. For this offence he was condemned as a heretic and executed. In his last words he urged his disciples to flee from the city and wait for the day when God would reveal the true religion.[3]

An old man from Niger, who eventually became a Christian, spoke of his meeting with one of these Muslim 'disciples of Jesus':[4]

> One day a man came from the north with a herd of sheep and goats ... He was sitting down. As I was a rather inquisitive person, I asked him where he came from. He told me that he had lived at Mecca since childhood. I asked him, 'Can you recite the names of the prophets which Islam recognises?' He listed the names of the known prophets. I said to him, 'I did not hear the name of Issa. Can you tell me about him?' He replied, 'It is true. I did not mention Issa. He had a power higher than ourselves. He is the master of heaven and earth, and that is why I could not mix his name with that of the other prophets.' He did not give any more details.

Time and again, in accounts coming from many places, we find mention of these nameless witnesses and of their strange spiritual journey. They are Muslim believers who, while remaining completely within their own religious community, fix their attention on Jesus until eventually their heart perceives something of his mystery as it is revealed in the Gospels.[5] Many of these people have never crossed the door of a Christian church. There may not even be a church in their country. They live as Muslims a solitary faith in which Jesus is their support and their way to God. When these 'Muslims for Jesus' encounter the Christian Church, either directly or through reading, they exclaim like Esmat-ul-Moluk, an Iranian princess and grand-daughter of a ruling prince: 'I have always been a Christian. I have loved Jesus Christ ever since I was a girl.'[6]

The sign of the crucified

There are other Muslims who find their way to Jesus, not through the Koran, but through their experience of the suffering and injustice which seems to be inseparable from the human condition. It is this which causes them to look at the cross of Jesus with fresh eyes. While classical Islam refuses the scandal of a crucified prophet, the wretched of the earth know from bitter experience that the just man may very well be oppressed, assassinated, crucified. A number of Palestinian poets recognise in the crucified Christ the image of their own suffering and humiliation.[7]

An Egyptian doctor, Kamil Husayn, has written a whole book on the drama of Good Friday, not to establish its historical character, but to bring out its deep meaning—the story of Jesus is the story of everyman.[8]

A Jesus who answers prayers

However interesting, ideas about Jesus need not lead to a personal relationship with him. These ideas may even be manufactured to fit one's own preconceived ideology.[9] One may be content to talk *of* Jesus, to argue *about* him, without truly meeting him and speaking *to* him. There are, however, those who truly meet Jesus. Sometimes it even seems that Jesus himself has taken the initiative and has come to meet them.

The strange story of a Pakistani girl

'I want to die. I don't want to live any more and that's the end of it.'

So spoke Gulshan Fatima, a Pakistani girl of sixteen, at three

o'clock on a cold winter's morning. The cry of despair was wrung
from her by her father's death.[10]

Fatima was born into a wealthy Shi'ite family, descended from
the prophet Muhammad himself. She received a strict and fervent
Muslim education. But Fatima was an invalid. When she was six
months old she caught an illness which paralysed her down one
side and made it impossible for her to move without help. Her
mainstay for many years was her widowed father who refused to
allow her to give up hope. In 1966 he took her to London to see a
specialist, but the medical verdict was that nothing could be done
for his beloved daughter. Then the family turned to religion. They
took Fatima to Mecca for the Great Pilgrimage in the hope that
God would cure her. Helpers brought her to the Black Stone itself
where she murmured again the prayer she repeated at every stage
of the Hadj: 'Please cure me and cure all these sick people.' Nothing happened. Her father still encouraged her: 'God is sending
you this trial. Let us not lose hope. Perhaps you will be cured at
some other time in your life.' His last words to his daughter were:
'One day God is going to heal you, Gulshan. Pray to him.'

It was at this turning-point in her existence that Gulshan uttered
her words of despair. One can indeed understand her feeling.
What followed is less easy to understand.

> I can't explain it, but I knew I was being heard. It was as if a veil had
> been lifted between me and some source of peace . . .
>   —Tell me why have You punished me so heavily?
>   —I won't let you die. I will keep you alive.
>   It was a low and gentle voice, like a breath of wind passing over
> me. I know there was a voice, and that it spoke in my language, and
> that with it came a new freedom to approach God, the Supreme Being,
> who until then had not given me any indication that He even knew of
> my existence.

When she renewed her complaint, the voice came again, vibrant
and low: 'Who gave eyes to the blind, who made the sick whole, and
who healed the lepers and who raised the dead? I am Jesus, Son of
Mary. Read about Me in the Koran, in the Sura Maryam.'[11] Gulshan
adds that she had no idea how long this exchange lasted. It might

have been five minutes, or half an hour. Then the call to morning prayer came. Everything was normal again.

From that day a new period began in the life of the young invalid. In her comfortable but solitary life, she continued to fight against despair and to ask 'why?' But she also began reading the passages in the Koran about Jesus, beginning with the surat 'Maryam'(no.19). This reading produced a growing faith and trust in Jesus, whom the Koran described as a prophet who healed the sick. Finding it difficult to understand all the finer points in the Arabic text, she obtained a translation into Urdu, her mother tongue.

Gulshan's searching of the Muslim scriptures was above all a prayerful search. She prayed to Jesus and asked him to cure her. Then she had a new experience. She found that the more she spoke to Jesus the more she felt attracted by him. Hers was no theoretical study of Jesus but a living encounter with him. She got into the habit of ending all her regular prayers with the invocation: 'Oh Jesus, Son of Maryam, heal me.'

Three years passed and then Gulshan had the experience which was to change her whole existence. One day while she was saying her little prayer to Jesus, a thought came to her: 'I've been doing this for so long, and I'm still a cripple.' She then addressed Jesus directly:

'Look you are alive in heaven,[12] and it says in the Holy Qur'an about you that you have healed people. You can heal me, and yet I'm still a cripple.'
I said His name again, and pleaded my case, in despair. There was no answer. Then I cried out in a fever of pain: 'If you are able to, heal me—otherwise tell me.'

She says that what happened next was difficult to explain. Her room was filled with light. Twelve figures appeared before her, surrounding a further figure who told her: 'Get up. This is the path you have been seeking. I am Jesus, Son of Mary, to whom you have been praying, and now I am standing in front of you. You get up and come to me.'

When Gulshan hesitated, the order was repeated three times. Finally she obeyed.

> And I, Gulshan Fatima, who had been crippled on my bed for nineteen years, felt new strength flowing into my wasted limbs. I put my foot on the ground and stood up. Then I ran a few paces and fell at the feet of the vision . . . The light shone into my heart and into my mind and many things became clear to me at that moment.

She then heard Jesus describing himself in terms she had never heard before: 'I am Emmanuel. I am the Way, the Truth and the Life. I am alive, and I am soon coming. See from today you are my witness . . . What you have seen with your own eyes you must take to my people . . . You must pray like this: Our Father . . .' .

When the vision faded she was healed. Her friends and family were astonished and at first overcome with joy; but their attitude changed to chagrin when Fatima insisted that her cure was due, not to the pilgrimage to Mecca and the intercession of Muhammad, but to Jesus.

Step by step, this young Muslim woman, who had never met a Christian and never read the Bible, discovered a new dimension of personal prayer, thanks to the Our Father. She had to face the growing mistrust and hostility of her family. In time she will be guided towards the Bible, then towards a Christian community and finally to baptism. She will be disinherited by her family and imprisoned. She will refuse to be intimidated and eventually become a journalist, only to lose her position when she refuses to return to the Muslim faith. She is now a speaker and 'evangelist' in the Methodist Church.

A saviour who really saves

Gulshan's experience is fairly typical. She offered her distress to Jesus, while leaving him free to intervene to save her from what was crushing her. This, in itself, was a very practical and down-to-earth way of proclaiming that Jesus is a saviour.

Some further examples will show us how, for Jesus, action

comes before words. He first helps and then makes himself known, just as he did with the crowds in Palestine.

MERAT-US-SULTAN (1876–1948)

Merat-us-Sultan was a well-connected Iranian officer. He enjoyed rapid promotion and was chief of police in Tabriz in 1912 at the time of the Russian invasion. He was obliged to flee through the snows of Armenia and eventually found refuge with an Armenian priest who sheltered him for over a month. When the time came for him to leave, the priest said: 'I have prayed to Christ for you every day. I am sure that he will protect you until you are reunited with your family. But are you willing, in the depths of your heart, to promise Christ never to forget him and to give yourself to him as your Saviour when you arrive home?'

The fugitive was soon arrested, and after a period of imprisonment was one day told that he was to be executed on the following morning. He passed a disturbed night, and it was only then that he remembered his promise. He addressed himself to Jesus: 'Save me! If thou art alive, save me! Save me, and I will devote my life to thy service.' After this prayer he experienced a great peace. He repeated this prayer from his prison to the foot of the scaffold when suddenly the order arrived to set him free and hand him back to the Iranian authorities.

After a first moment of gratitude in which he addressed a prayer to God and to Jesus, Merat-us-Sultan resumed his normal activities and forgot all about his promise—until one day a year later he was reminded of it by a Christian friend. He fell to his knees and, surrounded by some Iranian converts, put himself and his life into the hands of Christ. He rose up a Christian. He was baptised in 1920 and resigned from the army to offer his services free as an administrator in a mission hospital. Later on he became a preacher and died in peace in 1948.[13]

SAVED FROM DRUGS

Another not dissimilar story is that of an anonymous Iranian.[14]

Born in 1951 into a simple Muslim family, this young man spent a normal childhood among friendly neighbours. He had no particular interest in religion, nor in the classes on the Koran which he was obliged to follow at school. Several members of his family were pious Muslims, but his parents left him free, and he did not go to the mosque and neglected the prescribed prayers. His friends included an Iranian Christian family.

His difficulties began when first his brother and then his sister were accused by the new regime of being left-wing atheists. His brother was imprisoned, his sister lost her job, and he himself was directed to a disciplinary camp for his military service. He began at this period to think about God, but still did not pray in the Muslim manner and was regarded by his officers and comrades as a renegade. One of his comrades was a Christian and this seems to have awakened his interest in Christianity, although he did not at this time take any positive steps towards the Christian faith.

When his service was over he spoke of his growing sympathy for Christians, and received the expected insults from his Muslim acquaintances.

When I returned home, I renewed contact with my old friends, including certain Christians. I had never spoken to them of Jesus, just as they, regarding me as a Muslim, never asked me about my religion . . .

For two years I had been taking drugs. I wanted to stop but could not. Then I prayed to Jesus for help and I managed to stop. This made me think that he could really rescue me. From this time I started to pray, very simply but from the heart. On the major Christian feasts, I would go to the church but stayed at the door, full of hesitations and conflicting desires . . .

In the midst of these trials and difficulties, the call which I felt was transformed into a search for Jesus Christ. I do not know why but I trusted him and regarded him as my support. I must add that, at that time, Jesus was my friend and nothing more. But how could I continue my search unless I got to know him properly? One problem was that I did not even know that the Gospels existed in Persian. This was regarded as a Muslim language, and I could not imagine that a priest could speak it.

Quite suddenly I decided to ask for baptism. You may well wonder how I could possibly take such a decision without having read the Gospel or sought anyone's advice. How could I have the slightest knowledge of Jesus? How could I know that baptism was important?

I should say in response that I had seen a number of films about Jesus on television and these had given me an idea of his life and teaching. I had also found some Christian pamphlets on a variety of subjects in the houses of Christian friends and had read them eagerly.

Evidently what had influenced this young man was not Christian teaching, about which he knew practically nothing, but the person of Jesus with whom he entered into direct contact.

A SOLDIER FROM NIGER

Antoine Douramane was born in 1903. He is now a catechist in his native Gorouol area of Niger.[15] Douramane is a local form of Abd-ar-Rahmân, a Muslim name, and our subject was indeed a Muslim from a community in which African traditional beliefs were very strong.

Douramane spent a long period in the army, and this was where he met Christians from Benin who spoke of God as a Father and of Jesus who came to show men the way to God. He felt strangely attracted to Jesus and attached himself to the chaplain. He found 'a signpost on his road to Jesus' when he accompanied the latter on a visit to an apparently dying man. That same evening the man who was supposed to be dying was cured and busy telling everyone that the sacrament of Jesus had brought him back to life. From that moment wherever he was sent by the army, Douramane took every opportunity of studying the catechism and he was finally baptised in 1929.

Once he left the army he returned to his home village and felt an urgent need to reveal to his people the faith which burned within him. Little by little a small Christian community formed around him. He did not teach doctrines about Jesus but simply invited people to communicate with this Jesus who gave 'the power of God'. One of his listeners, Paul Assane Daouda, has recounted the result:

> I was a Muslim and against the Christians. I spoke ill of them. Then one day it came to me that I was only behaving in this way because I was unwilling to change my life. Yet I saw the evil I was doing and my heart was not at peace. Then I began to consort with the young

catechumens of my age and little by little Jesus took hold of me. I no longer wanted anything but him.

One day people said to me: 'We cannot cultivate, the ground is too dry, we have had no rain for twenty days. We have used all our charms, the marabouts have prayed, and still no water has come.' I don't know what it was that pushed me to speak but I replied:

'I am a Christian. There are many of us here who believe in Jesus and follow him. We are going to ask him to come to our aid. If his name possesses the power of God, you will see rain before day break.'

Soumana Bakarou, the marabout, replied: 'If it rains before tomorrow, we shall know that it is due to Jesus and we shall give him everything.'

Night fell without a cloud in sight. Everyone retired to his hut, except for the catechumens. Led by me, they started praying, determined not to stop until rain fell. In the middle of the night, quite suddenly, flashes of lightning appeared in the east. A moment later the storm broke over Dolbel and the rain poured down. The people were overjoyed. In the morning Soumana Bakarou came to see us:

'It is true,' he said, 'you are really the people of Jesus and power is in him. May God hear your prayer.'[16]

The power of the name of Jesus

How rare are events like these? A number of recent books testify to the same kind of 'divine response' in the most diverse societies: gangs of young New York drug addicts,[17] drug-and-prostitution derelicts in Hong Kong,[18] Timor peasants in the Indonesian archipelago.[19] All these stories show us people without any contact with the Christian tradition. The persons concerned knew absolutely nothing about Christian doctrine, but they met Jesus when *they let him help them* in their distress.

With the help of Jackie Pullinger, the abandoned drug addicts of Hong Kong discovered that, if they called on a certain Jesus, of whom they had never previously heard, they could be freed from the slavery of heroin. That is all they knew about Jesus.

Few of the junkies had had any exposure to Christianity before coming off drugs. Far from being a hindrance this actually helped them. Now they would arrive saying:

'I have heard how Ah Kei (or some other friend) has changed. He says it's Jesus who did it. I think Ah Kei is the meanest addict I know. If Jesus can change that one he can change me too.'

Their faith did not depend upon any understanding of theological concepts but upon the seeing of Jesus working in others and the willingness to let him work in their lives too. Each time they prayed they were answered and their faith grew as they were healed . . .

Most of our boys began to understand Jesus with their minds only after they had experienced him in their lives and bodies.[20]

It was of course in exactly the same way that the Palestinian crowds, and even the Apostles themselves, 'discovered' Jesus. They first experienced the extraordinary presence and power of this wandering rabbi; then they came to love him; and then, loving him, they followed him in order to get to know him and to listen to him. But it was not until Pentecost that the mystery of Jesus was finally grasped and proclaimed.

The spiritual journeys of these Muslims can in this way be seen as perfectly normal: they experience the power of the living Jesus before they accept Christian teaching about him. If this surprises us, it is because we have been Christians all our lives and have followed the opposite path. We began with the catechism where we learned about Jesus before we had had any experience of his presence.

Experience of the power of Jesus is only the beginning. The disciple has to pass from knowing the power of Jesus to knowing the person of Jesus himself. How can this be brought about?

From the power of Jesus to Jesus himself

A beginning can be made by meditating on the passages in the Koran which speak of Jesus.[21] These only amount however to ninety-three verses out of a total of over six thousand and they give only a very meagre sketch of the mission and teaching of Jesus. The Muslim in search of Jesus must therefore look elsewhere.

Muslim sources

Muslim mystics have produced a number of anecdotes about Jesus. Unfortunately most of them have no connection with the Gospels, nor even with the ancient Christian Apocrypha. The Muslim stories about Jesus seem to have been taken from stories told of the Desert Fathers. In Islam these tales were transferred from the monks of the Egyptian desert to Jesus. Jesus is presented above all as a poor ascetic who preached renunciation of the world. Here are some examples of Muslim sayings about Jesus:

> Jesus said: Devotion has ten degrees; the ninth is silence, and the first, flight from people.[22]
>
> The disciples asked Jesus to teach them how to win God's love. He told them: Make the world your enemy and God will befriend you.[23]

Other stories present the vocation of Jesus as an exemplary search for absolute poverty:

> It is written that Jesus, Son of Mary, never settled down and was for-ever wandering from place to place. When asked why, he replied: Per-haps I might set foot one day where a saint has trod and, stepping in his tracks, find intercession from sins.[24]
>
> At the ascension of Jesus the angels assembled. He sat down and his garment was torn into three hundred pieces . . . Then the angels searched in his undergarment and found there a needle. God then said: By my glory, if he had not had this needle I would have caught him up into my innermost sanctity and would not have been happy to grant him only the seventh heaven; but now this needle is a veil between him and me.[25]

These stories about Jesus are hardly cited by ordinary Muslims and they are probably not known outside certain esoteric mystic confraternities. It is unlikely that somebody will look into that type of literature to find Jesus.

The Bible

The Bible is the normal and natural place for finding out the truth about Jesus, but it is not always easy for a Muslim to get hold of one. The Koran indeed praises the Bible, calling Jews and Christians 'People of the Book' and describing it as 'Guide and Light'.[26] However, Muslim commentators and doctors of the law have implanted the idea that the biblical writings have been falsified and that they are a danger for the faith.

In some Muslim countries the importation of Bibles is forbidden. Elsewhere their importation is surrounded by so many regulations that it becomes practically impossible to offer them for sale. Such biblical bookshops as there are are subject to harassment and continually threatened with judicial closure. Nevertheless, the presence of a Christian community in a Muslim country, whether native or foreign, means that there are Bibles in circulation, often in the form of booklets containing a single Gospel or a collection of a few important passages.

Qassim is an Iranian shoemaker, originally from Meshed. One day he bought some cheese in the market. When he got home he discovered that the cheese was wrapped in paper which had been torn from a book. He read the page: it was a story about a master of a vineyard who hired workers at various times of the day and then gave them all the same pay as if they had all worked for a full day.[27] Qassim enjoyed the story, and the next day he went to the cheese-seller to ask for the following page. The day after that he bought what remained of the book from which these pages had been torn: it was a New Testament. A little while later he went to see a priest to find the whole of this fascinating book. It was reading the New Testament that determined him to ask for baptism.[28]

Khalil was the imam, or leader, of a mosque in Niger. Today he is a Christian in the same village. He told the following story:

> It was just four years ago today that I got caught up with the Christian religion. It all started when I read John's Gospel. One day I was strolling in the market at Zinder and I came across a man sitting down and selling books. I bought this little book from him for forty African francs. When I got home I started reading and came to the passage where it says: 'Darkness and death are relatives, and light and life as well.' And it was said: 'Jesus is the Light, he is the Life; darkness is from the devil, light is from God.' I said to myself, 'I am on the side of Jesus, on the side of this light.'[29]

We should not be deceived by the baldness of this testimony and others like it. The calm, modest and simple narrative is in the

African manner, but it conceals an interior turmoil produced by the words of the Bible. The whole personality undergoes a shock which can only be expressed in words like, Well now, that is true, that is really God speaking!

Still under the influence of the words he had read in the prologue to John's Gospel, Khalil found a stranger who obtained a Bible for him in Arabic. He read it and loved it, especially the Gospel, which he read from beginning to end. He continues his testimony:

> At that time I was the imam, I was the one who led the prayer in the village. When the people noticed that I was reading the Bible, they said: You have become a Christian, you are ruined! They rejected me and would not allow me to lead the prayer any longer. I said to them: I have seen the way of truth. Formerly I was in sin. I have read in the Gospel that Jesus is the liberator. He takes upon himself the weight of our sins.
>
> It was the beginning of my new way. And now here I am. I have many sufferings, but I know that Jesus bears them with me.

Whatever their religious education, many converts speak of a moment when the Islamic scriptures, hitherto experienced as so spiritually nourishing, seem in need of a new light which can only be found in the Bible.

The witness of Christians

Most converts say how they felt the need to ask Christians whom they met for explanations about the Bible. They might ask them for the texts themselves if they found them too difficult to obtain.

When Gulshan Fatima had her vision of Jesus and the twelve apostles, he showed her a group of people singing canticles and said they were his people. One face stood out in the crowd. I looked closely at this man, who was sitting down. Jesus said: Go ten miles up to the north, and this man will give you a Bible.

Gulshan trusted this vision completely, and set off, saying that she was going to visit a friend. On the way she called at a mission and there discovered the man she had met in the vision. He was a

Christian pastor and he got a Bible for her. He was the first Christian she ever met.

Modern media

Muslims also have access to the life and teaching of Jesus, however distorted, through mass-circulation films like *Quo Vadis*, *Ben Hur* and *Jesus of Nazareth*. Radio and television programmes too, with all their other elements, issue for the most part from a culture originally Christian and, for those who are sensitive to the religious dimension, offer a kind of cumulative portrait of Jesus of Nazareth.

Ibrahim Deshmukh is an Indian doctor born in 1934 into a not over-religious Muslim family. He writes:

> While I was a medical student in Bombay, I saw two films, *Quo Vadis* and *The Ten Commandments*. Many people saw these films, including veiled women. I wondered at the time why there was so much more information in the Bible than in the Koran, although I learned later that the producers of the films had made additions to the biblical account.

In fact these films did not have a serious influence on Deshmukh. Much more important was his friendship with the woman who later became his wife. She was a Christian and introduced him to the Bible. He spent several years in solitary study of the Bible and the Koran, weighing their meaning and authenticity. This was all somewhat theoretical, but it assumed another dimension when he became aware of his need for God's forgiveness. This was the final stage in a process which eventually led him to become a Christian and dedicate his life to the service of the sick poor.[30]

In step with Jesus

Whatever the means it has taken, this discovery of Jesus leads to an experience of personal friendship with Jesus to which many converts testify.

Victory over drinking !

Jean Adda Boudaoud was born into an Algerian family which, like so many others, was cast up, destitute, on the shores of France by the war of independence in the late 1950s. The family lived in misery. Adda failed at school, could not find proper work, and, along with other members of his family, fell into drinking. Finally he turned into a wandering tramp. He was, however, of a reflective turn of mind, and he began to wonder if God could possibly exist, whether with the French or the Muslims.

Finally he obtained work as a labourer at Draguignan and came into contact with a young woman social worker. She was a believer and, so it seemed to Adda, radiated an extraordinary light and peace. He became friendly with her. Some years later she became his wife and it was through her that he discovered Christ. The birth of their first child marked the beginning of a new life in more ways than one:

> I felt the urgency of getting to know Christ, but the prince of darkness would not leave me alone. At the bottom of my heart I said to myself, Christ exists, he lives: for Elizabeth had told me that he had risen from the dead. That was how I came to abandon myself to Jesus Christ.

The alcoholism remained a problem, in spite of his efforts to follow the programme of Alcoholics Anonymous. He knew that his drinking was ruining his family but he was unable to stop. It was in this distress that he finally found Jesus:

> It was during that night that a still, small voice came to me saying: 'I too have suffered, I went as far as the cross; and it was one of my friends who betrayed me . . . We must forget and forgive. Now I am at your side, I am your great friend, the only one on whom you can count. Travel with me and I am there whenever you call. I am there to save the whole multitude.

It was then that Adda went with his wife to follow a retreat in a religious centre. A Christian retreat, like the Muslim *khalwa*, is a time of silence and prayer when one tries to place oneself totally at God's disposal. It was in this atmosphere of deep silence that Adda discovered the presence of God:

> I came because I needed to cherish the discovery of Jesus which I had made with my Elizabeth . . . so that we could walk in the light of Christ . . .
>
> August 29, 1977 was for me the day of deliverance, the day when I met God.
>
> Today I see, I feel a liberation. It is the presence of God. God who invites me to enter on the way of Christ in company with all my brothers and sisters who are on the same path . . .
>
> I allow myself to be led by you . . . My life, my thoughts, my cares, my debts, my joys, all that I possess: I hand them all over to you and you will look after them, for you are life and hope.

After his baptism, Jean Adda Boudaoud again took up his struggle against drink. He successfully followed a programme during which he discovered how to walk with God at every level of existence:

> Today is the fourth meeting of our group. The theme is sexuality. It is good to talk about sexuality in this calm way. I think and reflect about it, for myself and others. God needs me to be silent so that I can listen to him. I advance with him in a mysterious but real communication. The baptism which the Church gave me did not cure my alcoholism. The cure which I receive today makes me grow in my baptism.[31]

'A little change'

We have already met Dramane-Daniel Coulibaly, a young Muslim from the Ivory Coast. As he read the Bible and listened to preaching in church, he began to be aware of all the things in his life which were not in accordance with the call of God:

> But how to set about changing? It is very difficult. I thank God that I found the courage to pray. I entrusted myself to God. Sometimes I grew discouraged. I said, I pray but nothing changes.
>
> But then I said: Jesus is Saviour. I believe that. There is no other

Saviour. I also know strongly that he forgives. So he knows what is in me. He knows. I know too that it is not by doing extraordinary things that I shall find salvation. It is by his love. So I said, good, I shall carry on praying, in spite of my bad character.

I was conscious of a little change at the very moment that I no longer had the courage to pray. I could listen and accept things in a way that I could not do before.

My wife had suffered from my faults for a long time. Now she was conscious that I had changed, but she did not understand it and could not accept it. Nevertheless I found the courage to say to her: Look! I know that according to our customs, women are inferior to men. But I feel the need, because of my faith, to be your equal. [32]

Jesus, it appears from these experiences, is not simply a 'projection' of our dreams and fantasies. He calls. He demands choices, leading us where we would rather not go. Indeed, he reveals himself as a living person with his desires, his choices, his preferences. And each person is invited to put aside all his or her preconceived ideas and ambitions and to make room for Jesus as he is. Sometimes Jesus can demand us to make choices which are nothing short of devastating.

Converting to Jesus

Giving up amulets

Dramane Coulibaly tells us how he was obliged to make a choice between Jesus and the protective charms to which he was much attached and which are authorised by Islam.[33]

We Senufu are a people full of fear. Even our Muslim parents cannot trust in God alone. They make sacrifices and consult diviners. We are afraid of death, of being poisoned, of evil spirits. We consult diviners to foresee dangers and find remedies to avert them. We try and chase misfortune away by offering sacrifices.

I used to do these things. But then I heard these practices mentioned in church. I heard it said that Jesus can do everything, that God does not like seeing his position shared with others . . . That made things very difficult.

I continued to read and I saw that God can do everything for the one who believes in him. He is stronger than Satan, since he chased away the evil spirits from the possessed.

One day I went to church and came out very touched. I said: when I come before Jesus and am carrying these amulets, what does he think of me? I felt this strongly, I cannot say why.

This struggle against fear lasted several months. Dramane felt in his heart that Jesus was watching him and calling him to place his trust in nothing but him. It was only a year after his baptism that he finally threw away all his charms and found peace in trusting Jesus alone.

Renouncing hatred

Habib Wardan was a member of a Tunisian family which arrived in France when he was eight. They knew extreme poverty in a French slum and the child was obliged to leave and spend some time in a nursing home. It was here that he first heard of Jesus as he learned to read from an illustrated Bible. This Jesus, so sympathetic, so like the little shepherd boy that Habib had been in Tunisia, seemed a kind of fairy-tale character, a Peter Pan. This infantile religious experience came to an abrupt end when the Sister who was teaching him to read went rather too brutally to the point and told him that this Jesus was God himself! The little Muslim was so indignant at such a declaration that no one dared mention Jesus to him any more.

As an adolescent, Habib was a voracious reader. He had however no work and no future to look forward to and he made friends with drop-outs. It was from some of these that he heard of a group of Young Christian Workers and their chaplain. He joined them.

Their concern for justice and their rejection of the class system awakened in him an ardent desire to defend the poor and to change the world. He developed a hatred for the rich and prosperous, among whom he included Christians and the Church.

Probably without his being aware of it, Habib's ideas were derived from the ancient enmity between Muslims and Christians as well as from his own experience of rejection.

In meetings of the Young Christian Workers, I poured out my social rancour and spoke of the miseries of my people. My new understanding had filled me with hatred and anger, so much so that I forgot the convictions of those to whom I was speaking. To their talk of love, which seemed to me incomprehensible and derisory, I replied in terms of violent revolution. I noticed that the priest remained silent. He seemed doubtful about what I was saying but I went on with my inflammatory talk.

Confronted with such violence, the priest one day gave him a key to the premises and selected some texts from the Gospel which he advised him to read quietly.

It was a fine cold Sunday. The building where we met was empty and I went to the table where the priest had left the famous book for me. I sat near the window overlooking the peaceful garden. I felt strangely happy and calm, more at home here than anywhere else. I opened the book.

The life of Christ was there recounted with more details than I had heard from the Sister in my nursing home. There was no trace here of Peter Pan but only cruel days for his best friend. I was profoundly shocked to see how Christ willingly humbled himself under the daily burdens which I found so heavy, how he was willing to forgo his own will in a spirit of peace. I could not get over the poverty of Jesus. The constructors of the new world were drawn from the poor. The only things demanded of them were love and forgiveness. My heart was seduced. All my life I had had more sorrow in my spirit than love in my heart. Sitting there with Christ, in the silence of his matchless presence, I felt an exile no longer. His word contained the world and it could become mine. In an instant the whole of reality seemed to be reversed. A ray of light pierced the absurdity of my life. Christ was calling me with all the living force of fire.[34]

For two years Habib frequented this priest, reading both the Bible and the Koran, looking for the true word of God. The struggle continued. The ideal of Christ was beautiful but it had been betrayed by the Church, by Christians. And Habib's hatred returned.

Could he name me a single place where I could find authentic Christian life? I never believed that he would take up this challenge. But he gave me a name without hesitation. It was the name of an abbey in the mountains. If I liked I could go there and see people living according to the commandments of Christ.

The bet was accepted. Habib went and spent some time in this abbey. In silence and prayer he came to a new birth.

> For a long time after Christmas, a light remained burning in my Muslim heart. My eyes had surprised Jesus in the crib. God become a little child was the response to my presence here. For although I had lost my childhood, I knew that with Christ I could find it again. My religion was inadequate for maintaining this light within me. I had re-lived all the beauty of my childhood. I was in danger of losing an unspeakable treasure. Christ was offering me an Eternal Childhood. If I wanted to remain and to grow in the hands of Jesus, I must be planted in his ground. I must utter my Yes above the baptistry, in the heart of the Church.[35]

Through Jesus Habib gained victory over hatred and the revulsion which he still felt for the image of the Church left in his heart from past sufferings.

Some reflections

Of course the convert's story does not end with his or her conversion. There will be other stages on the road with Jesus. Each in his or her way has perceived the same call: 'Come to me, all you who are weary and burdened, and I will give you rest. Take my yoke upon you and learn from me, for I am gentle and humble in heart, and you will find rest for your souls. For my yoke is easy and my burden is light' (Matthew 11:28–30).

This passage is frequently quoted by converts as the key text in their encounter with Jesus. What then of Islamic teaching, of Christianity and its dogmas, of the divinity of Christ and the Trinity?

A constant factor in this type of conversion is that the relation with Jesus comes before questions of doctrine. The formulas of the faith only begin to make sense, either suddenly or little by little, when Jesus has been recognised as one who loves us and saves us.[36] Strangely enough, it was also the experience of Jesus' first disciples.

Can we recognise these new disciples when we meet them? Some of them may still be in the early stages of their evolution, like those men on the banks of the Jordan where John was baptising. Or they may already have spent months or even years listening to the teaching of the master. Some will amaze us with their stories of miracles, like the people whom Jesus cured in the Gospels. Others, finally, will be able to tell us of their faith in the risen one and of their experience of his Spirit.

Notes

1 In *Trenta Giorni*, May 1987, No. 5, pp.22–25.

2 A good summary of these may be found in Ali Merad's conference, 'Christ according to the Qur'an', delivered in Rome in 1968 and published in *Encounter*, no.69, November 1980. (*Encounter*, Viale Trastevere 89, 00153 Rome.)

3 The story of Mallam Ibrahim was given in an MA thesis written in Birmingham in 1981 by J.A. Idowu, *Jesus in the Qur'an, a Northern Nigerian Case Study*, pp.29–41.

4 See R. Deniel, *Chemins de Chrétiens Africains* (Inades: Abidjan, Ivory Coast, 1981), No.6, pp.10-11.

5 We are reminded of the Gospel scene when Jesus asks his disciples this question: 'But what about you ... who do you say that I am?' (Matthew 16:15)

6 See W.M. Miller, *A Christian Response to Islam* (Presbyterian and Reformed Publ.: Nutley, NJ, USA, 1976), p.116.

7 See Boutros Hallaq, 'La poésie arabe et le Christ', *Comprendre*, No.135, 17 May 1976. (*Comprendre*, 5 Rue d'Issy, 92170, Vauves, France.)

8 Kamil Husayn, K. Cragg, transl., *City of Wrong* (Djambatan: Amsterdam, 1959).

9 The figure of Jesus has been exploited by many a religious movement, even in recent times. In their controversies, Christians, Jews and Muslims have often used and misused the person of Jesus to score off their adversaries. Read M. de Epalza, 'Juifs, chrétiens et musulmans en Espagne (VI°–XVII° s.),' *Jésus Otage* (Cerf: Paris, 1987).

10 E. Gulshan and T. Sangster, *The Torn Veil: Christ's healing power breaks through to a Muslim girl* (Marshall, Morgan and Scott: Basingstoke, 1984). The details described here can be found on p.48 ff.

11 These words are a near translation of Koran 3:49 and 5:110 where Jesus' miracles are described.

12 From some Koranic verses, most Muslims draw the idea that Jesus has not been crucified, but has been raised up to heaven by God and that he will stay there until he comes back on earth to resume his earthly life before the end of the world.

13 W. McE. Miller, *Ten Muslims meet Christ* (Eerdmans: Grand-Rapids, USA, 1969, 1980), pp.68–86.

14 His witness is contained in a confidential document. The continuation of his story is given in chapter 8.

15 J.M. Ducroz, *Les Actes des Premiers Chrétiens du Gorouol* (Nouvelle Cité: Paris, 1977), pp.41–42.

16 *Ibid.*, pp.41–42.

17 D. Wilkerson, *The Cross and the Switchblade* (Pyramid Books: New York, 1962/1970).

18 J. Pullinger, *Chasing the Dragon* (Hodder and Stoughton: London, 1980).

19 M. Tari, *Like a Mighty Wind* (Creation House: Carol Stream, USA, 1971).

20 J. Pullinger, *op. cit.*, pp.159–160.

21 On the subject, see G. Parrinder, *Jesus in the Qur'an* (Sheldon Press: London, 1976).

22 J. Nurbakhsh, *Jesus in the Eyes of the Sufis* (Khaniqahi-Nimatullahi Publications: London, 1983), p.79.

23 *Ibid.*, p.81. It may be observed how far removed this 'teaching' is from the spirit of the Gospel Jesus who insisted that the love of God could not be earned, and who mixed freely with all classes of people and took part in their celebrations.

24 *Ibid.*, p.124.

25 R. Arnaldez, *Jésus Fils de Marie Prophète de l'Islam* (Desclée: Paris, 1980), p.213.

26 Koran 5:44,46,47,68.

27 Matthew: 20:1–16.

28 W. McE. Miller, *A Christian Response to Islam* (Presbyterian and Reformed Publ.: Nutley, NJ, USA, 1976), pp.113–114.

29 R. Deniel, *Chemins de Chrétiens Africains* (Inades: Abidjan, Ivory Coast, 1982–1983) vol.2.

30 I.O. Deshmukh, *In Quest of Truth* (FFM: Toronto, Canada).

31 A. Boudaoud, *Renaître, J'ai vaincu mon alcoolisme* (Salvator: Mulhouse, France, 1985).

32 R. Deniel, *Sur le Chemin Chrétien* (Vie Chrétienne, Supplement to No.274: Paris, 1984), pp.21–22.

33 A certain type of magic is accepted in Islam. Traditional ways are used to tell the future and to get in touch with the world of the spirits (the Djinn or genii). Islamic magic makes use of Koranic verses or of Divine Attributes combining them with considerations on the numerical value conferred upon each letter of the Arabic alphabet. These methods of fortune-telling and amulet-making enter into the training of the religious leaders in most Muslim countries and can be studied in well-known handbooks written in medieval times.

34 H. Wardan, *La Gloire de Peter Pan ou le récit du Moine Beur* (Nouvelle Cité: Paris, 1986), pp.135–137.

35 *Ibid.*, p.146.

36 One could read G. Diallo, *La Nuit du Destin* (Salvator: Mulhouse, France, 1969). This novel is based on the true story of a young Muslim from Mali who discovered Jesus during his studies in North Africa. The author was surprised to receive a number of letters from Muslim readers saying that they recognised themselves in the story.

CHAPTER 3

THIRST FOR TRUTH

Be not anxious. You must not allow the serenity of your fasting or your tranquillity of spirit to be disturbed by those who lack the light . . . Islam is transparently clear. Its divine principles and its teachings are luminous. Its texts are lamps which light the path of those who seek the truth which lasts and are searching for renewal in practical life.

From the Algerian daily *Al-Cha'b*, 5 June 1986,
on 'Islam and the Future'.

For better or worse, Islam has the reputation of being a religion of simple dogmas and strong convictions. Its adversaries use these characteristics to accuse it of fanaticism, while its defenders see in them the proof that it is the religion of pure reason and of evident truth.

What then are we to say of the substantial number of Muslims who explain their conversion to Christianity as the fruit of a search for the truth? Why aren't they satisfied with this 'luminous' Islam?

Influence of Muslim education

Many converts from Islam testify that it was in their family or in the course of the classical Muslim education that they received this passionate desire to know the truth which God has revealed to human kind.

The central message of Islam

From the beginning, Islam presented itself as revelation, as a clear word of God, source of certitude and security for the one who believes:

> 'Here is the book! It contains no doubt. It is a guide for those who fear God'(Koran 2:2)
>
> 'God sent the prophets to bring people the good news and to warn them. So he bestowed upon them the Book containing the Truth that He might judge between the people, and settle their disputes . . . God has directed believers to this Truth, about which others have debated, with his permission. God directs those whom he chooses along the right path' (2:213).

The whole teaching of Islam derives from the shattering experience which came to Muhammad on Mount Hira when he was forty years of age: there is only one God, creator, judge.

The Koran is full of invitations to reflect, to open the eyes, to recognise the evidence and draw the conclusions.

Judaism and Christianity tend to base their faith on historical events. For the Jews, reflection on the escape from Egypt produced the conviction that God is an all-powerful saviour; Christians discover the mystery of God's love in contemplating the life and teaching of Jesus and, above all, his resurrection on the third day.

All three religions in fact combine a degree of historical reflection and rational thought. But Islam places the greater emphasis on the latter. This shift of emphasis creates differences in the religious experience of these communities: while *events* reveal a God whose action remains always free and unpredictable, deductive *reasoning* offers the satisfying picture of a coherent world.

The slogan of a rational religion

Young Muslims are taught from their earliest years to recognise and respect the universal order which God has established and which he securely guarantees. The Muslim adult in this way develops a thirst for stable truth and a need for certitude and consistency.

It may be observed in passing that this feature of Islam is precisely what attracts some Western people: it offers security.[1]

Where is this truth?

We may proceed to enquire why some Muslims feel impelled to call in question this fine rational structure of Islam and end up by finding their truth in Christianity.

The divisions of Islam

Non-Muslims often imagine that Islam forms a single impregnable monolith. Some people, perhaps for ulterior motives, may present it as a formidable united front against Western identity. There are Muslims too who try to paper over the deep internal divisions of Islam and contrast it in this way with the divided Christian world.

In fact, however, Islam has been divided from the outset into a variety of sects: Sunnites, Shi'a, Kharidjites, each of which in turn is sub-divided into a number of factions, all convinced that they alone have the truth.

Sometimes the differences may be insignificant, but, as in Christianity, this does not prevent them from turning into bitter conflict. In East Africa there have been violent quarrels over the number of prostrations to be performed during Friday prayers; in West Africa the quarrel has been rather over the position of the hands during prayer.

We are not concerned here with the matter of these quarrels but rather with their repercussions in the hearts of Muslim believers, whom they often scandalise and disgust, even to the point of doubt concerning the foundations of their faith. As long as each group remains within its own limited territory, the problems of diversity can be contained. But once people start mixing with outsiders, group conformity becomes insufficient to sustain faith, and people begin to start posing the question of truth.

Stephen Masood, originally called Masood Ahmad Khan, was born in 1951 into a family of the *Ahmadiyyah* sect.[2] When Masood was still a boy of ten, he noticed that people from the surrounding villages treated his own people as unbelievers and pagans. This was brought home to him personally in a painful episode of his childhood. One day he heard an elder declaring in the mosque that if a man had real faith in the basic Islamic formula, 'There is only one God, and Muhammad is his prophet', he could walk on water. The boy took the man at his word and threw himself into the river. He was only saved from drowning by some fishermen who pulled him out of the water. When he explained to them why he had jumped into the river, they burst out laughing: 'Oh, you child of a pagan. Your father is a pagan, your mother is a pagan, your whole family is Qadiani Mirzai.[3] How can you, an unclean person, believe that God will hear you? . . . Get out of here, you unbeliever, and tell your family to become Muslims and then come back here and try again!'[4]

When the boy got home, he was in tears and said to his parents: 'But, Daddy, we . . . we are Muslims, aren't we? . . . we believe the Koran, we say our prayers five times a day. Why did that man say we're pagans?'

The question proved unanswerable. The explanations proffered by his parents and religious leaders in the Ahmadi community or by the other Muslim communities did nothing to calm his anxiety. Each group was utterly sure of its position, all had watertight arguments to refute the rest. As the boy grew, he began to be haunted by the desire for truth, and was more and more repelled by the attempts of his parents and their religious community to impose their version of truth by authority.

No degree of understanding was possible between the tormented young man who asked God to guide him to the truth and his community, which treated him as a rebel. Masood began to find his situation intolerable and finally, after being nearly lynched in his mosque, he fled. For a long time he had to hide from his pursuers. We shall see later how he finally reached certitude. But when he did, he explained: 'It was the Koran that had kept me searching for the truth.'[5]

Compulsion or conviction?

Masood's community responded to his questionings by attempting to impose orthodoxy by authority and, finally, by force. It was precisely this attitude which confirmed Masood in his doubts: for what kind of a truth is it which cannot compel assent through its own power?

While the controversy about the imposition of Islamic law was raging in Egypt, a Nobel Prize-winning novelist called Neguib Mahfouz wrote:

> I call God to be my witness, along with my conscience and my home-land, that I am suffering from an unease of mind and heart for which I can find no cure. My unease arises from a current which is threatening to overwhelm our intellectual and affective life with a brutality which grows stronger every day. I am sorry to say it is a current which is turning into a kind of intellectual terrorism which seeks to ban any divergent opinion.[6]

Faced with persecution or social pressure, people looking for the truth find no relief from their anxiety. On the contrary they feel their doubts justified.

The challenges of the modern world

Modern Islam is facing a challenge far more serious than sect-arianism: the confrontation between what may be called loosely modernism and fundamentalism.[7] The world press has made us familiar with the fruits of this confrontation: bombings, assassinations, censorship, occupation of mosques, attacks on unveiled women.

In the midst of this turmoil, it is not surprising that people are beginning to wonder where is the true Islam or, more broadly, where is the true religion. The conditions of modern life are exposing Muslims to another world and to other values: science and technology, the liberation of women, freedom of opinion. All these factors tend to undermine the authority or the centrality of the Islamic ideological system. 'All these different views of

Fasting, Prayer, Pilgrimage or Muhammad have not pleased me. These talks that Muhammad broke the moon are ridiculous, because science proves them as ridiculous.'[8]

In an attempt to dispel these doubts, many books have appeared claiming to show that all scientific discoveries can in fact be found in the Koran.[9] Other Muslims seek to reassure themselves by pointing to the—often exaggerated—number of Western converts as proof that people brought up in modernity can still accept the final validity of Islam.

The malaise however remains, since a thousand details daily arouse new doubts suggesting that Islamic faith and modernity are incompatible. At this point, some begin to look elsewhere for a way to reconcile faith in God and all that is good in modern thought.

The mystery of evil

Another reason may induce a Muslim to look for truth outside his or her tradition. Its root lies in the feeling that evil and suffering—and more particularly innocent suffering—are not accounted for in traditional Islam, and are often presented under a simplistic form of triumphalism.

This is how A. Al-Maududi, a renowned Muslim writer, describes the real Muslim:

> His life will be a life of purity, piety, love and selflessness. He will be a blessing for mankind . . . such a man will be a power that one will have to reckon with. Only that man can succeed for nothing in the world can stop him or bar the way to him.
>
> He will be the most honoured and respected of men . . . the most powerful and the most efficient . . . He will be the richest . . . He will be the most revered, the most beloved, the most popular of men . . . Such is the life of a true Muslim.[10]

Everyday life gives the lie to that sort of picture. There are plenty of pious and sincere Muslims who have to endure failure, unemployment, humiliation. How can a believer not feel that traditional teachings fail here? How can Islam explain the mystery of evil and suffering? We find here an echo of the question raised by the book of Job in the Bible.

Saliha, an Algerian Christian, speaks of her first steps towards faith in Jesus after she had caught a glimpse of a cross:

> The years went by, and I carried on with my religious practices like everyone else: the daily prayer, the ablutions ... Yet in the depths of my heart I felt disappointment. I started to read books of philosophy to help me to an understanding of the mystery of the evil in the world. I believed in God. But where did evil come from, and how could it be met? God seemed so far away.

Some people find in Christ another way of combining faith in God with the problems of evil, suffering and death.

From polemics to faith

'Evil is not always safe (from God's influence),' wrote Paul Claudel, and a frequently noticed feature of religious history is the movement from violent opposition to fervent faith. St Paul is the most famous example of this phenomenon, but we also find it among converts from Islam.

Qazi Maulvi Sayad Safdar Ali (1830–1899?)

On 10 April 1854 a famous debate took place in the Anglican mission in Agra, India, between a Christian missionary, K.G. Pfander, and a Muslim leader, Rahmat Ullah Kairânawî. The latter, helped by an Indian doctor who had studied in England, won what appeared to be a famous victory by forcing the Christian missionary to admit that there were textual uncertainties in the Bible.[11] For the Muslim audience, the slightest variation in the text showed that God's original message had been tampered with by men and that one should never read this unreliable Bible.[12]

The 'great controversy' of Agra produced some very unexpected results. The Muslim champions had sought to use European rationalist principles to discredit the Bible, and this approach eventually inspired a judge called Sayyid Ahmad Khan (1817-1898) to study the Bible. He published three volumes of biblical commentary, then set himself to apply those same principles to the Koran and to Muslim traditions. His work led to the whole modernist trend of Indian Islam.

Two other young Muslim scholars were so struck by this discussion that they found in it the starting point for a search that eventually led them to Christianity. One was *Imad-ud-din*, of whom we shall speak later; the other was *Sayad Safdar Ali*.[13]

Safdar Ali was the son of a Koranic judge and a descendant of the Prophet: hence the name 'Sayad'. He received from his father a careful education in all branches of Muslim learning: Koran, Traditions, Law. He also studied Persian, Arabic and Urdu, indispensable for Indian Muslim scholars.

While pursuing these classical Muslim studies, Safdar also studied in an English school which finally enabled him to obtain a post as school inspector. He thus received a double education and this caused him some difficulties:

> During this period, I spent some time in perusing some of the religious books of the Hindus, and became acquainted with the articles of their creed, with the mode of their worship, and with their traditions and fables. The metaphysical books of the Greek philosophers also, in their Arabic versions; and moreover the controversial and polemical works of atheists, sophists and deists, and other profound and mysterious subjects, passed under my review.
>
> Although I was aware that many of the stories and statements of the Koran and Hadis were plainly at variance with the fundamental principles and undoubted facts of true science, especially in the case of physics, astronomy, the healing art, and the phenomenon of creation; and though I was disturbed in mind on this account; yet I fortified myself with the common saying, 'What has reason to do with revelation?'
>
> And this I did the more easily in that many of the institutions, precepts, and narratives of the Mohammedan religion were very superior to the creeds, and systems, and fanciful speculations above referred to.

Safdar Ali was thus situated when he listened to the famous debate at the age of twenty-five. It did nothing to ease his difficulties, and he turned to an intensive search of mystical experience as it is taught in Islam. He was hoping in this way to go beyond the popular beliefs with which he felt uneasy.

> The teaching of the mystics on the future life, whether things damning or things saving (the source of all which instruction is the Holy Scriptures)—were so agreeable and delightful that, although I appeared to be rigidly strict in conforming to the rites of Mohammedanism—which indeed, the Sufis insisted upon—yet my soul altogether revolted against these external ordinances, and meditated very gravely respecting inward amendment, and purity and holiness of heart.

Putting aside the theoretical problem, Safdar drew up for himself a programme of mortification and fasts, with complicated exercises combining meditation, the recitation of a mantra, and concentration on breathing which in the end brought on serious cardiac irregularities. At the end of all these efforts, he found himself more ill at ease than ever. 'I was more desolate than ever, for I found here no one to whom I could reveal the secret of my heart with any hope of sympathy.'

The young inspector was contemplating making the pilgrimage to Mecca as a way of easing his inner pain when by chance he came across a Bible, along with the book of that same Pfander whom he had heard in the great debate five years before. He decided to use these two books to confront his great problem and to reassure himself of the validity of Islam and the Koran.

Pfander's book, *The Balance of Truth*, examined the Muslim accusation that the Jewish and Christian Scriptures had been falsified. The author showed that the Koran itself invited Muslims to believe in the Bible and to study it. For two years Safdar Ali read all the books he could find on the controversies between Islam and Christianity.

At first, he found all his fears concerning the Koran confirmed and, to his great distress, began to lose faith in Islam. Even worse, he began to realise that his experiments with mystical experience had been no more than self-seeking and that he had never really encountered God at all. At this point he met a Hindu mystic who had been converted to Christianity and whose common sense and balanced judgement made a great impression on him. He asked his new friend to become his spiritual adviser, and, on his suggestion, began to read the Bible, not now to satisfy his intellectual curiosity, but to try and enter into God's perspective.

Little by little he came to understand that he must *surrender* himself to God along this new way which had been shown to him. He was aware of the hostility of his companions, he was afraid of cutting himself off from his family. Finally, in spite of raging fears in his heart, he decided to ask for baptism, and found at last joy and peace.

Although abandoned by his wife and family, he remained faithful to his origins while becoming also a pillar of the Christian Church in India. He retained his Muslim name, his way of life, his relationships. He carried on too with his work as inspector of schools, while writing a number of Christian books. He died towards the end of the last century.

Chaudari Inayat Ullah

More recent is the witness of an Indian member of the Ahmadiyya sect which we have already met. Ahmadiyya missionary activity was modelled on that of Christian missionary societies. It translates the Koran into various languages and sends preachers all over the world to convert people to Islam. Their writings and sermons are remarkable for their violent attacks on both Christians and other Muslims.

It was in this atmosphere of violent controversy that Chaudari was brought up. He had also read the New Testament in Urdu with pleasure while he was a child, although he could see in it nothing more than a fable.[14] It was while reading a Christian book in 1924 that he began to experience religious doubts. For the first time he tried to see the point of view of a non-Muslim author and found it disturbing: for a moment, he had doubted the truth of Islam.

Hardly had he recovered from this experience than he found himself faced with another incident: a Muslim had suggested that the Koran puts Jesus above Muhammad. The suggestion was received with horror by the members of the sect, and Chaudari was shocked by the violence of the hatred which it aroused. His shock increased shortly afterwards when he read an anonymous text about love which seemed to him almost inspired. It was only later that he learned that the text was in fact the thirteenth chapter of Paul's First Letter to the Corinthians.

In the meantime however he had become a vigorous campaigner on behalf of his sect, and his only contacts with Christians were in the course of religious polemics, some of them taking place in writing, others orally.

It was to arm himself for a debate on the subject of Christ that he committed to memory all the arguments of his community against Christ and Christianity. The better to prepare himself, he had placed two books on his table: the New Testament and an Ahmadi handbook of polemics. Suddenly, seeing things as a whole, he began to examine objectively the arguments presented by his handbook:

> This was the first day in my life that I had regarded these accusations with justice. There remained no limit to my amazement when I saw that all these accusations contained no truth. I thought, 'Of course Christianity is not a true religion, but no one has the right to accuse anyone falsely.'
>
> As I took both books in my hands this was the first day I had ever felt shame for the Qadianis.[15] 'Why have they brought false accusations upon Christ?' This thought came to me again and again.

Chaudari now set himself to read the New Testament in a spirit of fairness. The more he read, the more he felt that he was a sinner, while the holiness of Christ pierced his heart.

> I saw also that the Christian religion was not a religion of the body, but a true road to the holiness of the heart. Understanding all this I still did not wish to leave my dear ones and relatives, but on the other hand my heart was very uneasy. It seemed to me that Christ was calling me from one direction, and in the other direction relatives were forcing me.
>
> At last salvation, the desire for eternal life, and the infinite love of Christ won the victory over all else, and I decided to become a Christian.

Chaudari then placed at the service of Christ his abilities as a preacher and a missionary.

Jean Mohammed Abd-el-Jalil (1904-1979)

Even more remarkable is the pilgrimage of this young Moroccan from Fez who became a Christian and a Franciscan.[16]

> For the benefit of those who do not know me, I beg to present myself. I am a Moroccan, from the town of Fez, from a poor but honourable family of devout Muslim believers, strict on faith and morals. The family was originally from Andalusia, but had lived in Fez for nearly four hundred years . . .
>
> I was twenty-three and studying at the Sorbonne. I had spent nearly three years in religious enquiry and finally I decided to ask for baptism in the Catholic Church.

Before coming to Paris this young man had studied in the secondary school in Rabat and then, at his own request, in a school run by Franciscans. He explains himself that at this period he had no interest in Christianity:

> The Muslim is so convinced of his faith and of the rightness of his religion that he feels no interest in other religions. He already possesses the Muslim judgement on them, and especially on Judaism and Christianity. To become a Christian would mean going backwards, just as it would for a Christian to become a Jew. There must be therefore something vital, and not merely intellectual, before the religious curiosity of a Muslim is aroused. This is what happened to me.

As a matter of fact, Mohammed's curiosity is aroused because of two factors: his friendly relations with some authentic Christians, and his feelings of hostility towards their religion: 'I went to study Christianity in its citadel, so to speak, in the Institut Catholique in Paris. My sole purpose in taking this step was to find arguments against it. Rather like St Paul, I suppose.'

The reason for such a decision is to be found in the very first days spent in France by the young student. On first arriving in Paris, Mohammed stayed for a while with Franciscans and then found lodgings with a sincere Catholic woman in Viroflay, who received him as a member of the family. He soon involved his hosts in religious discussion and made no attempt to hide his violent hostility towards Christianity. 'One day the lady of the house lost patience and told him: you know nothing, you have not even read the texts, shut up!'

Stung by this attack, Mohammed started to read the Gospels, and was at first pleased to find there only an extension of his Muslim faith. At the same time, he seemed to lose his taste for religious controversy: 'The words "against" or "anti" have been excluded from my vocabulary . . . From my first contact with the Gospel, I have thought I ought to take seriously the words of Jesus who announced that he had not come to condemn but to save.'

While continuing his literary studies at the Sorbonne, he also followed courses at the Institut Catholique, and he was struck more by the personality than by the ideas of the Christians he met:

> One of the greatest graces of my life has been to meet, to converse with, and even to love, exceptional personalities. Two of them were geniuses: Louis Massignon and Pierre Teilhard de Chardin.
>
> Marshal Lyautey, one of the greatest twentieth-century Frenchmen, treated me like a real friend . . . I also had the grace of meeting Jacques Maritain. As I hope anyone who reads my words will perceive, I use words carefully, and I do not speak of 'grace' unadvisedly. When I first met Jacques Maritain face-to-face, and we were alone together in his 'sanctuary' of Meudon, I did not experience him at all as 'Heaven's beggar'—may he forgive me for writing thus of him while he is still alive, if he ever comes to read my words—but truly as Heaven's radiance, a 'beginning of glory'—such was his sweetness, his purity, his humility, his peace, his trust in God.[17]

Maritain was not the only Christian whose intellectual and moral stature made an impression on Mohammed while he was in Paris.

> It was meeting lay people, including especially my teachers, which led me to put the question, 'Is there not perhaps something for me in Christianity, something which can transform my life more than Islam has been able to do? . . .The great virtue which I noticed among these

people was their charity. They really tried to be useful to others, they were solicitous about other people: this was what really struck me. I proceeded to ask a second question: 'Why is this religion so strong?'

Three years were spent in studies, three years of frequent contacts with Franciscans, with Lyautey and with these Christian friends who walked in step with him through his search for answers yet showed respect for his struggles and hesitations. He felt that he was enveloped in a cloud of prayers offered for him by friends who placed him in the hands of God. The philosopher Maurice Blondel, who was going blind, offered the loss of his sight to God for the young Moroccan. Finally he came to the conclusion that God was truly beckoning him, and he asked for baptism in 1928. He became a Franciscan the following year and was ordained priest in 1935. He was appointed to teach in the Institut Catholique in Paris in 1936, and remained there until 1964.[18]

Like most converts, Abd-el-Jalil was for a long time rejected by his family. When reconciliation finally took place, a rumour, totally false, was spread about that he was returning to Islam. In fact he died faithful to the Christ in whom he experienced the fullness of the faith which he had initially received from Islam. It was for this reason that he never abandoned his Muslim name, but wished to be known as Jean-Mohammed.

The world of the Bible

Far from remaining 'a dead letter', the Bible often seems to operate like a living thing. There are those who begin to read it in order to find ammunition against Christianity, but sooner or later the Scripture pierces their armour and knocks on the door of their heart with God's eternal question: 'And you, how are you responding to this summons?' Here are some witnesses who speak of the impact which the Bible has had on them.

Dr Abdul–Qayyum Daskawie

Dr Daskawie was from Pakistan. He was born in 1903 in Sialkot into a learned Muslim family of Arab extraction. His father's brother was a well-known lecturer and author who, among other things, compiled the first Urdu dictionary. His father was a teacher.[19]

Although his family belonged to the Muslim élite, the young Abdul-Qayyum was sent to a Christian college which had a good reputation both for its discipline and its academic standards. He now remembers with amusement the religion classes from which he escaped while the teacher closed his eyes in prayer, or which he only attended in order to ask impertinent questions. His studies ended abruptly in 1920 when Mustapha Kemal Ataturk deposed the Ottoman Sultan, soon to deprive him of the title of Caliph. Indian Muslims were in turmoil and the young Abdul-Qayyum decided to abandon his studies.

He now had time to explore his father's library and he found there a book of anti-Christian polemics written by his uncle. He also found a Bible and proceeded to go through his uncle's book, verifying each quotation from the Bible as he went along. He was particularly struck by the differences between what he believed and what was in the Gospels.

I was particularly impressed by what was said about God and his relation to man. How could there be a God who would wait for the return of a prodigal son? And in any case how could God be a father to man?

Such problems agitated my mind. If I mentioned them to anyone in the family, I knew I would get into serious trouble. I sought the help of a Christian classmate who took me to the Rev. R. McCheyne Paterson, a man of eminent piety and learning. We talked for some time and agreed to meet again.

As my study continued I was entranced especially by the idea of a God of love, a love all-embracing, pure and holy, absolutely different from the love that was so much talked of in our circles; but its full significance was beyond me. The sermon on the mount with its simple yet baffling statements was even more bewildering.

But the things which at this stage I could not accept were the Trinity and the atonement. I did not desire to doubt the faith of my fathers, but I was attracted by this new philosophy of life.

The story might have ended there if his family had not learned of the visits which the young man was paying to the Christian pastor. Without asking for an explanation, his father attacked him one evening, beat him and threw him out of the house.

> A cousin said, 'You were once my brother; now you are an enemy.' My money and keys had gone ... Now that I was cut off from my family, any hesitation I had about my faith in Christ came to an end.

The refugee found shelter in a mission far from his native town.

> Night had come and it was very cold; so I matched my faith against the cold and the thinnest of covering, waiting for the dawn. There was no light to cheer me, but I was filled with an unspeakable joy which kept me warm.

In solitude and poverty, Abdul-Qayyum was obliged to earn his living by teaching Urdu. A few months later, still only eighteen, he asked for baptism. Shortly afterwards he resumed his studies and eventually became Dr Daskawie. He thus concludes his testimony:

> Most people, after reading this account, will ask whether all this lone-liness, privation and suffering had been worth while. In other words, what have I gained by becoming a Christian?
> In the first place, it is not what a man gives up but what he finds that really counts. Would you have offered condolences to the merchant in Jesus' parable who was rejoicing over his great find? I am the man whose ploughshare turned up the treasure and the merchant who was looking for the pearl. The good life in Christ, the knowledge of God that he has brought, and the indestructible hope that he has given me, more than compensate for any trouble I have suffered.

A strange story among scholars

In August 1861, a venerable Muslim leader[20] from Damascus, Ahmed Abd-el-Hâdî, received a letter from an old friend in Aleppo, a Christian.[21] It was a short enough letter, but it drew the attention of the Sheikh to the fact that the Bible, contrary to pop-ular Islamic belief, could not have been altered or falsified, since the Koran itself confirmed its teaching and recommended its read-ing. This letter did not produce any new arguments in the controversy which has divided Christians and Muslims for centuries. It was remarkable only for the fact that it led Abd-el-Hâdî to invite a group of learned Muslims, friends of his, to discuss its contents and to formulate a response.

These men, who occupied important positions in the local government or in the Muslim community, then spent several months rereading the relevant passages of the Koran to discover the real meaning of what was said about the Jewish and Christian Scriptures. For readers who may not be familiar with the Koran, here are two of the passages which these religious men considered:

> We have in truth revealed the Torah wherein is to be found a Direction and a Light. (Koran 5:44).
>
> We have given [to Jesus] the Gospel, wherein is to be found a Direction and a Light to confirm what was said before him in the Torah: a Direction and a Warning addressed to those who fear God. May the people of the Gospel judge men according to what God has there revealed. (5:46–47)

Their careful studies and discussions increasingly impressed these Muslim thinkers of Damascus with the importance of verses such as those above. The most ancient manuscripts of the Bible pre-date the Koran by three centuries, so that these Koranic verses could not refer to a text of the Bible differing from the one we have today.

The searchers therefore turned to the study of the Bible, in obedience to these texts from the Koran in which they had placed their faith and which they had been studying from their youth. Their reactions differed. Some felt that the safer way was to return to Islam as they had always lived it. Others however discovered in the Bible the message of the coming of a Saviour, Jesus, of pardon, and, little by little, of the divinity of this Saviour, his death and resurrection.

At this point, relatives and neighbours became upset and these Muslim scholars were put in prison. Syria at this period was part of the Ottoman Empire, dependent on the Turkish Sultan. The local officials would have been glad to gloss over the affair, but some of the prisoners' colleagues insisted on pursuing it. Eventually they brought the youngest of the prisoners, Omar al-Hâris by name, to imply that he had doubts about the divine origin of the Koran. It was sufficient to accuse him of insulting the Koran and the Prophet. This unfortunate prisoner, seemingly filled with an inexplicable joy, was condemned and beheaded, while his companions were deported to Lebanon.

International opinion was aroused, and the Sultan of Istanbul ordered that the exiles should be allowed to return to their homes after two years. Ahmad Abd-el-Hâdî, who was responsible for starting this whole disturbing episode, was already elderly and he died five years later. Both he and his companions had been baptised in Lebanon and they lost no opportunity for explaining their new faith to other muslims.

Steven Masood

We have already heard the testimony of this young Pakistani Ahmadi. The divisions in Islam had sown the seeds of doubt in his soul, and he had set off on a quest for truth which had earned him the hatred of his family and friends. Eventually he was obliged to flee in order to escape death.

Masood's search for the truth was accompanied by persistent prayer for God to be his guide. After one of his violent quarrels with his father, one part of himself felt that he should let the matter rest and seek only to live in peace; but another voice echoed through his soul: 'This is not the truth, and you know it. Unveil the truth.' He remembered his religious examination in school: 'I have written; but I do not believe.'

> Again I thought, 'Of what value will it be to you if you prove that the Ahmadi way is wrong? Where will you go then? To conventional Islam? But Islam is also divided . . .
>
> I was thirsty and depressed. I went through to the kitchen and drank a large glass of water, then left the house. Outside the moon was full and the shadows of the town were comfortable and familiar. The fresh air seemed to sweep away the cobwebs of my mind and I walked on to the edge of the town, away from the subdued bustle.

There I sat down on a big stone and looked at the moon. I felt full of praise for the wise creator who had made all things so wonderfully. The stars and the moon seemed so perfect and clean when compared with the problems of my world, there in Rabwah town.

In my heart I felt a quiet urge to tell God everything. 'Take your problems to him,' my heart seemed to say. 'He is the great creator and he can reveal himself to you. He is the God who can solve your problems. He can do it, for you have a desire to know him.'

At this thought, tears came to my eyes. I spread out my hands to the starry heavens and said from a sincere heart, 'O God, great creator, I call upon you to help me. I beg you to lead me to the light and the truth, or else change me so that I will not want to know the truth any more. Why are you silent, O God? I hear about you. I read about you. Now I need to hear you. I need you to lead me.'

I could say nothing more but just wept, alone in the moonlight. Slowly I got to my feet and walked back into the town. And something strange happened. I felt so clearly that I was not alone. Someone was with me on that night walk and I came back with new strength to continue my search for the truth.[22]

This prayer was at the centre of his life during the harsh years which followed. Obliged to leave his family, Masood became a servant in another family, and then, at the age of twenty, was taken in by another orthodox Muslim family.

He spent all his spare time reading the Koran and its commentaries. He too was struck by the verses which speak of the Scripture revealed to Christians and Jews.

I thought of how many times I had recited those words like a trained parrot, but today when I concentrated on them, the words of these verses touched my conscience to the depths. Suddenly, I had a great desire to read the Bible again, to start with a new attitude, a new beginning. Yes, I was aware that they said it had been corrupted and changed. I knew Muslim scholars had warned me that studying the Bible would corrupt and dissolve my faith. But in my heart I knew differently.

If my faith was worth anything at all, then it would survive. It was not like a piece of brittle sandstone that would crack and shatter into a thousand pieces if it was dropped! If you really trust the true God, I told myself seriously, then you will be all right. There and then I resolved to read and study the subject further for myself. I would compare the Qur'an and the Bible.

After all, I reasoned, if the Qur'an admonishes me to have faith in the Bible, then clearly it could not have been changed in Muhammad's time.[23]

As his studies proceeded, Masood discovered the message of the Bible: the message of Christ, of his death, resurrection and divinity.

With each new discovery, he felt more keenly the disagreement between the Bible and official Islam. Rereading the Koran to find the truth, Masood each time discovered a confirmation of the Bible, although this meant giving the Koran an interpretation different from that offered by official Islam. He felt repelled by people who abused their authority to demand blind faith in their own interpretations.

Here, for example, are his reflections on the miracles of Jesus:

The next evening, I opened my Bible at random and read these words:

And many other signs truly did Jesus in the presence of his disciples, which are not written in this book: But these are written, that ye might believe that Jesus is the Christ, the Son of God; and that believing ye might have life through his name (John 20:30–31).

These words seemed to have been written specifically for my need, but again the deity of Jesus stuck in my throat and I could not easily accept it. Miracles! Faith! Eternal life! What sort of man was Jesus Christ, I wondered. More than ever, I resolved that I would study this great life and see where it led me. I knew that the Qur'an mentioned the miracles of Jesus, though they were not always the ones that the Bible mentioned. The Hadith speaks of Muhammad turning the moon into two pieces . . . But the Qur'an definitely stated that Muhammad did not perform miracles! . . .

My mind went to verse 7 in Sura 13 where it is written: 'Those who disbelieve say, "If only some portent were sent down upon him from his Lord. Thou art a warner only."

And further, in Sura 29 verse 50, it is said of Muhammad: 'And they say, "Why are not portent (miracles) sent down upon him from his Lord?" Say, portents are with Allah only and I am but a plain warner.'

In other words, the Prophet Muhammad never claimed to do miracles. But it was clear that miracles were as natural to Jesus as breathing! I was uneasy as I thought this over.

Only God could do miracles. Christ did miracles. Did I dare to draw the logical conclusion—that Christ was God?

My heart trembled in prayer: 'O, creator God, show me the straight path, the path of those whom thou hast favoured, not the path of those who earn thine anger nor of those who go astray.'[24] I wept as I prayed these words from my heart.

At that moment I felt as though someone was in the room and that he wanted to say something to me. I looked around eagerly, but there was no one there that I could see. Yet ... yet someone, something, was calling to me. I looked down at my Bible where it lay open on the desk and took it up. It was open at a different place to the one where I had been reading. With disbelieving eyes I read these words:

Ask, and it shall be given you ... For every one that asketh receiveth, and he that seeketh findeth; and to him that knocketh it shall be opened (Matthew 7:7–8).

God had spoken to me! It was he who had led me to these words. I trembled as I realised that he had accepted my prayer and that he had given me the answer.[25]

Little by little this study of the Bible, constantly confirmed by reading the Koran, led Masood to the conviction that he had finally found the truth. He asked to be admitted to a Christian church. He met the distrust which converts so often find. But his conviction was now strong enough for him to endure both the final rupture with his Muslim friends and the solitude in which he was left by a closed and selfish Christian community.

The consistency of the Christian message

Disunity aroused doubt in the heart of Masood, but faith came back when he found agreement between the Koran and the Bible.

Other converts have trodden a similar path, but it is the *internal consistency* of the Christian view of the universe which is, for them, the hallmark of evident truth.

Monsigneur Paul Mulla (1881-1959)

Such was the case with Mehemet Ali Mulla-Zade, a Cretan of Turkish origin from a liberal Muslim family.[26]

Son of a doctor and local politician, the young boy received a particularly careful education. He received his basic training, including knowledge of the Koran, from a private tutor engaged by the family, and by the age of fourteen he could speak five languages: Turkish, Greek, Arabic, Persian and French. He was sent to Aix-en-Provence, in France, for his secondary studies, and completed a four-year course in three years. He amused himself by asking questions intended to trap the chaplain during religion classes. In 1900, still in Aix, he registered in the faculties of law and philosophy. He speaks, in the third person, of his years in secondary school:

> In this secular establishment, no one was interested in bringing the little Turk into contact with a religion against which he had anyway already been warned. At first the boy's peculiarities brought him into conflict with his schoolfellows: his abstention from pork and wine, his sensitivity about European attempts to take control of the Ottoman Empire and of the Muslim world generally, the fez which he continued to wear with his school uniform as a distinctive sign and to protect his faith, made him the butt of jokes on the part of his fellow-students, who used to make fun of Muhammad's hanging coffin or of his wives or his Paradise or his fatalism. He replied to the taunts of his comrades by accusing them of worshipping three gods, or by comparing their mass and altar to a chemistry laboratory.[27]

Behind this mask however all was by no means secure:

> I lived my interior life in a kind of solitude. It had begun when I was about six. One evening I felt impelled to make a commitment before God to follow in all things what I called 'the right thing'. It was a first conversion or option which welled up out of my heart with an intensity which, while it may not have determined all my subsequent choices, passed judgement on them. It made an indelible mark on my consciousness ... I developed a moral appetite, a need for moral consistency, which made me, in childhood and adolescence, deeply

shocked at the behaviour of adults whose actual conduct so often belied their professed principles. It remained thenceforth my only genuine religious disposition, the root of everything pure, healthy and solid in the depths of my soul.

What then was this shocking inconsistency which Mehemet Ali perceived in adults?

Many of my co-religionists, including my parents and even my teachers, habitually neglected the five-times daily ritual prayer, while teaching me that it was a serious obligation. The same applied to the abstention from wine.

Not being able to count on men, I could only have recourse to God. But my idea of God was too vague and uncertain to provide me with a solid basis . . . In my better moments, I turned to him as the Sovereign Law-giver to bind myself before him in a promise I made to myself . . . For the most part God was a vague presence in my consciousness, a colourless Supreme Being or First Principle whom most men only acknowledge then immediately remove from their consciousness as they seek to live a wholly godless existence.'[28]

It was while the young man was completing his secondary studies that he was introduced to the first elements of philosophy. To him it was a wonderful discovery. He glimpsed the possibility of a new perspective, combining recognition of God, the moral responsibility of man and the building of a better world:

In this way I began to discover another Europe than the Europe of godless humanism: a Europe where religion was no longer a relic on the margin of life, or an atrophied organ, but a living force and the spring of action. I said to myself that I was no longer alone. The regeneration of my homeland would have to be spiritual or it would never recover at all.

The decisive turning-point came in the following year when he met the work and the person of Maurice Blondel:

I quickly perceived that I was in the presence of a high-minded thinker who was at the same time an old-fashioned believer.

I remember still the thrill of opening his doctoral thesis in the university library. In my last year at school I had been very conscious of the need to achieve some kind of reconciliation between the two philosophical currents which had led to empirical positivism on the one hand and to immanent idealism on the other. What was needed was a dynamic spiritualism embracing the whole of human life and thought, proceeding *from the exterior to the interior*, then *from the interior to the highest*, in a kind of mental journey towards God . . . And here I found my wishes more than fulfilled, for I recognised in Blondel a philosopher who started from the very depths in order to rise to the greatest heights. Here was a Sorbonne thesis beginning with the most radical negations and ending in peace and tranquillity with a sign of the cross. I therefore applied myself to the study of a thought so original.

Mehemet-Ali spent several years reading the works of Maurice Blondel. At the same time he became friendly with some students and Christian families who manifested that consistency between life and doctrine which he had found so lacking at home.

His intellectual research was accompanied by moral development and by a growing desire for intimacy with God. He even found a spiritual director who was able to help him to respond ever more faithfully to the call of God in his daily life. In 1905 he asked for baptism and Maurice Blondel agreed to stand as his sponsor. He took the name of Paul. However, the decision to ask for baptism was so stressful that he had to spend several weeks resting!

Mehemet-Ali fully understood the consequences of this decision, so foreign to the views of his family. He even spent a year in Crete trying to explain it to them. On his return he knew that he was called to the priesthood, and he was ordained in 1911. He first taught philosophy at Aix and then moved to Rome where he taught Islamics at the Oriental Institute until his death in 1959.

Hassanayn Hirji-Walji

Quite different was the spiritual pilgrimage of this young Ugandan Asian.[29] Much of the commercial life of East Africa is, or was, in the hands of the Indian community, which is divided between Hindus and various Islamic sects. The family of Hass was among those who were expelled from Uganda by Idi Amin Dada in 1972.

Hass Hirji-Walji had received a fervent Islamic education. He said himself that he had read the whole of the Koran nine times before he reached the age of ten, and he enjoyed taking part in competitions to recite it by heart. His story resembles that of many immigrants, living originally as a minority in Africa but knowing no other country, and then suddenly turned into refugees. After a few terrible months, the Hirji-Walji family settled in the United States. They were received by a Lutheran parish which provided them with a furnished house and fed them for several months.

Far from being in the least seduced by Christianity, the young Hass began studying electronics with only one idea in his head—namely, to convert Christians to Islam. He even spoke at student gatherings to this end. He insinuated himself into a Christian prayer group at the university in order to get to know Christians better and thus be able to convert them. At a meeting in which Billy Graham invited the participants to seek forgiveness for their sins, the young Muslim was so incensed to see so many students exposed to such teaching that he shouted at the preacher during a moment of silence: 'You will be the first to go to hell for teaching a false religion!'

Hass's missionary zeal led him to ever more frequent contact with Christian students. These seemed better disposed than unbelievers. Irritated by suggestions occasionally made to him that he should consider becoming a Christian, he continued to compare the two religions ... still with the aim of converting his Christian friends.

Little by little Hass began to perceive what the Christian message really was:

> As a Muslim, I had to work hard to try to gain salvation. The Christian faith is entirely opposed to a system of works. God requires only faith, complete trust and confidence in the saving merits of the Lord Jesus Christ. By faith one appropriates to himself what Christ has already done for him. Salvation is free! Islam has nothing to compare with this.

Previously I had spurned Christianity as an easy religion. I thought Christians were lazy. I accused them of not being able to fast for a month as I did during Ramadan. There appeared to be no laws for Christians to keep or duties to perform. It seemed foolish to me. But yet, the pieces of the Christian puzzle were coming together and my perspective was beginning to change. I started to wonder which religion might really be more in keeping with the character of God.

As he grew aware of this religious evolution, Hass decided to break with his Christian friends in order to save his Muslim faith. He isolated himself for three months and devoted himself to a renewed study of Islam. He found it so painful however to be cut off from his Christian friends that he accepted an invitation to join them for a weekend retreat, telling himself that he would take part as a witness to Islam.

Hardly had the weekend begun than he felt himself assailed by renewed doubts:

> I did not have the feeling of 'belonging'. . . . It was that our outlook on life, although so similar, was yet *so different*. It was that 'something' which I had sensed all along. Their lives for the most part possessed a special savour, a certain kind of liveliness that was hard to pin down. And I knew that it was somehow linked to their faith. Simply being in their presence made me feel well . . . What was I to make of a false faith that bore such positive and wholesome fruit? One could not argue against it.[30]

Before the weekend was over, young Hass was deep in spiritual crisis. He felt more and more strongly that he was being called to make a decision, and to allow himself to be guided by God who was putting before him . . . Jesus. On the one hand, there was his education, his spiritual and cultural heritage, his family; on the other, this call, this offer of life, this Jesus. Helped by a female friend, he became aware of the call and, with her help, expressed his painful acceptance:

> Dear Lord Jesus . . . I open the door of my life to you and I invite you into my heart. I ask you to come and take over my life and forgive all

the sins I have committed. I pray that from now on I will do everything that is according to your will.

It was so hard to pray this prayer, yet there was another power enabling me to say it. I could have stopped at any point—especially when I saw the faces of my beloved family—but something else kept me going.

'Jesus,' I continued after Carol, 'I thank you that you have already come into my life and that you have already forgiven my sins just as you have promised.' As I prayed these words of thanksgiving, full of faith that what I was saying was true, an unspeakable joy began to blossom forth within me until it flooded my entire being. It was a joy I'd never known existed. And with it came a transcending peace which dispelled all fear of what might come upon me as a result of yielding to the risen Christ. Jesus, the sovereign Lord, enveloped me in a love so overwhelming that I was assured of his very presence. I knew I was weak in myself and my assurance rested not on any determination or stubborn will of my own, but on a quiet peace which came from God.'[31]

Some days later Hass Hirji-Walji told his family what had happened and how he had become a Christian. At first he was thrown out of the home and had to live by himself, but in the end he and his family were reconciled. We have already seen the way in which, one day in the middle of the town, he was attacked and stabbed by a Muslim commando, and only saved at the last minute when the children came out of a nearby school (p. 24). He is now married and the father of a family.

When asked why he had abandoned Islam when he had found it so satisfying and fulfilling, Hass replies: 'It is a question of truth. The answer is that Christianity and Islam forced me to choose one or the other. I was faced with conflicting truth-claims. I had to come to terms with what I had come to know of the teachings of Christ and the Bible. We have to follow truth. And Jesus is the truth.'[32]

Notes

1 L. Rocher and F. Cherqaoui, *D'une foi l'autre*, pp.24–25,51,81,ff.
2 The members of this sect, founded in the nineteenth century by Mirza

Ghulam Ahmad (1830–1897), are very active propagandists of Islam, although they are regarded as heretics and even as non-Muslims by the Muslim world in general.

3 That is, 'Ahmadi'.

4 S. Masood, *Into the Light* (STL Books/Kingsway: Eastbourne, 1986), p.20.

5 *Ibid.*, p.182.

6 Published in the Egyptian daily, *Al-Ahrâm*, on 4 March 1976 with the heading 'Dumb demon'. Quoted by E.S. Sabanegh in MIDEO, 14, 1980, p.364.

7 These two trends should not be pictured as organised parties or schools. They exist as tendencies that may divide members of the same family, and may even tear apart the heart of a single individual. Some may be 'modernists' on certain topics, and 'fundamentalists' in other matters.

8 Witness given by a Pakistani convert in S. Syrjanen, *In Search of Meaning and Identity, Conversion to Christianity in Pakistani Muslim Culture* (Annals of the Finnish Society for Missiology and Ecumenics, No.45: Vammala, 1984), p.102.

9 See, for example, M. Bucaille, *La Bible, le Coran et la science* (Seghers: Paris, 1975). There is an English translation. Convinced that this line of reasoning reduces the Koran to the status of a riddle for half-baked students, some well-known Muslim thinkers have criticised that approach. For instance, Dr Bint Al Shati' in *Al-Ahrâm*, 7 January 1972, p.7. (French translation: 'La Foi et la Science, la logique de la science entre l'authenticité et la prétention', *Comprendre*, No.61, 21 June 1972; and Dr K. Hussein, 'Le commentaire "scientifique" du Coran: une innovation absurde', MIDEO, 16, 1983, pp.293–300. In much the same way, from 1900 until now, some Christians have tried to defend a 'scientific' approach to the Bible, called Concordism.

10 A. A. Mawdudi, transl from French ed. by Gaudeul, Dr J.M, *Understanding Islam* (Leicester, 1973), pp. 27–28. One can find other sources in Islam which let one understand that sufferings may, for a time, befall the believer. A tradition, ascribed to Muhammad, even states: 'If you love God, get prepared for trials.' This type of teaching, however, is not placed on a par with the promise of prosperity in this world and in the next.

11 The clincher in their argument concerned a passage in the New Testament where a comment added by a copyist in 1 John 5:7 has often been thought to belong to the text itself.

12 The Muslim community has always tried to keep the Koran free from textual changes. Yet history shows that there were initially several versions of the same Koran which were destroyed under 'Uthmân's rule (644–656), and that, at one time, as many as fourteen different schools, all recognised as canonical, taught how to read and pronounce differently the same Quranic text (Qirâ'ât).

13 His life story can be found in D.P. Rajaiah, *Lights in the World, Life sketches of Maulvi Safdar Ali and the Rev. Janni Alli* (Lucknow Publ. House: Lucknow India, 1969).

14 His witness was published in *Moslem World*, 32, 1942, pp.69–75.

15 Another name for the Ahmadis.

16 For a good presentation of his spiritual evolution, see P. Assouline, *Les Nouveaux Convertis, Enquête sur des chrétiens, des juifs et des musulmans pas comme les autres* (Albin Michel: Paris, 1982) pp.104–114. See as well 'Un Franciscain doublement fidèle: J.M. Abd-el-Jalil (1904–1979)', *Se Comprendre*, 80/2, 21 February 1980. All quotations given here come from these sources.

17 These words were written by Father Abd-el-Jalil in 1980 in an article in which he also disagreed with Maritain's judgement on the course of the Church since the Second Vatican Council.

18 He wrote many articles and books principally dedicated to Christians and helping them to discover the deeper dimensions of Islam. These works seem to reveal how Father Abd-el-Jalil could experience his Christian faith as a fulfilment of Islam.

19 His testimony is in R.W.F. Wootton, *Jesus more than a Prophet, Fifteen Muslims find forgiveness, release and new life* (Inter-Varsity Press, Leicester, UK, 1982), pp.58–62.

20 There is no priesthood in Islam. But the Muslim community is served by a sort of 'clergy': a class of men trained in the various disciplines of Islamic learning. Members of that 'clergy' are called 'Sheikh' or 'Mollah' (the equivalent of our Reverend), Imam (the one who leads the prayers), Ulama (scholars).

21 Details of that story can be found in a book written in Arabic by an anonymous Syrian author, *Al-Bâkûrat al-Shahiyya* (Sweet first fruits) (Light of Life: Villach, Austria).

22 S. Masood, *Into the Light—A young Muslim's search for truth* (STL Books/Kingsway: Eastbourne, 1986), pp.55–56.

23 *Ibid.*, p.120.

24 This prayer is a quotation from Koran 1:7.

25 *Ibid.*, pp.130–131.

26 C. Molette, '*La VERITE où je la trouve' MULLA ZADE, Une conscience d'homme dans la lumière de Maurice Blondel* (Téqui: Paris, 1988).

27 *Ibid.*, pp.43–44.

28 *Ibid.*, pp.41–42.

29 H. Hirji-Walji and J. Strong, *Escape from Islam* (Kingsway: Eastbourne, UK, 1981).

30 *Ibid.*, p.78.

31 *Ibid.*, pp.85–86.

32 *Ibid.*, pp.107–108.

CHAPTER 4

WITHOUT FAMILY

The rampant individualism of the West sometimes leads Europeans to look with nostalgia on what they see as the strong family life of Muslim societies, their hospitality, the strong ties uniting their groups. Even Christian pastors may occasionally be heard exhorting their flocks to imitate the community spirit of Muslims. Like eighteenth-century European writers, some tend to idealise the openness and tolerance of Muslim society.[1]

How then are we to explain the fact that there are 'refugees' from Islam who seek admittance into the Christian Church precisely because they feel the need for community? Are such persons to be regarded as abnormal and anti-social?

The ideal

It is quite true that Islam proposes an ideal of fraternity and equality. The Koran wished to replace the old Arab tribal ties by a solidarity based on faith: 'Believers are only brothers' (49:10). The tradition expands this vision: "*Believers are as equal as the teeth of a comb; an Arab is not superior to a non-Arab, and vice-versa, nor a black man to a red, and vice-versa. Men differ only in their degree of piety*."

The ideal is clear. Yet the actual organisation of Muslim society creates institutionalised inequalities: between men and women, between slaves and free, between Muslims and non-Muslims.[2] In practice, furthermore, Muslim believers have been unfaithful to their ideal, just as Christians have been to theirs. Muslim societies have often known internal strife, civil war, abuse of power, various forms of censorship and consequent purges, injustices of every kind.

Experience of disunity

Some Muslims become profoundly dissatisfied with their experience of community. This may be due to some aspects of the ideal or to a failure to put this ideal into practice. Whatever be the reason, there are Muslims who have suffered profound social traumas, and they are not always completely healed by the discovery of Christianity.

Violence

In an age when people are becoming more sensitive to basic human rights, it is particularly scandalous that abuses of these rights should be perpetrated in the name of religion. Christianity has its share of such abuses. So has Islam.

INDONESIA

We have already spoken of the wave of conversions in Indonesia, as many as two and a half million, which followed the massacre of communists and their sympathisers in 1965. There is no doubt that these atrocities triggered the movement towards Christianity.

Yet the actual motivation of the converts had not much to do with these events. Research into the initial motivation of these converts[3] has shown that only a fringe group mentioned 'reaction to events' as their initial motivation. As for the others: 17% confess to having tried to protect themselves from the suspicion of being communists; another 20% seem to have given their religion as Christian because they were required by law to declare their religious allegiance. The majority (63%) however spoke of a spiritual hunger (disappointment, anxiety, inner emptiness), or of some particular feature of Christianity, like the Church or the Bible, which attracted them.

While feelings of disgust, as well as fear, may trigger off the decision to convert, the conversion itself is essentially interior and more profound.

This is particularly clear in the case of conversions which take place a long time after the events. An Indonesian explains:

> I went to the mosque every afternoon to pray, but it was no use. The situation did not allow me to worship, because every day I heard slander, felt pressures, and heard threats to those of us who had been communists. One day they called together all of us who had been involved with the communists and then, one by one, they left us standing alone. Then from a far distance they said things that really offended us. After about two years I began to be very unhappy with the actions of the Moslems, and so when I heard there were Christians in a nearby village, I decided to go and see what they believed. I was very impressed by Jesus' teachings on love. The Christians were very different from the Moslems, who were cruel and showed hate toward their fellowmen.[4]

KHALIFA AL GAFSI

In his book on new converts, P. Assouline describes the trial of a Tunisian who was condemned to twenty years' imprisonment for killing his child whom his wife, a Spaniard, wished to take away with her. He explained that he had been carried away by anger: 'Muslim fanaticism and Spanish fanaticism: there is no difference.' He had been sickened by fanaticism, and the behaviour of his wife opened up an old wound and caused him to lose control of himself. The answers he gave during his trial, as poignant as they are incoherent, make us perceive how he felt driven from Islam into Christianity:

> An experience in my village in Tunisia made a big impression on me. One day when I was about fifteen, a group of pious Muslims took hold of a Tunisian who had been talking to a Catholic priest. They stoned him in the middle of the street until he was covered in blood. I was a practising Muslim, but I could not stand that . . .

Later on, once arrived in France I decided to stay there. I wanted to become a Catholic ... I cannot give an explanation. I love this country, I love these people, I love their religion ...

When I was working as a labourer in Evreux, I was given hospitality by a good Catholic French family. They were wonderful. The parents seemed to me to be an ideal couple. I wanted to be like them.

As the public prosecutor tried to make him say that he only wanted to be baptised so that he could stay in France, he protested, but could only say: 'These things, you can't explain. It's something inside you.'[5]

Corruption

Corruption, like virtue, seems to be spread fairly evenly all over the human family. When however a sensitive person, especially a child, meets corruption in a religious leader, faith and trust can be destroyed, and that religion itself becomes intolerable.

Michel Larbi (1852-1911) was an Algerian from Kabylia. He speaks of a childhood experience:

My father was very attached to amulets. Indeed he was practically covered with them. Naturally the marabouts were always welcome in our house and they exploited us unmercifully. One day when I came home from herding goats, I was surprised at the fine smell of cooking coming from our house. When I went in I found my mother Halima preparing a splendid couscous, with butter; even more extraordinary, for we were far from rich, a big cock had been killed.

'Is then today a feast day?' I asked.

'No, my son,' she replied.

'What is this fine meal for then?'

'It is not for us, but for a marabout who has promised your father to direct him towards a hidden treasure.'

And right enough off went the marabout with the dish. I began to cry with rage, and then threw stones after him. My aversion for marabouts began on that day. It has been growing ever since.[6]

During the great famine in Algeria in 1868, the parents of Amar, as Michel Larbi was then called, both died. The misery was so widespread that traditional family solidarity broke down completely. There were children wandering about everywhere, young vagabonds begging in order to survive and chased from the villages with stones.

Amar was picked up by the French authorities, along with hundreds of others, and placed in one of the orphanages opened by Archbishop Lavigerie of Algiers. After his baptism some years later, Amar recounted his first impressions of Christians: '*In my childish head, I could not help contrasting the way I had been treated by my fellow-Muslims with the charitable behaviour of the Christians.*'

Eventually Amar entered the seminary and became a member of the missionary congregation founded by the same Archbishop Lavigerie. At the heart of his conversion there were his experiences of two religious communities: on the one hand, the rapacious marabouts and the rejection meted out to the orphans by their own people; on the other hand, the substitute Christian family where the orphans were not only housed and fed but also treated with affection. Many of the orphans were later to speak of this. Until his death, Father Michel Larbi retained this contrasting vision of the two communities, one of them signifying for him corruption and rejection, and the other generosity and hospitality.

Educational traumas

With *Nureddin Ishraqiyyah* we come to a story which reminds us of many young Christians who have bad memories of their years of education in religious institutions. Too often the outcome has been that their religious faith, far from being strengthened, has been extinguished.

This story concerns a Lebanese Muslim, the son of a teacher. He was born in 1931, and the family was continually on the move as the father received different appointments. Like all Lebanese of his generation, he had some superficial acquaintance with different religious communities. In particular he was aware of Christians and he paid occasional visits to their churches and witnessed their ceremonies.

When he was sixteen, he was directed by his father to a

boarding institution for Islamic studies. He made no complaint at first, but as time went by he felt more and more homesick, and resented the rules, the minute and suspicious regimentation, the traditional instruction, the archaic teaching methods. He was disgusted by the system of secret informers and by the petty black-marketeering in which some of the teachers were involved. He went to Egypt to finish his studies and found the atmosphere no better there. His exasperation led him to tear up his diploma when he received it.

He then decided to leave home and go and seek employment as a teacher abroad. Deeper than this merely external exile, another flight was taking place in his heart. It found expression in a recurring dream in which he felt that he was being called to leave the path he was on and take a road leading to a church. This and other dreams of the same type kept recurring over a period of years. It was only in Libya, after twelve years of hesitation and reflection, that he found the courage to admit the attraction he felt for Christianity. Another year passed before he responded finally to what he knew was God's call.[7]

Family divisions

As divorce becomes more frequent in the Western world, people are discovering its negative effects on the psychological development of children. The Muslim world has not escaped this scourge. As is well known, divorce is common in some Muslim countries. Polygamy and divorce are permitted by Islam, and it is not surprising that women and children can come to see in religion itself the source of their unhappiness.

The unwanted ones: illegitimate children and their mothers

In the Muslim world, illegitimate children are rejected. Muslim countries, like those of the West, have seen in recent years a decline in traditional values, and this has led to a vast increase in the number of children born out of wedlock.[8] Whatever steps governments may take to alleviate the situation, single mothers and their children are still rejected by society.

Islamic society is essentially patriarchal, based on the family unit of which the father is the head. There is no place within it for the fatherless child or the husbandless mother.

Fadhma Aït Amrouche (1882–1967) describes with great dignity and sensitivity her situation as an illegitimate child.[9] Her mother could ultimately only protect her child from the malice of her neighbours by placing her in an orphanage.

After a disastrous experience in a religious orphanage, Fadhma entered a combined orphanage and secular school. After successfully completing her education, she decided to become a teacher. This proved to be impossible. In the end she found employment in a hospital run by religious sisters, and at the same time she found in the missionary community a new family. She remained deeply injured by her experiences, hyper-sensitive to any suggestion of contempt or gossip.

When Fadhma married a Christian Kabyl teacher, she adopted his religion, with which she was already familiar. Her conversion however seems to have been more to a new community than to a new faith. For better or worse, the missionary world of fathers and sisters became the wider family within which the couple and their children developed. Both husband and wife retained links with their families of origin, but little by little they drifted away from them as they made new friends and developed different interests and convictions.

Fadhma does not cover up the faults in the missionary world which she thus entered, but at the same time she makes it clear that it was a world in which she, outcast though she was, found acceptance and respectability.

Not a few young Muslims in Western European countries go through similar experiences. Life in France often means that the traditional family institution is undermined, and parents may react by seeking to exercise tyrannical supervision over their daughters and by forcing them into arranged marriages. One result of this situation is that girls devote all their efforts to their studies in order to achieve independence; some have recourse to dissimulation, others even run away from their families, in a general atmosphere of sexual permissiveness. Associations have been formed to help girls who have incurred family displeasure and ostracism in this way.

Some single Muslim mothers, recognising that they can never be accepted in a Muslim community, approach the Church and ask for baptism for their child. Clearly, their motives are mixed. There is a religious motive, but it is fed by the natural human need for community—here, the Christian community. And yet, there may lie some incipient stirrings of faith if there is trust in the ideals of that community.

Orphans and the handicapped

We have already spoken of the religious pilgrimage of a number of young Muslim orphans. The 1868 famine in Algeria produced thousands of orphans, and in our world today there are still many children who find themselves without parents as a result of war or natural calamity. Only a minority find in this tragic experience an interior call to the gospel.

Christian churches on the whole can say with honesty that the help they offer to the needy does not lead, and is not intended to lead, to winning 'converts'. The vast resources expended on humanitarian aid by Christian agencies produce no return in terms of conversions. This is of course absolutely as it should be; for what value could one attach to a bought conversion?

At the same time however individual choices must be respected, and some homeless or sick people, perceive in the help they may eventually receive that this help sprang from faith. Human persons, meeting for material reasons, may be led naturally to deeper friendship and to the exchange of ideas.

Sghir ben Mohammed ben Halima (1860–1909) was orphaned at the age of four. An uncle seized the inheritance and drove out his nephews. The boy was taken in by a parish priest and later sent to an orphanage. When he was eight he decided to adopt the religion of those who had befriended him. In spite of the taunts of his fellow-orphans, he became a Christian. Eventually, as Joseph Roch, he became a priest.[10]

Little *Mohand* (1882–1909) followed a similar path. His mother was destitute and received help from a neighbouring mission. The boy grew up with the mission, accompanying the fathers on their visits and excursions, and defending them when they were criticised. No doubt Christianity was his family before it became his faith, but his faith was no less fervent because of that. He spent long hours in prayer in the chapel, years before he became a Christian. He finally became a religious, taking the name of Brother Valentin.[11]

One may say that, in cases such as these, changing one's family has effected and brought about a discovery of the Christian faith. It is hardly a question of changing one faith for another, for these young orphans had little opportunity of reflecting on the beliefs of the religion into which they had been born. When they awoke to a conscious and personal religious faith, they did so in a Christian environment—the only one in which these children felt comfortable.

Torn asunder across borders

We have looked at people who have been rejected by the Muslim community. But there are also those who feel suffocated because Islam lays too strong a claim on them, even against their wishes.

There is, for instance, the situation of children born into mixed households. Choosing one's religion, even in the case of the child of a mixed marriage, should never be presented as a decision that we take through our own initiative: we do not choose a message because it is pleasing to us; we respond to God's choice, we answer his call as it is addressed to us. This is why it is probably better for the children if parents can agree in which of the two religions they are going to bring up their children. In this way, children hear from the beginning a message that is spoken to them and which calls for a response from them.[12]

At the same time, this response must remain a personal matter. It cannot be determined by others, whether family, government or religious authority. Ideally, especially in a mixed household, children should be helped to discern what is God's call for them. Such discernment however is not easy, since the child is subject to many external pressures, including the pressure of family affection.

Sometimes parents and children try to avoid the necessity of personal choice by passing over the religious problem in silence.

Such attempts however are rarely successful. God knocks on the door of every human soul and demands a response. He may make us feel uneasy, and lead us through a real identity-crisis until we recognise who we must be in response to his call.

THE MARTYRS OF CORDOBA

These ninth-century martyrs are an interesting example of religious choice.[13] Between 850 and 859, fifty persons, officially Muslims, each on his (or her) own initiative, proclaimed before a Muslim judge their Christian faith and their violent rejection of Islam and of Muhammad. One after another they were condemned to death and executed.

What is interesting in the present context is that a considerable number of these martyrs were either the children of mixed marriages or belonged to official circles in which Christians and Muslims spoke the same language and lived the same kind of life. It seems that some of them did not know to which religious community they really belonged: their names could be both Latin or Arabic (Zohra or Rosa; Kâmil or Perfectus). Eventually an inner call made their ambiguous religious situation unbearable, and they were impelled to proclaim their personal faith in the most vehement and outspoken way possible.

This phenomenon happens in modern pluralistic societies where people of different religious traditions are again living side by side. Some of the children born in France to North African immigrants, as well as young people in general who have been deprived of religious and moral education, may experience some unrest of a purely social and cultural nature. But there are also cases in which unrest stems from a divine call to religious faith in a way that needs to be seriously discerned.

PARALLEL EDUCATION

Something should be said at this point about young people who have been brought up simultaneously in a Christian and a Muslim environment.

Pierre Rabhi was born in 1936 in southern Algeria. He has left an account of his childhood in a fairly well-off, traditional Muslim family.[14] When he was about six, his father became convinced that the key to the future lay with education, and the boy was entrusted to a European couple, both teachers. The consequence was cultural dislocation, as the boy had to learn a totally new way of life in matters of dress, housing, cleanliness and time-keeping. He became virtually European during school terms, and then returned to his traditional Arab life during the holidays.

Pierre thus belonged to two families, both of which showed him great affection. Not surprisingly, he became confused. He confesses to having 'suffered very quickly for not knowing which family he belonged to'. 'It was the beginning of the unbearable pain of a divided heart', for when he was with one of his families he felt homesick for the other. He felt keenly the hostility of Muslims towards Christian values and beliefs and was treated as a renegade by his Muslim comrades. He yearned to see reconciliation between the two communities and the two religions. One day his uncle, a Muslim imam, received a visit from two White Fathers, and the boy was comforted to see how friendly the meeting turned out:

> Naturally, I could not follow all the discussions, and my childish interest waned as the relations between the Muslim and the Christian visitors became simply normal. But I could not help feeling a certain satisfaction at seeing religious and racial prejudice give way to a more flexible attitude towards the 'Rumis'. In my child's mind, the people who loved me, my new parents in the south, stood for the whole of their race, and I had acquired a certain facility in forgiving their brothers in the faith.[15]

The child found the continual coming and going very wearisome, and he longed for stability. But he had to complete his studies: that was his father's wish. Finally a psychological choice had to be made between the two cultures:

> I had my Certificate of Primary Education, and my European 'parents' had entered me in a private Secondary School. I could no longer use my native tongue, and to tell the truth I hardly wanted to. Unconsciously I had made a decisive option ... Integration into the

European world was by no means smooth, and I still put up a defensive façade. But my soul was changing. As my religious prejudices began to evaporate, I no longer felt the need of a weapon to confront ambiguous situations. Under the guidance of my 'mother', I devoured European literature and developed a taste for European music. Little by little my aesthetic sense underwent alteration, and the interests and attitudes deriving from my origins were overlaid by those of European civilization. I became accustomed to French food, French customs, French feasts, French language, French art, French thought. Total immersion in French culture wrought a transformation. Yet I had no sense of being disloyal. I was only responding to my own deep need for consistency. Finally the alteration was complete, at least in appearance.[16]

This acute piece of personal analysis shows how Pierre is inwardly torn asunder, although his choices and behaviour masked the fact for a long time:

Deep in my soul I had a permanent sense that my past was in conflict with my actual present and my probable future. Out of necessity, I had to live with endless compromises, I struck and stabbed again and again the colourful and careless bird that kept claiming its right to live.[17]

Little by little the religious world of Islam lost its hold on the inner life of the growing boy. When he began to discover the Bible and the Gospels, he was transported with delight. The aesthetic appeal grew into religious faith. He experienced a real conversion to Jesus Christ and asked for baptism. But the psychological trauma of a sundered soul remained.

The collision of the two cultures which surfaced violently during the Algerian War did not ease the young man's interior conflict. Living now in France, with a French wife, Pierre sought peace by fleeing civilisation to live a life closer to nature in a remote farm in the Ardèche. Was it a kind of return to the world of his childhood? The 'recovery of a dream', as he expressed it? By living a primitive life in the natural world, a neutral environment, he escaped the clash of cultures.

In a similar way, he sought to avoid the clash of Christian and Muslim religious dogmas by adopting the accomodating belief system of Krishnamurti.

> Is my choice-less self to be seen as the fruit of an act of love between two civilizations, or of the rape of one by the other? Which culture should claim his allegiance, the quasi-feudal culture of Islam or Christian modernity? Was he to crush the 'primitive' or the 'educated' self? Was there a way out, apart from simple denial of one of the two cultures, for one like myself who could no longer belong to my original land but who could neither ever belong totally to the country who received me?
>
> This was the question which tormented me until I realized that such conflicts and ambiguities were typical of the sufferings that befell the entire planet. Krishnamurti taught me that all the paraphernalia of religions and nationalisms, all the ideologies and the cult of flags, diplomas or competitions, were no more than elements of division in the human family, pretexts for perpetuating the endless killing which is still a characteristic of human life.[18]

Clearly the schism in the soul of Pierre Rabhi was not healed. He does not resolve the conflict. He escapes it by denying the validity of both Christianity and Islam. He sees organised religions in general not as roads to truth, but only as factors of division.

The conclusion seems to be that attempts to replace one culture by another lead to religious relativism, almost to agnosticism. The only way to avoid that inner division is to hearken to the voice of the living God when he summons a man or a woman to take a particular route.

HASSAN DEHQANI-TAFTI

A similar pilgrimage, though also very different, has been described for us by a man who became an Anglican bishop in Iran.[19] Hassan was born in Iran in 1920 of a Shi'ite father and a mother who had secretly converted to Christianity. The mother died when the child was five, after commending him to her missionary friends, and asking them to do all they could to bring him up as a Christian.

The growing boy thus found himself caught between a father who wished him to be a Muslim and the dying wish of his mother evoked by missionaries. Like Pierre Rabhi, his childhood, particularly between the ages of ten and twelve, was a continual coming and going between Christian schools and his Muslim family of origin. He describes how his father several times decided to withdraw the child from Christian schools, but changed his mind after consulting Koranic oracles.[20] The boy suffered a short but particularly painful experience in a Koranic school which may have turned him against Islam. At the age of twelve he took a firm decision to become a Christian.

In contrast with Pierre Rabhi, his decision was more directly religious than cultural. Hassan's missionary educators had insisted above all on the religious dimension, and becoming a Christian did not mean that he had to adopt another culture: Iranian he was, Iranian he remained.

Choosing a different religion did not therefore involve a psychological and cultural rupture. Indeed his membership of two cultures, Iranian and European, was a positive advantage, for Hassan was able to translate liturgical and biblical texts into Persian, and felt proud of it. He even tells us that the worldly prestige of his dual cultural situation gave rise to a personal pride which was only healed by what he calls his second conversion in which he was enabled to offer to God his whole existential situation, with all his shortcomings and weakness.

It was undoubtedly this profound anchorage in God and in God's call—deeper than the cultural level—which gave such solidity to the conversion of Hassan Dehqani-Tafti and steeled him under persecution. He became an Anglican priest and then a bishop. In 1979, during the Islamic Revolution, one of his sons was murdered for his faith at the age of twenty, and he himself narrowly escaped assassination in his bedroom. Finally he was driven into exile.

Traumatised or converted?

When we consider these 'refugees' from Islam, a question comes to mind: Is dissatisfaction with one religion a valid reason for seeking entrance into another? Can a religious community be justified in accepting as 'converts' those who cannot stand their brethren in the faith, even if it is for legitimate reasons?

The answer is clear: dissatisfaction with one religious community is not a sufficient reason for seeking admittance to another. Negative experiences in Islam are no substitute for a positive experience of Christ and his Church. Experience has shown that an over-hasty or superficial acceptance of a religiously discontented Muslim by the Christian community can lead to a dead end.

An example of a change of culture thinly coated with a veneer of religious conversion is provided by the story of an Arabian princess, *Salme, daughter of Sultan Sayyid Sa'īd* of Zanzibar, who became Emilie Ruete.

Born about 1840, and brought up in her father's harem, Salme fell into disgrace after her father's death for having intrigued against his successor in favour of one of her brothers. One day a young German trader passed by. He fell in love with the young princess, she was agreeable, and one night they eloped. They stopped in Aden. Salme was swiftly baptised, the pair were quickly married, and off they sailed to Hamburg. Three years later the husband died, and Salme, now called Emilie Ruete, had no other choice but to survive as best she could as a German lady. Years later she decided to return to Zanzibar, much to the embarrassment of everyone, not least her brother the Sultan. She did not even think of becoming a Muslim again nor did she wish to take up residence on her island of origin. She simply returned to Germany, and wrote her memoirs concluding disenchanted: 'I had fled from home as an Arab in every respect and a good Muslim. What am I today? A bad Christian, and hardly even a half-German.'[21]

We can see how a conversion, and even a life, can end in failure when the change is merely cultural and not a true exodus in faith in response to a divine call. We should however not lose sight of the fact that the Holy Spirit can make use even of these experiences to awaken a soul to faith. There may be a search for the community where God can be found. Dissatisfaction with home can turn into a thirst for the living God. Let us push the argument further:

'It is not the will of my Father that one of these little ones should be lost' (Matthew 18:14).

It often happens that a person has been so hurt in his or her religious community that he or she develops a positive antipathy towards everything which this community represents: God, faith, ritual, prayer. But can't God direct such a wounded soul towards another community so that the life of faith and of prayer may revive?

The case is the same, whether it is a frustrated Christian who becomes a Muslim, or a frustrated Muslim a Christian. The Christian who believes that God is love (1 John 4:8) shouldn't be surprised that it may be part of the divine strategy to prefer reviving love to all doctrinal considerations. As for Jesus, his passion shows us that he preferred to be misunderstood and betrayed rather than leave us to be lost.

Notes

1 On this tendency to idealise Islam, see M. Rodinson, 'The Western Image and Western Studies of Islam', J. Schacht and C.E. Bosworth, *The Legacy of Islam* (Clarendon Press: Oxford, 1974), pp.9–62.

2 On this subject, one could read R. Levy, *The Social Structure of Islam* (Cambridge University Press: Cambridge, 1927/1965).

3 A.T. Willis, Jr, *Indonesian Revival, Why two million came to Christ* (W. Carey Library: Pasadena, Ca., USA, 1977), p.223ff.

4 *Ibid.*, pp.50–51.

5 P. Assouline, *Les Nouveaux Convertis, Enquête sur des chrétiens, des juifs et des musulmans pas comme les autres* (Albin Michel: Paris, 1982), pp.117–220.

   A similar case can be found in L.L. Vander Werff, *Christian*

Mission to Muslims: the Record (W. Carey Library: South Pasadena, Ca., USA, 1977), p.39, where a Muslim Scholar is shocked by the way in which a group of murderers use the Koran for their purposes. Later he was converted to Christianity by the Gospel text of the beatitudes.

6 Miss. Afr. Archives (Rome). *Notices Nécrologiques*: P. Michel Larbi (1852–1911).

7 Nur-ed-din Ishraqiyyah, *Al-Dâ'i' yagidu tarîqahu ilâ l-salîb* (Lost, he finds his way to the cross) (Centre for young adults: Basle, Switzerland), especially pp.70–75.

8 It has been calculated that between 1965 and 1979 this number increased fifteenfold in Algeria, cf. K. Zeghloul, 'Précaires existences—des milliers d'enfants sans foyer, abandonnés à un sort précaire', *Algérie-Actualité*, No. 853, 1982.

9 Fadhma A.M. Amrouche, *Histoire de Ma Vie* (F. Maspero: Paris, 1968).

10 Miss. Afr. Archives (Rome). *Notices Nécrologiques*: P. Roch Sghaïr Ben Halima (1860–1909).

11 Miss. Afr. Archives (Rome). *Notices Nécrologiques*: Fr Valentin Mohand Ramdan n'aït Saâdi (1882–1909).

12 That is why the Roman Catholic Church (*Canon Law*, 1086,2 and 1125–1126) insists on the need to bring up children of mixed households in a climate of practical faith, and not in a sort of religious vacuum.

13 A. Cutler, 'The Ninth-century Spanish Martyrs' Movement and the Origins of Western Christian Missions to the Muslims', *Muslim World*, 1965, pp.321–339; or N.A. Daniel, *The Arabs and Mediaeval Europe* (Longman/Librairie du Liban: London-Beirut, 1975) pp.23–48.

14 P. Rabhi, *Du Sahara aux Cévennes ou la reconquête du songe* (de Candide, ed., Lavilledieu, France, 1983)

15 *Ibid.*, p.72.

16 *Ibid.*, pp.99–100.

17 *Ibid.*, p.102.

18 *Ibid.*, p.11.

19 H.B. Dehqani-Tafti, *Design of My World, Pilgrimage to Christianity* (Seabury Press: New York, 1982).

20 This custom, called *Istikhâra*, consists in opening the Koran at random in order to find God's answer to a particular problem. This answer can be found in the first sentence one reads, or in comparing

the relative recurrence, on that page, of two letters, the first of which signifies approval and the second disapproval.

21 E. Ruete, *Memoiren einer arabischen Prinzessin* (2 volumes, Berlin), reviewed by A. Barine, 'Mémoires d'une princesse arabe', *Revue des Deux Mondes*, February 1889, pp.817–851.

CHAPTER 5

GOD'S COMMUNITY
(1) THE SEARCH

You ask what it is in Catholicism that most warmly, most profoundly and most vitally attracts me. Why does it retain my allegiance? It is not God the Father, nor the Spirit of peace and grace, nor Jesus, nor Mary: my faith is not yet mature enough to attain these realities directly. What enables me humbly to approach them, what I feel most vividly and passionately in Catholicism, is My mother, the Church!

Paul-Mehemet Ali MULLA ZADE to a friend, in Molette,
La Vérité où je la Trouve (Téqui: Paris, 1988), p. 201.

Twentieth-century Western Catholics may find these words astonishing. They know the Church from within, they may say, and they are only too aware of its weaknesses and imperfections. They cannot but feel uneasy when they sing words which seem to be addressed to them by a hostile world: 'I seek the face, the face of the Lord, I look for his countenance in the depths of your hearts . . . But what have you done with him?' Modern films and books tend to present the history of the Church as a long series of either inquisitorial witch-hunts or compromises between the leaders of the Church and the rulers of this world. It is therefore a surprise to hear that two-thirds of the converts to Christianity say that they were attracted to this faith by the Church.

Masks and false trails

All things human are complex and even ambiguous. We are composed of different dimensions, and all of them are reflected to some degree, often unconsciously, in everything we construct.

Inevitable ambiguity

The religious search does not take place in a kind of social and psychological vacuum, unmixed with secondary motivations which may have nothing to do directly with faith. No 'cradle Christians', including priests and religious, can pretend that they remain loyal to their faith solely out of pure spiritual love. However disinterested he or she may be, the Christian remains a human being in whom generosity and egotism live side by side. There is no doubt a thirst for God, but this does not eliminate the need for earthly food.

It would therefore be both unrealistic and unfair to demand of those who seek to enter our churches a superhuman purity of intention. A recent book[1] describes the experiences of a German journalist who spent several months disguised as a Turkish worker. Insecurity, illegal employment, the use of foreign labour for dangerous tasks: all these injustices which form part of modern European society, often without our being aware of them, are strikingly brought out in this book.

One of his chapters is devoted to his encounters with the Church. Several times the journalist approaches a priest and asks for baptism. On each occasion he is rebuffed. The author interprets the refusal as a form of racism, part physical and part spiritual. One may however suggest another explanation: the refusal of complexity.

In each of these encounters with a priest, the journalist presents three interconnected requests: the request for baptism; the regularisation of his union with a German girl whom he has made pregnant; and the extension of his residence permit. It may have been above all this complexity which led the priests to see request for baptism as no more than a device to obtain an extension of the residence permit.

The ambiguity of the request for baptism prevented the priests from taking it seriously. The only priest who showed sympathy offered to supply a false baptismal certificate so that the applicant might obtain his other requests. There is often present in Church circles a kind of super-spirituality which imagines that faith can only be authentic when it is the product of wholly spiritual motives. In fact, however, there can be no wholly unmixed spiritual motives. But the spiritual motives may be, or at least may eventually become, the central factor. Even in matters of faith, motives are always mixed.

When we dwell too much on the secondary motivations, even with a view to rejecting them, we only increase their importance. Purity of intention is not reached by pruning away secondary motivations but by focusing one's attention on the essential.

Islam and 'integral religion'

While people in the West tend to separate faith and politics, faith and science, faith and technology, Muslims, by tradition, often favour a type of society where all these elements are not kept apart. Not surprisingly, this tends to produce regimes in which religious faith and politics are indistinguishable.

We may quote as an example some words from an Egyptian fundamentalist thinker, Omar Talmasânî, written in 1976: 'Islam recognises no distinction between religion and State, between Scripture and sword, between law and society. The Muslim who does not practise his religion in its entirety has not understood his religion.'[2] Islamic education instils the ideal of a society which is the expression of faith in God and of the worship due to him. Naturally, religious aspirations often take the form of a search for the ideal community in which the religious dimension can find full expression.

Negative image of the West

At the present time, many people are aware that their community does not correspond to their ideal, and they may therefore cast their eyes on the wider world to see what is the situation in other communities.

Very often Muslims judge Christianity by modern Western culture. They see in Christianity no more than 'big power' imperialism, callous wealth-seeking, modern technology, the media, pornography, alcoholism, the permissive society: in short, decadence.

The confusion between modern Western culture and Christian faith provoked this reflection from an Indonesian Christian during a meeting between Christians and Muslims:

> All of us in Indonesia feel a terrible frustration arising out of a deep sense of alienation on the part of both Christians and Muslims. The Christian in Indonesia is always identified as a puppet of outside powers, rather than as a citizen of Indonesia. But what we Christians of Indonesia yearn for is to be regarded as Indonesian just as we regard our Muslim brothers as Indonesian.[3]

The same mentality is reflected in the common Muslim propaganda, often found for example on the lips of Colonel Qaddhafi, that Islam is the religion of Africa, while Christianity is the religion of the West and of imperialism. It is quite understandable that a Muslim in search of a new faith-community may be put off by this popular identification of Christianity with the West and its moral corruption.

We have already spoken of the pilgrimage of Chaudari Inayat Ullah from religious polemics to the discovery of the love of Christ. He speaks of how his conversion was retarded by a meeting with two 'Christians':

> I happened to go to a mission station. The missionary of that place was not there, but I remained that night waiting for him. Two 'Christian' young men lived there. They were both of such a kind that their loose actions gave me a loathing for Christianity, and I rose up very early and went home. Previously for some period of time I had been very antagonistic to Christianity, because my faith was upon one (the founder of the Ahmadiyyah) who said, 'I came into the world to break the cross,' and who in his eighty-five books had opposed the Christian religion more than all else. And I well remember that I also was constantly debating with Christian preachers. Then also for some time

back there had been born in my heart doubt concerning Islam. But those two young men pushed me so far from Christianity that I understood that the tree itself could never be sweet whose fruit was so bitter. Accordingly, once more, I made a firm resolve to oppose Christianity.[4]

We have seen how further reading, and encounters of a different kind, finally led Chaudari to revoke his decision and to receive baptism.

The heritage of old hatreds

The negative image of Christianity so often presented to Muslims goes back centuries. In the sixteenth century St Francis Xavier lamented the example of Christianity given by the Portuguese in India. Even earlier, some Muslim polemicists had busily produced an almost racist caricature of the Christian as cruel and corrupt. In 855 the famous Arab writer Jâhiz (776-869) was commissioned by the Caliph of Baghdad to compose a refutation of Christian teaching. He did not however deal with Christian teaching but sought to undermine the popularity of Christians and Jews in his society by presenting them as cunning, unchaste, cruel and degenerate:

> Another cause for the admiration accorded by the masses to the Christians is the fact that they are secretaries and servants to kings, physicians to nobles, perfumers, and money changers, whereas the Jews are found to be but dyers, tanners, cuppers, butchers, and cobblers. Our people observing thus the occupation of the Jews and the Christians concluded that the religion of the Jews must compare as unfavourably as do their professions, and that their unbelief must be the foulest of all since they are the filthiest of all nations. Why the Christians, ugly as they are, are physically less repulsive than the Jews may be explained by the fact that the Jews, by not intermarrying, have intensified the offensiveness of their features.

We need not dwell on the comparison he proceeds to draw between the consanguineous marriages of the Jews and the breeding of animals. He then speaks of the cruelty of Christians who, he says, castrate their boy infants, mock Muslims, and make converts everywhere:

> And the Christian, though cleaner in dress, though engaged in more refined professions, and physically less repulsive, yet inwardly is baser, filthier, and fouler; for he does not practise circumcision, does not cleanse himself from pollution, and in addition eats the flesh of swine. His wife, too, is unclean. She does not purify herself from the defilement of menses and childbirth; her husband cohabits with her in her courses, and, in addition to all this, she too is uncircumcised. In spite of their evil natures and over-ruling lusts, their faith offers no restraints against passion such as eternal hellfire in the world to come or punishment by religious authority in the world we live in.
>
> How indeed can one evade what harms him, and pursue what profits him if such be his faith? Can such as we have described set the world aright? Can anyone be more fit to stir up evil and corruption?[5]

We must admit that texts such as these are rare. For the most part the Muslim anti-Christian polemic concentrates on dogmas and laws. It is, however, useful to cite such texts as the above to show the ancient hatreds and antagonisms between the two communities. It is no help to ignore these hidden feelings.

Popular culture, both Christian and Muslim, has passed on these prejudices from generation to generation. Everything, from food and drink to personal hygiene, has been turned into an offence and an obstacle to mutual respect. The disgust has to be recognised before it can be dealt with. We must neither feel guilty about these revulsions nor try to defend or justify them lest they turn into permanent racism.

It is evident that Muslims who begin to take an interest in Christianity have to overcome a mountain of mistrust and revulsion. They cannot do this on their own. The same of course applies to Christians in countries with a long history of anti-Muslim prejudice and who wish to approach Islam in a spirit of good will.

The heritage of the Koran

Something needs to be said about remarks in the Koran concerning Christianity and other religions with a scripture.

Many people are under the impression that it is from the Koran that Muslims learn to despise Christians and treat them as 'infidel dogs'. This, however, is untrue. It is not principally the Koran itself but the writings of Muslim apologists which have created these anti-Christian attitudes at a popular level, and even among intellectuals. The Koran gives rather a complex picture of the disciples of Jesus.

A positive image, in these two passages:

> You will observe that those who are closest in friendship to the believers are those who say, 'Yes, we are Christians'; for you find among them priests and monks who are not puffed up with pride. You will see tears in their eyes when they hear what has been revealed to the Prophet and recognise therein the Truth. (5:82–83)
>
> [After the prophets] we sent Jesus, son of Mary. We gave him the Gospel. We have planted in the hearts of those who follow him meekness and compassion. We did not ordain the monastic life, but they instituted it themselves, motivated solely by the search for the satisfaction of God. But they have not observed it as they should have done. (57:27)

Then follows the recognition that human beings are not perfect:

> We have rewarded those among them who have believed, while many of them are perverse. (57:27)

Towards the end of the life of Muhammad, the attitude towards Christians becomes much more negative and we see the beginning of the long history of confrontation between the two communities:

> O you who believe! Do not take as your friends either Jews or Christians. They are each others' friends. He among you who takes them for friends is one of them. God does not guide an unjust people. (5:51)

Fight: against those who do not believe in God and the Last Day; against those who do not declare unlawful what God and his Prophet have pronounced unlawful; against those People of the Book who do not practise the true religion. Fight against them until they have been humiliated and paid the tribute.

The Jews have said: Uzaïr is the Son of God! The Christians have said: The Messiah is the Son of God! Such are the words which come forth from their mouths. They repeat what the unbelievers have said before them. May God destroy them! They are so stupid! They have taken as their lords, instead of God, their doctors and monks, as well as the Messiah, son of Mary. (9:29–31)

All this does not prevent the Koran in earlier verses from inviting Muslims of all times and countries to respect the faith of faithful Christians, and even to see in the plurality of religions a plan of God which will continue until the Last Day:

May the people of the Gospel judge men according to what God has revealed therein. The perverse are those who do not judge men according to what God has revealed.

If God had wished, he could have made of you a single community. But he wanted to test you by the gift which he has made to you. Try to outdo one another in good deeds. You will all return to God, and then he will enlighten you about the differences between you. (5:47–48)

It is clear that there are texts in the Koran which by no means convey an entirely negative image of the Christian community. When the Christians encountered in daily life are sympathetic and visibly believers in God, more weight will be given to the positive statements about Christians in the Koran, while the negative statements will be seen as addressing the particular context in which Muhammad lived rather than the present situation.

When all this has been said, however, it remains true that the religious atmosphere has been so poisoned by polemicists on both sides that the positive statements about Christians in the Koran, however often cited, may have little practical impact.

Christian France

This heading may look strange. However, it should be borne in mind that there is sometimes a double element in the phenomenon of conversion: there is both the discovery of Christian faith and a fascination with the world of European culture. The two are not easily separable.

Augustin Iba Zizen (1898–1980), a Kabyl and a Christian, ended his career in France as a lawyer in the Council of State. He left two books in which he described the cultural, religious and political elements in his life-experience.[6] He very clearly describes two parallel conversions: on the one hand his passionate love for France, which led him to enlist in the First World War, eventually becoming an officer; on the other hand he had a yearning for intimate friendship with God which attracted him to Christianity. This is what he has to say about the first of these conversions:

> Bernanos has said that converts are a disturbance. I must be a very disturbing person, for I am a double convert, to Christianity and to France! Without denying anything of my roots, I accepted with both hands what was offered to me by my French school. I decolonised myself by pronouncing myself the equal of all those about me. There were stormy periods, no doubt. I swallowed as best I could the bittersweet potion offered to us by French colonialism, as I have explained in my first book . . .
>
> I proceeded on my way without ever ceasing to be dazzled by what I had received from France. I have loved France. I have fought for her. Shame on Poirot-Delpech for what he says when speaking about Romain Gary: 'Patriotism like this looks very odd in our day. You hardly meet it among those who are French by accident of birth; it is now the preserve of writers who have chosen their fatherland for themselves. The trouble with filial piety is that it does not come from a free choice.' I scorn such scorn. Whether I am a disturbance or not, I have two mother-countries: one, Kabylia, according to the flesh, and the other, France, by choice and according to the spirit. I find disagreeable the fashionable ideology which takes pleasure in running down France and calling it wicked, egotistical, sectarian, racist, incorrigible. I know from experience that some sons of France deserve to

be so described. But I know also the treasures which she has opened
to me.

He speaks of the great monuments: Notre Dame, la Sainte
Chapelle, the Louvre, Versailles, Chartres, Mont Saint Michel:
'the whole land, with its cathedrals, its museums, its laboratories,
its learned men and its saints: how can one belong to such a
country and not realise what it represents?'[7]

He was stunned by the tragic massacres in Setif,[8] but he was
still able to speak of the real France, the France of its ideals:

> I willingly concede that the collective crime of May could shatter the
> convictions of an enthusiast for France. Can I respect myself and still
> love her?
>
> There was a moment of doubt, I will not deny. I needed all the
> powers of my reason, all the vitality of my first enthusiasm, all
> the drive received from my father and my first teachers, all my powers
> of self-mastery, to avoid the apostasy of flinging into the fire every-
> thing that I had previously worshipped . . . I had set France so high in
> my mind and so deep in my heart!
>
> In my indignation, all the dark pages of French history rose up
> again in my memory: the killings of the Cathars at Monségur, the
> shameful night of St Bartholomew, the September massacres and the
> atrocities in the Vendée during the Revolution, the walls streaming
> with blood after the firing-squads of the Second World War . . .
>
> Should all these horrors be laid specifically at the door of France,
> or should we not rather recognise in them humanity itself run riot?
> Moreover—as Péguy is my witness—there have always been
> admirable sons to redeem the sins: the burning charity of St Vincent
> de Paul, the names of Schoelcher and of Charles de Foucauld: these
> are only examples of so many whom it would be wearisome to
> catalogue.[9]

All this is a valuable reminder that in judging a culture we should
contemplate its best fruits and not its dregs. Religion too can only
be truly judged by its saints. It is in this spirit that L. Massignon
invites Christians to know Islam by its saints and mystics and not
by the excesses of some of its adherents. Each religion and each
culture attempts to tame the natural savage in humankind by

injecting certain ideals, like liberty, equality and fraternity, and certain principles of order and harmony and organization. It is in these ideals and these principles, and not in a human nature left to its natural barbarism, that we find the real identity of religions and cultures.

Augustin Iba Zizen truly idealised French culture:

Born a child of Kabylia, and a subject of France,[10] I soon developed all the neophyte's enthusiasm for everything that had made France what she is, beyond all the dark pages of history. From my adolescence, I seized every opportunity to identify myself with France. I defended her with all my heart, and that earned me the right to belong to her as a citizen.

This passion may be incomprehensible to less ardent spirits, whose commitment is only partial and who consider confrontation more important than enthusiasm. But my generation was the first to have the opportunity of drinking fully from the springs of this culture. Its name was France, and we gazed upon it as upon a marvel. We did not distinguish, as later generations were to do, between the culture and the country which dispensed it. The only problem for me was how not to lose a drop of what was offered. And when came the time of rupture, I was too deeply immersed in a country for so long regarded as my own that I could not change my allegiance. And yet, for all that, it was also impossible for me to break with my native Kabylia.[11]

Unlike Pierre Rabhi, Iba Zizen did not feel that two rival worlds, and two different cultures, were competing for his allegiance. France was culture, its values were the supreme values. His kabyl roots did not draw him away from this ideal. We shall see shortly that a spiritual quest, as deep as it was tenacious, was at the same time secretly in progress in the depths of his spirit, relegating the cultural debate to second place.

Socio-cultural prejudices

A scandal or a fascinating model: Christianity has been seen as both these things also in terms of social standing.

We have already seen how *Habib Wardan* still saw Christianity as the religion of the rich and powerful, even after his discovery of the

Young Christian Workers had brought him into contact with Christians who threw in their lot with the poor.[12]

Yet in certain Muslim countries, far from being the religion of the powerful, Christianity is above all the religion of the poor and despised. In Pakistan, most Christians belong to the lowest castes: the sweepers, the scavengers, 'the tribals'. In Saudi Arabia and the Gulf, the Christians are poor immigrants who have come from the Philippines or elsewhere in search of work.

In this latter context, the Muslim who comes to Christ knows that he is going to drop to the bottom of the social ladder. The struggle continues after conversion, for the convert finds it very difficult to associate religiously with a group with which he can neither identify himself nor establish normal social relations. A Pakistani speaks of his hesitations when he was contemplating conversion: 'It is difficult: our society is what it is. Whenever anyone tells my family what has happened to me he will say: Your son has joined the rag-pickers and sweepers. He will not say, he has put his faith in Christ, but, he has become a sweeper.'[13]

Bilquis Sheikh is a Pakistani lady of high rank whose husband was at one time Minister of the Interior. We shall see later how she experienced the fatherly tenderness of God and, little by little, heard the call of Christ echoing in her soul. When she arrived at the moment of decision, she made the following reflections:

> And I thought of my daughter Tooni. Surely this young woman had enough worries already. And there were my other children; although they lived far away, they too would be hurt if I 'became a Christian'. And then there was my Uncle Fateh, who had watched so proudly the day I was four years, four months, four days old and began learning the Koran.
>
> And there was beloved Aunt Amina and all my other relatives, some hundred 'uncles', 'aunts' and 'cousins'. In the east, the family becomes biraderi, one community, with each member responsible to the other. I could hurt the family in many ways, even interfere with the opportunities of my nieces getting married, as they would have to live in the shadow of my decision if I chose to join the 'sweepers'.[14]

'Tailor-made' conversion

There are Westerners over whom the 'mysterious' East, with its rituals and spirituality, exercises a strange fascination. In a somewhat similar way, there are Muslims who are fascinated by Christianity. They find it strangely exotic in comparison with the sobriety of Islam. Sacred art, religious music, liturgical hymns and vestments: all these things can be the beginning of a journey towards Christ.

Then there are those who can accept the Christian message, but are reluctant to enter the Church for reasons of national or cultural identity, or because they are repelled by the cultural forms of Western Christianity. When one has been the victim of racial hatred one may even become passionately attached to one's culture of origin.

Hence a variety of spiritual journeys combining very differently faith and culture.

From nationality to faith

Mohammed arrived in France just before the Algerian War. He belonged to a devout family and was himself a fervent Muslim.

> His comrades often reproached him, 'You are always going to the mosque, and never to the pub.' After four or five years, he became less assiduous in his attendance at prayers. One day he assisted at the burial of a Christian friend and thought, 'I would like a burial like that.' Immediately after the ceremony, he bought a slice of bacon. He had never eaten pig's meat before, and found it good. Mohammed is no longer a true Muslim. From time to time he goes into a church to pray, without knowing too well which God he is praying to.[15]

After a failed marriage, this humble, plump little man wandered about French society, wanting to become part of it, yet at the same time looking for his roots. He felt French. He did not ask for Algerian nationality after independence and did not set foot in Algeria for fifteen years. But he could not shake off his homesickness. He bought records of Arab music and finally decided to return to Algeria. His family was willing to arrange a good

Muslim marriage for him if he would renounce his French nationality. Mohammed reacted vigorously: 'Keep your girl. As for me, I am keeping my nationality.' Later on he was annoyed when he heard one of his brothers say to his wife, 'That is no business of yours. You do not belong to the family.'

He entered into a civil marriage with a Portuguese woman by whom he had three children. On the day of his son's birth, he was so overjoyed that he said to his wife, 'Ask me anything you like.' She replied that she would like to have a Church marriage. He could not refuse, and it was while he was preparing for the ceremony that he discovered Christian faith. The parents were married in church on the day of their son's baptism. On Easter Sunday 1987 Mohammed himself was baptised.

Here was a case in which religious conversion only followed after several years of gradual integration into French society. The conversion was not produced by that integration, but the social experiences of burial, marriage and baptism of the child.

From faith to nationality

There can also be a movement in the opposite direction. At first the converts may have no thought of separating from their community or country of origin. But when family and friends regard their action as an intolerable act of treason, they have no alternative but to go into exile and look for a country which will accept them.

Such was the case of *Paul Mehemet Ali Mulla*, whom we have already met.[16] He asked for baptism after discovering Christianity through the work of Maurice Blondel. After his baptism in 1905, he spent a year with his family in Crete trying to explain his decision. He was unsuccessful and returned to enter a seminary in France. At this point, he met a politician from his own country, one of the leaders of the opposition to the Ottoman regime. Speaking of himself in the third person, he gives an account of the interview:

Just before he was due to receive Holy Orders, he paid a visit to Ahmed Riza, a Turkish statesman living in exile in Paris from where he opposed the despotic regime of Sultan Abdul-Hamid. Some months later, after the revolution of the 'Young Turks', this man would return to Turkey. He was a convinced secularist, yet he made it clear to the seminarian, courteously but firmly, that, as long as he persisted in a way of life which his people were not yet in a position to understand, there could be no place for him in a liberal Turkey.

Seeing no hope of an immediate return to his home country, the young priest therefore remained in France.[17]

This situation led him to apply for French citizenship. He worked first in Aix and then in Rome instead of returning home. For others, the outcome was more tragic.

Nabil is a young Egyptian who fell ill while he was on a visit to Lebanon. He spent the long days in hospital idly turning over the pages of a book. It happened to be one of the Gospels. Gradually the text began to capture his attention and he started meditating on it. The slow process of conversion extended over several months until finally he asked for, and received, baptism. He wrote to his family in Egypt to explain the step he had taken. The response was swift. He was found half-dead in a Beirut street after his family had sent killers to defend the honour of the family. In hospital he was found to have sustained eighteen fractures. He survived and tried to live with his family in Egypt. It proved impossible, and he is now wandering from town to town, pursued by his brother, and living as a fugitive.[18]

Even more dramatic was the end of *Qamar Zea*, a young Muslim from southern India. After her conversion to Christianity she became Esther John and fled to Pakistan where she studied nursing. Eventually she found employment in a Christian mission. After receiving, and rejecting, an ultimatum from her family, she was found dead in her bed with a broken skull in 1960.[19]

These examples are not intended as specific reproaches to Islam. All religions have known similar outrages, and the ideologies which replaced religion have been guilty of even worse excesses. The massacres perpetrated by Stalinism in Russia, by National Socialism in Germany, by Maoism in China and by the Khmer Rouge in Cambodia outdo any atrocities of Christian inquisitions or of the 'most Muslim' Tamberlaine

(1336–1405).[20] We have sited these cases simply to help us understand how conversion to the Christian faith may eventually force a person to seek another nationality.

Faith, yes! Culture, no!

Under the eye-catching headline '*Zohra, a Christian Muslim*', a journalist recently described the position of an Algerian woman of thirty-six married to a Frenchman who had become a Muslim. She was captivated by the figure of Jesus, and fell in with some Christians who were trying to live the Gospel. She asked for baptism and received it, twelve years before the journalist came across her. Her decision did not cause a rift in her family:

> At first things were not easy. They were afraid that I was no longer their daughter. I did not rush them, and we spoke of what had happened, frequently and affectionately. My father is very good and a firm believer. One day he said to me, 'Listen, do what you have to do, it is God who calls, and he calls as he wishes.' I was able to be baptised when I was twenty-five, but I did not cease to be a Muslim.

When the journalist expressed surprise and asked how she could be a Muslim and a Christian at the same time, she replied:

> I understand your question, but I do not like it. I am a believer. I dislike the expression 'Christian and Muslim' because it does not do justice to my quest for God. My faith is one; I do not take a bit from here and a bit from there, practising this particular Muslim rite and this particular Christian rite. I am in search of God, and whenever I find something which will speak to me of him and bring me into his presence, I embrace it. But I know now that it is Jesus above all who is that 'something'.

Zohra accepted the doctrine of Jesus as Son of God, and even studied at the Institut Catholique in Paris. At the same time, within her Christian faith, she retained a certain sensitivity, a certain spirituality of the transcendent, which she owed to her Muslim upbringing:

I believe that the intimacy with God which comes through Christ and the Spirit is only possible to the degree that one maintains a certain distance. In this respect, perhaps you are right, I remain very Muslim. For me, spreading the mat before prayer and making the ablutions are marks of respect which I absolutely need. Your easy-going manners in church make me uncomfortable. Knowing that God is near, that he came among us, does not mean that we should lose sight of his transcendence.[21]

Zohra remained faithful to the Muslim ritual of the five-times-daily prayer. She shows us that it is possible to retain one's original culture, even one's religious culture, while fully living the Christian faith. Islam, as she lives it, is not a body of doctrine in opposition to Christian doctrine, but a movement towards God which finds its fulfilment in Christ.

Other converts also feel called to become Christians while retaining their Islamic culture. A distinction thus emerges between Islam as a faith, some of whose beliefs may be incompatible with Christian belief, and Islam as a culture, which the Church can adopt, as she can adopt any culture, in order to live the Christian faith in a new fashion.[22] This is no doubt a new phenomenon, and it may be at first confusing for members of both communities; but one would be wrong to assume automatically that people who try to combine Islamic culture with Christian faith are merely syncretists, playing a double game and seeking to have the best of both worlds.[23]

The refusal of unnecessary rupture

More and more, new Christians are trying to adopt a way of life which does not cut them off either from their family or from their culture.

After his baptism, *Habib Wardan* explains how he resumed his life in the midst of his people:

In the district in which I lived, I met no Christian, and I would go and receive Communion several towns away, for the Islamic community which was my cradle remained in my heart. I would never affront my people by letting them see me mix with another crowd of faithful.[24]

Sakina was the daughter of a Shi'ite mullah from India. She discovered Christian faith at the age of fifteen when she was living in a religious boarding-school in Paris. At first she was refused baptism on the grounds that she was too young. When she was twenty, she asked again and was again refused, this time because she was living with a young man, a Christian, whom she intended to marry. She was however reluctant to make the open breach with her father which a public religious marriage would inevitably provoke. The priest who was helping her explained:

> Sakina was still only twenty and was not willing to oppose her father, nor to make a gesture of independence which would have led to a rupture. She was not prepared to proclaim to her family, 'Whether you like it or not, this is how things are, and I am going to marry Jean-Marc.' I tried to explain to her that if she was not ready to break with her family by proclaiming her marriage, neither was she ready to make a similar break by being baptised.[25]

He adds that, although at first angry, Sakina came to understand the justice of this temporary refusal of baptism. She received the sacrament a couple of years later.

We cannot pass judgement in cases like these without knowing all the details, but one can surely say in general that an unwillingness to break with one's family is by no means always a sign of cowardice or immaturity. One can be perfectly adult and yet not wish to break with one's parents unless absolutely driven to it.

The first Christians had no difficulty in accepting that converts might be known to their brethren in the faith without informing their own family. Christians were only required to make a public statement of their faith when faced with a demand incompatible with that faith.

There may, of course, be cases in which the new convert is unable to keep silent about his or her convictions. A faith which is not publicly acknowledged can more easily be eroded, and one might even say that some ruptures can be positively helpful.

There are thus many different choices possible. They will all express authentic conversion provided only that in the end faith takes over. Each has to respond to the particular appeal which God addresses to him or her, to integrate into the community which God indicates, to adopt the style of life which God wishes. All this calls for discernment: the search to discover the personal vocation of each human person.

Notes

1 G. Wallraff, *Ganz Unten* (Verlag Kiepenheuer; Köln, 1985). French translation: *Tête de Turc* (La Découverte; Paris, 1986). The particulars mentioned here are to be found on pp.54–81.

2 Omar Talmasânî, in *Al-Da`wa*, No.3, September 1976, pp.2–3 (editorial), quoted by O. Carré and G. Michaud, *Les Frères Musulmans* (Collection Archives, Gallimard/Julliard; Paris, 1983), p.117. On the Muslim Brothers, one could consult *Etudes Arabes* (publication of PISAI, Viale Trastevere 89, 00153 Rome), No.61 (1981–82), No. 62 (1981–82).

3 Professor Ihromi, Indonesian theologian at the Chambésy meeting (June 1976), cf. *International Review of Mission*, No.260, October 1976, p.445.

4 Chaudari Inayat Ullah, 'My conversion from Islam', *Muslim World*, 32, 1942, pp.69–75.

5 J. Finkel, 'A Risâla of al-Jâhiz', *Journal of American Oriental Society* (New Haven, 1927), pp.311–334. See, in particular pp.327–328, 333.

6 A. Iba Zizen, *Le Pont de Bereq'Mouch, ou le bond de mille ans* (La Table ronde: Paris, 1979), and *Le Testament d'un Berbère, Un itinéraire spirituel et politique* (Albatros: Paris, 1984).

7 A. Iba Zizen, *Le Testament d'un Berbère*, pp.18–19.

8 At the end of the First World War on 8 May 1945, riots took place in the region of Constantine (Setif, Guelma, etc). According to the newspapers, 103 Europeans were massacred. Reprisals were carried out by the French army on such a scale that official sources reported 1,500 Algerians killed. Nationalists later advanced a number of 45,000 victims. Historians (R. Aron) suggest a more likely estimate of 6,000 dead.

9 A. Iba Zizen, *Le Testament d'un Berbère*, pp.163–164.

10 In colonial times there was a difference between the *French subject*, born in a French colony and living under French authority, and the *French citizen* who enjoys the fullness of all civil rights.

11 A. Iba Zizen, *Le Testament d'un Berbère*, pp.189–190.

12 H. Wardan, *La Gloire de Peter Pan ou le Récit du Moine Beur* (Nouvelle Cité: Paris, 1986). The same solidarity with the poor can inspire a conversion to Islam, that of V. Monteil, cf. L. Rocher and F. Cherqaoui, *D'une foi l'autre, les conversions à l'Islam en Occident* (Seuil: Paris, 1986), p.125.

13 S. Syrjänen, *In Search of Meaning and Identity, Conversion to Christianity in Pakistani Muslim Culture* (Annals of the Finnish Society for Missiology and Ecumenics, No.45, Vammala, 1984), p.112.

14 B. Sheikh, *I Dared to Call Him Father* (Word: Waco, Texas, 1978, 1980), p.54.

15 A. Salles, 'De l'Islam au Christianisme (1) La foi et les racines', *La Croix*, 4 March 1987, p.15.

16 See chapter 3 for the beginning of his story.

17 C. Molette, 'La VERITE où je la trouve', *MULLA ZADE, Une conscience d'homme dans la lumière de Maurice Blondel* (Téqui: Paris, 1988), p.58.

18 The facts are given by G. di Fazio, 'Storia di Nabil; che volle farsi cristiano', *30 Giorni*, 10 November 1986, pp.30–35.

19 R.W.F. Wootton, *Jesus More than a Prophet, Fifteen Muslims find forgiveness, release and new life* (Inter-Varsity Press: Leicester, UK, 1982), pp.47–51.

20 Timur Lang, of mixed Mongol and Turkish blood, 1336–1405, led a sort of 'crusade' to restore Islamic orthodoxy from India to Turkey. In so doing he ordered countless massacres wherever he went, sparing no one, Christian or Muslim.

21 A. Seve, 'Zohra, Musulmane Chrétienne', *La Croix*, 1–2 January 1988, pp.8,13.

22 For an example of this distinction, read Mohammed Talbi, 'Islam and the West: beyond confrontations, ambiguities and complexes', *Encounter*, No.108, October 1984.

23 On this: H. Fesquet, 'La double appartenance religieuse ouvre-t-elle une nouvelle voie à l'oecuménisme?', *Le Monde*, 29 July 1981, where Zohra's case is presented under the name of Aïcha.

24 H. Wardan, *La Gloire de Peter Pan ou le Récit du Moine Beur* (Nouvelle Cité: Paris, 1986), p.149.

25 A. Salles, 'De l'Islam au Christianisme, (2) L'intégration difficile', *La Croix*, 5 March 1987, p.14. Sakina's story aroused indignation among readers of the newspaper. As an answer, the priest who had been her counsellor felt it necessary to give this word of explanation in *La Croix*, 10 September 1987, p.12.

CHAPTER 6

GOD'S COMMUNITY
(2) THE DISCOVERY

When faith takes over

'What helped me most to discover God's call was finding Christians, real Christians, in whom the grace of God was truly present.' One hears such a declaration from many converts. In their encounter with the Christian community, there comes a moment when something within them exclaims: 'Surely the Lord is in this place, and I was not aware of it . . . This is none other than the house of God' (Genesis 28:16–17).

And yet, regular contact with the Christian community may have involved many of them in risks and difficulties. But the final discovery is worth all the trouble and all the pain. As the gospel says, it is only after he found the hidden treasure that the man was able to give everything he had in order to buy the field (Matthew 13:44). The converts may at first harbour mixed motives or contrary feelings; when they come to experience the presence of God in that community everything else becomes secondary or even harmful. Initially imperfect motivations fade away as the essential dawns.

The religious experience may not be immediate or sudden. Very often it will be more in the nature of a process, demanding a long period of hidden gestation before finally coming to birth. It is hardly necessary to add that those who have been baptised as infants are invited to make the same discovery; retreats, recollections and prayer meetings are just means to that end.

Radiant witnesses

There are Christians who seem simply to radiate peace, forgiveness and devotion. Meeting such persons has often proved decisive for converts.

We have already met the tragic person of *Khalifa al Gafsi*, accused of murdering his son. Let us look again at the words in which he explains his conversion: 'When I was a labourer in Evreux, I was welcomed by a practising French family. They were wonderful. They seemed to me to be the ideal married couple. I wanted to be like them.'

We have also heard how Father *Jean-Mohammed Abd-el-Jalil* was inspired by his meeting with Jacques Maritain and other professors, especially lay persons, at the Institut Catholique in Paris. It was the faith of these people, and especially their capacity for love, which led him to ask the crucial question: 'Is there not in Christianity something for me, something capable of transforming me more than Islam has been able to do? . . . Why is this religion strong?'

Dr Sa'eed (1863-1942), a Kurd from Iran, provides us with another example of the shock experienced by a young Muslim on meeting an authentic Christian.[1] He was the son of a devout and charitable mullah, who went around visiting the sick, including lepers. The boy received a sound religious education in the Koran and Islamic tradition, and learned Persian and Arabic in addition to Kurdish.

He became a devout Muslim. The converse of his zeal for Islam was strong antipathy towards all other religions. When invited to a Christian house, he considered it an act of virtue secretly to slash with a knife the carpet on which he was sitting and chatting. Or he might feign clumsiness in order to smash a vase or a plate.

When he was still only thirteen he began to help his father with the calls to prayer. When the father died, he took over as director of the Koranic school, while continuing his own religious studies under a scholar of note.

Little by little, the young man began to be aware that, underlying his religious zeal, was a desire for perfection which he never seemed able to attain. At sixteen he joined a group of mystics which emphasised the need for contrition and purity of intention. He remained with the group for three years but did not find peace.

At this point a Protestant pastor, Kasha Yohanan, a Syriac-speaking Iranian, asked the young Sa'eed to give him private lessons in Persian. This did not however in the least reduce Sa'eed's antipathy and contempt for Christians, whom he refused to offer the classical Muslim greeting of peace.

One day he arrived earlier than usual at the house of his pupil and found the pastor at prayer with two friends, reciting psalms and then offering spontaneous prayer for their friends and enemies.

Sa'eed was now himself a mullah, and he often received clients looking for amulets, sometimes intended to protect them from their enemies, or even to injure those enemies. He was struck at hearing the Christians actually praying for their enemies, and he began to observe them more closely to see if their conduct corresponded with their words:

> From day to day I found myself more drawn to the pastor, his love, his truthfulness, his pious life, his meekness, and his honesty affected me deeply. I used to listen to his conversations with as many as came to him. I weighed every bit of it in the balance of reason. I could see how true his points were and how weighty his arguments, but above all, his life was a decisive witness to what he said.[2]

Dr Sa'eed's nephew adds: 'It was the influence of this Christian character that introduced a change in Mullah Sa'eed's spiritual outlook. For the first time he became aware of the magnitude of his own shortcomings.'

While continuing to teach Persian to the pastor, the young tutor kept returning to the theme which tormented him—sin, repentance, salvation—and tried to understand the Christian teaching on the matter. One day he had a conversation with the pastor about ritual purification:

If there were but a single drop of blood on our clothes, our prayers would be void, because blood is unclean.

Then what about the blood that courses through your whole body?

That is inside us, and since we judge the outward state, that does not matter.

But in prayer the Christian is not concerned with the exterior, for true prayer proceeds to God from the heart and is not affected by the outward condition.

Confronted for the first time with a radically new system of thought, the young Sa'eed began to experience doubts about the relevance of his beliefs, and even about the truth of Islam and of its prophet. He fought these doubts with outrage and anger at himself, but one thought surfaced again and again as he reflected on the pastor's life:

How was it possible for an unbeliever to be so virtuous a man? Then the true picture of his inner self, stripped of all its punctilious piety, flashed on his mind like a hideous phantom, ugly and repulsive. He shuddered. He remembered the word of his Prophet: 'Ye are the best folk that hath been raised up unto mankind.'[3] As he contrasted his life with that of Kasha Yohanan, this assertion did not accord with the facts and only added to his dismay.

For a time, Sa'eed took a vow to keep away from the pastor, sealing the vow by burning his legs with a live coal. He remained faithful for a few months, but then his despair became intolerable. Finally he prostrated himself in prayer in a dark alley-way of the city and asked God to lead him where he would. When he rose to his feet, he knew with certainty that he must resume his contact with the pastor and study the Bible and the Koran until light came into his heart.

He pursued this course for four or five months. He soon came to believe that the prophecies of the Old Testament clearly pointed to Jesus as the Saviour, the Son come to save the world. He intensified his research, not without arousing the suspicions of his elder brother who gave him a beating and broke a stick over his head. On that day, filled with sorrow, he prayed alone in his room:

> O merciful God! In thy presence I am less than the dust in which I lie—a helpless sinner in need of thy pity. Let my tears of penitence move thy heart of love. I beg for mercy, though deserving only judgement. Wash me, cleanse me and receive me for the sake of thy Son.

As this prayer makes clear, Sa'eed had already accepted the essential Christian message. His faith was still, however, somewhat theoretical. The decisive turning-point came one afternoon in mid-October when suddenly the words of Isaiah rang through his soul: 'Arise, shine . . . for your light has come, and the glory of the Lord rises upon you' (60:1). The words echoed and re-echoed within him until every fibre of his being throbbed to the joyous call. Now he knew. His search had come to an end. He had arrived.

The pastor had not come to stay. He left, and soon Sa'eed was left alone with his new Christian faith in a wholly Muslim city. For a while he tried to accommodate his faith within the religious practice of Islam, reciting the Our Father and the Creed while praying in the mosque. Eventually, however, he was unmasked and denounced and he had to flee for his life.

He studied medicine and later practised in Iran, known to all as a Christian and enjoying a great reputation both as a doctor and as an evangelist.

A similar testimony is given to us by an orphan girl entrusted by her family to an orphanage run by religious sisters:

> At the orphanage we were brought up in the Muslim religion of our parents. A Muslim mistress taught us the Koran.
>
> When I was fourteen or fifteen, I began to wonder about the sisters who showed us such attention and affection. Their charity, their generosity, their dedication, puzzled me. I wanted to get at their secret. I said to myself, 'Allah is master and judge, but the God of the Christians is goodness and love.' Somehow I managed to get hold of a copy of the Gospels. I had to read it in secret, for if the sisters had known, they would not have let me keep it.

When I was twenty-five I decided to go to France where I would be more free. I was a Muslim and had no intention of being anything else, for I did not wish to cut myself off from my family. But Christ attracted me. After several years of reflection and struggle, I began my catechumenate and was finally baptised . . . Only a few people knew what I had done. Several years later I told the two sisters who had brought me up, asking them not to tell anybody else.

There are several interesting points in this account. The secret surrounding the discovery of the Gospel is typical of several neighbouring Muslim countries. Also remarkable is the desire of the sisters to respect the Muslim family and to avoid any suggestion of proselytism, to such an extent that they were ignorant of the conversion of their former pupil and have been the last to be informed about it. It is noteworthy too that the young girl understood that the attitude of the sisters reflected the conception of God which was their inspiration.

This lady now lives in France and is married to a Christian Frenchman. It was after meeting him that she realised that she had a story to tell. For a long time she kept her new religion secret, and with good reason, for when her conversion and future marriage became known to the authorities of her country of origin, they refused to supply her with a birth certificate.

Edith Samaou Komoi is a young woman from Niger. Her father was a Christian catechist and her mother a Muslim, although still deeply attached to the traditional religion. The daughter remained between the two religions, although with an inclination to that of her father:

I was fourteen when Jean Adama Seidou came to our house, asking for me to marry him. I was happy to take him for a husband, but my mother opposed the match because he was a Christian. My father however took my side and the marriage went ahead. Today my mother accepts the marriage because she knows that I am happy.

It was while living with Jean that I really came to know Jesus. Jean often spoke of him to me, but I was especially impressed by the way Jean lived with me and with others. I used to think that it was impossible for a man and a woman to live together without fighting and quarrelling. I had never seen a harmonious marriage before, but now I had a happy home myself and saw other happy Christian homes. I said, God is great! Jean even admitted his faults to me and told me the truth. A Songhay never behaves like that. In all this I recognized that it is God who counts for Christians and that Jesus gives people a strength which they could never otherwise acquire.

However, if today I believe in Jesus, it is not simply because of Jean, but because Jesus himself has taken hold of me. Now, even if I wanted to, I could never abandon him.[4]

An acquaintance with African philosophy helps us to understand this emphasis on 'strength', or force. In theology we call it 'grace'. The diffusion of films like *Star Wars* has made the idea of force familiar to young Europeans, and it could be usefully applied in catechetics.

Nasser Lotfi was an officer in the Iranian Air Force.[5] He now lives abroad as a Christian missionary. His conversion goes back to his childhood. An American engineer had rented a room in the boy's home, and instead of paying rent it was agreed that the tenant should give lessons to Nasser, the oldest child. Nasser soon noticed that the American spent all his spare time reading the Bible, and that he shared his food, down to the last morsel, with the poor of the neighbourhood. He also often spoke of Jesus and of Christianity to the Muslims he met. Nasser's astonishment soon changed to admiration. He listened to the American telling Bible stories and learned them by heart. On one occasion the stranger was insulted and had stones thrown at him after he had spoken of Jesus, and Nasser came to his defence.

When Hassan, the father of the family, heard that his son was defending this foreigner against Muslims, he expelled the boarder from his house and arranged to have him deported from the country. Nasser was then twelve and again he took the side of the American, declaring that he too was a Christian and believed that Jesus was the Son of God. For this declaration he was beaten by his father who brought him three times before the judge and denounced him as an apostate. Finally he was thrown out of the house in the depths of winter, wearing nothing but his shirt, and the doors were closed upon him.

The boy took refuge with the old family maidservant, who lodged him in her hut and fed him for three years. When she died, he left the town and joined the army, eventually becoming an officer, in spite of having been imprisoned for his faith.

No doubt there are radiant believers in all religions, including Islam. These stories are only offered as evidence that the daily example given by the Christian community in the world is by no means always negative.

The courage to invite

Many converts speak of how they have been helped by Christians who found the courage to invite them to take part in the activities of their community or to simply come and see.

Brahim was born in France of North African immigrant parents. When he speaks of his conversion, he tells of the long years during which he pondered in solitude the mystery of life and faith, walking the streets in winter and strolling along the beach in summer, waiting for someone to speak to him at last and invite him to speak himself. Finally he found the opportunity when he came across a group of young Christians who were preaching in the streets. They spoke about God and seemed happy. There must be many others like Brahim who are waiting for someone to approach them.

We have seen how *Habib Wardan* accepted an invitation to join the Young Christian Workers. He was then able to discuss his problems with other young people and to hear how the Christian faith had helped them. It is perhaps not widely known that at the present time the Young Christian Workers in France have within their ranks a significant number of young Muslims. There is a similar organisation in West Africa, called Young Believing Workers, which tries to meet the needs of thousands of young people, mostly Muslims, who are only waiting for an invitation to join such a movement in which they can try and use their faith to confront their problems, without necessarily becoming Christians.

Joseph Issifi Bosso was born in Niger in 1912. It was in 1980, when he was a farmer and a catechist, that he told his story to an enquirer.[6] His religious pilgrimage had begun under the influence of a marabout who was his maternal grandfather:

> He taught me, and instructed me in prayer and in reciting the Koran. I acquired a taste for Islam. I spent all my time with the marabouts who came to see my grandfather and I did what I could to help them . . . I was completely devoted to Islam and never dreamed of being anything else but a Muslim. If I went by myself into the villages, I would instruct people who did not know Muhammad or how to pray.

When he moved to another village, he lived next to *Antoine Douramane*, a former soldier who had become a catechist. Joseph explains how his new neighbour took the initiative:

> There was no marabout in the village and I was the only person with any religious instruction. The marabouts who came to Fantyo used to lodge with me. While I was still a comparative newcomer, Antoine called me into his house. Soon I started meeting him every evening and he began to instruct me in the Christian religion. He used to say to me, 'Issifi, I can see that you are an honest man and that you are looking for God but have not yet found him as you should. You should make the comparison yourself: you have been brought up in Islam, and know it sufficiently; now I am going to tell you what I know about Jesus.'

Antoine thus took the initiative. He first of all issued the invitation and then, when he felt that the moment was right, began a dialogue in which he claimed the right to speak about what he knew, namely, Jesus. Issifi remained free to take his own decision, as he explains:

> Finally I said to myself, 'What Antoine says to me seems to be the truth, but suppose I decide to join the Christians . . . Even if my marabout was wrong, I would praise him and talk about all the things he could do. When he received money or other gifts, he would

share with me. If I choose the way of Christ, the marabouts will be against me. I will have to think about the matter carefully.

One day I went to see a Muslim friend, Seydou, and said to him, 'The words of Antoine seem to me to be true, but I do not yet know what to do.' Seydou said, 'What Antoine says is the truth, but it is hard to live like a Christian.' I went away and thought.

Finally the day came when Issifi decided to take 'the Christian way' and he asked Antoine to give him Christian instruction. Far from feeling that Antoine had put pressure on him, he felt completely free, for no one had told him what he should do:

> Everyone who came and heard me speaking of Jesus said, 'Issifi, we urge you not to take this path, it is not your place, Antoine has deceived you!' I said to them, 'Before, when I was a pupil of the marabouts, I followed you right and left, I was like your slave. Now I want to follow Jesus. There I am completely free, I am liberated.' All the people gathered round to see what was going on and some gave me black looks. They were so angry that I could not look at them.

Mahmoud Jalily (1882–1969) was an Iranian civil servant who worked in the Ministry of Finance. He was a pious Muslim but suffered from a spiritual malaise which he sought to cure by pilgrimages and by what we would call retreats. He had never had any direct contact with Christians until he entered his son in a school run by missionaries.[7]

In November 1930 this son brought home from school an invitation for his father to attend a conference by a visiting speaker in the mission chapel. Without really knowing what it would be about, Mahmoud decided to attend. It did not take him long to sense the religious atmosphere. He began to hum the hymn tunes, while telling himself that these people did not belong to his world of the royal court. The speaker then presented a summary of the Christian message: human sin, and God's forgiveness offered through the person of Jesus. As the speaker proceeded, Mahmoud felt himself more and more moved:

> All the events of my life, passed before my eyes like a moving picture, and as I gazed on my past deeds I saw myself condemned. I

had been like a blind man. Then when my eyes were opened I saw all the filthiness of my life.

Most of the audience left, but Mahmoud remained seated, overcome by the realisation of how much he needed a saviour. Only a few others stayed behind, wishing to hear more, and the speaker then invited those to stand up who were willing to allow themselves to be purified by Jesus. Without hesitation Mahmoud stood up, followed by his son, and said:

'When I entered this room I thought I was the best man here. But now I know there was no greater sinner in the meeting than I. I believe in Jesus Christ as my Saviour, and I will follow him as long as I live.'

He explained later:

I do not know how it was possible for me to confess before those people that I was a bad man, for all my life I had tried to make people believe I was a good man. Truly an unseen power lifted me to my feet and enabled me to confess my sins. When I did so, at that very moment I experienced in myself joy such as one would have who was relieved of a heavy burden. I felt that I was no longer my former self, I was a new being. On that night I was born again! That troubled heart found quiet, that self-esteem was changed to humility, that enmity to friendliness. Instead of avoiding people I wanted to come near them. For me the world became new. I had found what I had so long sought.

Without the invitation to the conference, Mahmoud Jalily would never have had the opportunity of finding what he was lacking. We might compare his experience with that of *Hass Hirji-Walji*, the young Asian expelled from Uganda. He was helped by Christian fellow-students, who constantly told him how much they appreciated his presence at their meetings and prayer gatherings. Very many converts remain grateful to a comrade, a friend, a stranger, who had the courage to say to them, 'Come and see, and judge for yourself.'

French Christians are often reluctant to invite a non-Christian to take part in their liturgy or religious meetings. They speak of the evil of proselytism and of respect for others. And no doubt with good reason. But respect does not mean a kind of religious apartheid in which everyone remains enclosed in their own world without ever hearing another point of view. To welcome another, to offer him or her hospitality, implies a willingness to invite him or her into one's own world, and this need by no means exclude religious discussion. The invitation may be accepted or rejected. Mutual respect means accepting both these responses.[8] If the response is positive, one should not of course resort to any kind of pressure; if it is negative, the invitation should still stand, and perhaps be repeated. The door should never be closed.

The people where God acts

We have already considered some of the elements in the Christian community which strike new converts from Islam. Let us now look at some others.

THE MIRACLES

All religions have tales of miraculous divine interventions. It is true that, according to Islamic orthodoxy, the only miracle performed by Muhammad was to transmit the most divine book in the world. Nevertheless, popular Islam attaches to the life of the Prophet copious miraculous prodigies. In a similar way the tombs of Muslim saints attract crowds of pilgrims and are credited with miraculous healings and feats of protection.

Christianity, with the tradition of the Gospel miracles and the intercession of the saints and martyrs, is no stranger to this aspect of Islamic devotions. Indeed when Christians first encountered Islam, they used miracles to prove the truth of their religion in opposition to that of Muslims. The latter, in response, developed an answer in kind. Each community has used miracles as evidence of the truth of its religion.

A VIRULENT PAMPHLET

When I worked in the pastoral ministry in a small town in East Africa, I often visited both Muslims and Christians. There would be long conversations in which people related the latest gossip.

One day a Muslim trader handed me a booklet written in Mombasa, in neighbouring Kenya, entitled *Why I am not a Christian*, intended to help Muslims to preach to Christians.[9] The author begins by explaining that Jesus was only sent to the lost sheep of Israel, so that one could only profit from his teaching and enjoy his protection if one was a Jew. He then considers the text at the end of Mark's Gospel in which Jesus sends his disciples to preach to every creature: 'And these signs will accompany those who believe: In my name they will drive out demons; they will speak in new tongues; they will pick up snakes with their hands; and when they drink deadly poison, it will not hurt them at all; they will place their hands on sick people, and they will get well' (Mark 16:17–18).

The author of this Muslim pamphlet comments:

These are the signs which Jesus established to distinguish a true from a false Christian. So there you are, my Christian friend: if up to now you have been unable to pick up a serpent, or to speak any language which takes your fancy unless someone has first taught it to you, or to expel demons by invoking the name of Jesus, as Jesus told you to do . . . Well then, know with certainty that you are not a true Christian: you are deceiving yourself and wasting your time. And I believe that you will die before you are able to perform any of these feats. If you cannot perform them, you have no right to call yourself a Christian, as Jesus himself proclaimed. That is why I have decided not to be a Christian. For I cannot take up serpents either . . . and I have no inclination to try . . . And what about you, Reader? Would you like to try?[10]

The virulent tone is typical of polemical literature, Christian as well as Muslim. The short passage we have quoted will suffice to give an idea of the level of this sort of writing, which selects from the Scriptures what suits the author's purpose. A few words are picked out which he can make fun of without making any attempt to penetrate their real meaning. What this extract does show is the author's notion of a miracle: not a ray of the divine pity on our miseries but an absurd circus trick with a religious label. Above all this passage reflects the writer's conviction that miracles do not happen, at least among Christians. In all this he is reflecting popular Muslim opinion.

JOSEPH SALLAM (1877–1947)

With this background, one can understand what a shock it was for a young Muslim from Alexandria, studying in a Christian Brothers' School in that city, to hear one of his teachers reading from Henri Lasserre's book on the miracles of Lourdes. Ibrahim Sallam came from a very pious, middle-class family. He wanted to become an imam in a mosque or a teacher of religious studies. He began his education in a Koranic school at the age of three, and became very fervent in the faith: 'I felt that I was on fire and I told God of my joy in discovering that he was so great, powerful and merciful. All along the way to my school, my heart was overflowing with sentiments of love of God.'

Sallam's father died in 1887 and his elder brother took over as head of the family. It was he who placed Ibrahim in the Christian Brothers' School three years later. He speaks of his first impressions of Christians:

> Warnings and prejudices collapsed. The disinterested goodness of the dear Brothers; the interest which they took in all their pupils, regardless of race, nationality or religion; their fervent and solid piety, shown both in their words and their deeds: all these things belied the suspicions which Islam instils into its adepts concerning Christians.

On the other hand, the elements of the Christian catechism which he heard made little impact:

> Islam, or the religion of one God, one in his divinity and in his person, seemed to me at that time the only true religion, corresponding to sane reason. I found a lively joy in this faith and I never ceased to thank God that I was born into a Muslim family . . .
>
> In 1893 I entered the senior school. At that period classes extended from 7.30 am until 7.30 pm. At about 7.00 pm one evening in May, the month of Our Lady, our very dear Brother Fidelis, may his blessed name never be effaced from my heart, noticing that his pupils were

tired, invited us to listen to something very interesting. It was the work of Henri Lasserre on the miracles of Lourdes.

This was the first time that I had heard of miracles taking place within the Catholic Church. Their authenticity was beyond dispute. These were not miracles taking place in some dark age, beyond the scope of verification. Doctors of every religious belief and none attested to their truth, after rigorous scientific examination. How could one possibly doubt them? I had always been taught that Christianity was not the true religion. But could God be with Christians if they did not belong to him, if they were not his own disciples, his worshippers in spirit and in truth?

When I returned home, my soul was in turmoil. As usual, I made my ablutions and said the daily prayers, but then I went straight to bed without eating. My mother tried to discover the cause of my distress, but I could not open my heart to her that evening.

The next day the very dear Brother Fidelis, no doubt oblivious of the drama taking place in my soul, continued reading from the same book, and the following day likewise. I felt that I was being battered by truth. Finally Our Lord, knowing my heart, took pity on my misery, and condescended to pour the light of faith into my mind and heart, that light of which no one is worthy: it is a pure gift of the mercy and generosity of God. Enlightened and consoled, I made an act of faith in the truth of Christianity.

I now only had to carry out its prescriptions.[11]

It should be observed that the young man did not envisage a miracle simply as a sign of God's compassion for the sick. Like many believers, both Muslim and Christian, he regarded a miracle as a proof of the truth of dogma.[12] This emphasis on truth remained one of the strong points of his thinking throughout his life. We may note too the sadness he experienced as long as he resisted the light he had received: a sadness replaced by consolation once he decided to accept the light, whatever the cost. Another convert, Ignatius of Loyola, experienced a similar swing between sadness and consolation, and he made these feelings the criteria for judging the authenticity of God's calls.

For three more years, the soul of Ibrahim Sallam was divided between positive faith in the truth of Christianity and continuing emotional attachment to Islam. Later he would take a more discriminating approach to both religions, and perceive both the strong and the weak points of each. The principal factor which would eventually integrate his faith and his feeling was his growing love for Jesus.

During this period of his religious development, Sallam entered into discussion with his Muslim comrades. He soon encountered opposition within his own family. He tried to calm things down by continuing Muslim rituals while secretly reciting Christian prayers, but his honest, open temperament would not allow him to carry on living this double life. He finally abandoned his country and became a priest in a society of missionaries of Africa where he exercised his ministry until his death in 1947.

THE LITURGY

Christian liturgy is another source of fascination and bewilderment for a Muslim whose ritual prayer exudes sobriety in words and gestures. It is true, however, that in popular Islam, and in certain Sufi brotherhoods, Islamic religious rituals may be accompanied by music and dancing.

The liturgy of the Eastern Christian Church has retained and even developed rites which derive from the pre-Islamic culture of the Middle East and owe nothing to Islamic culture.

As a result, the rituals used by each of the two religions feel foreign to the believers of the opposite community. Each of the two worlds has cultivated its difference to the point of provoking a negative reaction in the believers of the rival religion. In spite of all these factors, the experience of the Christian liturgy can be for some persons the beginning of the road to Christian faith.

Kailung was a young Filipino of eighteen who had left his native village to do his secondary studies on the island of Jolo.[13] One day he was invited to a Christian religious service. He was so attracted by the prayers that he kept returning. Eventually faith took root in his heart and he was baptised. The solidity of the new faith he had received was severely tested: he was rejected by his family and made the object of threats, including an attempt on his life. The account of his adventures suggests that it was his very firmness in the face of death which persuaded his brothers to sheathe their daggers when they were on the point of stabbing him.

For *Moussavi*, on the other hand, a member of a non-practising Muslim family in Iran, the discovery of the mass one day in Paris was actually the final stage on the road to Christian faith.[14] He was twenty in 1982 when he secretly procured a Bible in Tehran: 'What interested me was Jesus. He did not force people to be converted and to practise their religion. In Iran I was forced to pray. I did it to avoid trouble. But it had no meaning.'

Moussavi's reaction to social pressure was one factor which alienated him from Islam. Another was the violence perpetrated in the name of the faith during the Islamic Revolution in Iran:

> It disappointed and disgusted me. I will never be able to forget the young man of twenty who had his fingers cut off for stealing. All his life he will think of nothing but revenge . . . I want to have nothing to do with this God who proposes Holy War. I want to believe in a God who forgives.

When he arrived in Paris, he was therefore already looking for a new community and another message. He was in fact looking for Christ, whom he had discovered in reading the Bible. He wrote to a priest and then asked to assist at a mass. The priest agreed and Moussavi went into a church for the first time. In 1983, a year after his arrival in France, Moussavi discovered a new community in the Scouts of France. He now belongs to a catechumenate group in which adults from different religions are preparing for baptism. He still feels the need to belong to a religious family: 'It is hard. As long as you are not baptised, you are not really a member of the family, you are different from the others.'

We have already met *Nureddin Ishraqiyyah*, the young Lebanese man who was put off by his experiences in Islamic educational institutions.[15] He fled from his community of origin and felt an attraction to Christianity. He was a sensitive child, something of a poet, naturally moved to worship the God whom he perceived in the beauties of nature. He visited Lebanese Christian churches with his Christian neighbours and came to love the Eastern liturgy, with its hymns and icons and splendour.

From an aesthetic appreciation of the forms of Christian worship he progressed to an understanding of the Christian message. We have seen how he experienced the call of Christ first in dreams and then in a growing discovery of the love of Christ crucified and risen, the conqueror of hatred.

He describes how, in the hours before he took the decision to become a Christian, he was inspired by artistic beauty: a statue in a park;[16] Tripoli Cathedral in Libya symbolised for him the freedom of Christianity in its quest for beauty. He decided to go to mass on the following Sunday and found his decision confirmed; he felt at home, overcome by the atmosphere of prayer, transported by the splendour of the Christian liturgy. The liturgy, both in its form and in what it represented, was for him both the beginning and the end of his religious pilgrimage. Truth and beauty went hand in hand.

Hussayn Behzad was an Iranian painter, well known for his miniatures. Unfortunately his life was ruined by drug and alcohol addiction. When one of his Christian friends invited him to a religious service, he was able to see in Jesus the one who could transform and liberate him. After deciding to become a Christian, he was able gradually to overcome his problem and his art flowered. He died a Christian in 1968, many years after his conversion.[17]

A RELIGION WHICH TRANSFORMS

The story of this artist, liberated from drugs and alcohol, provides us with a further example of the attraction of the Church: it is a place where people can be transformed and freed from their weaknesses, provided they accept the strength which Christ wishes to offer them.[18]

It is possible that many 'cradle Christians' fail to discover this strength. One often meets disappointed and sceptical people who expect little from their Saviour: hope can be almost dead. As a result they do not offer him control of their lives, they deprive him of the space he needs to deploy his power and to bring them to an experience of personal transformation.

In Islam, human weakness is countered by urging people to accept and observe the Law, the *Sharia*. For one educated in this tradition, the Christian message comes as a great surprise. Christ offers not commandments but a presence, the presence of the Holy Spirit who comes into our hearts and grows there secretly, producing fruit by his own power.[19] Jesus described this action of the Spirit in terms of a vine: 'I am the vine; you are the branches. If a man remains in me and I in him, he will bear much fruit' (John 15:5).

The passage from a law to a 'power' involves a complete reversal of perspective, and for many it is the most important point in their discovery of the Church.

Jean-Baptiste Daoudou Birgi was a young Nigerian. Although a Muslim, he was one of the leaders of a voodoo-like cult known as Heuka in which his role was to dance and enter into a trance when he would be possessed by a spirit who spoke through his mouth. One of his musicians was converted to Christianity, and Daoudou started questioning him. He heard him speak of Jesus and of his power:

I began to perceive that the truth was with Jesus. When I came home, I wanted to leave Heuka, but this was very difficult because people came to consult me, and since I now refused to listen to them they would insult me. But I realised that it was no longer right for me to deceive them. That is why I held fast. I saw that my life 'had become upright'. Previously I had followed Muhammad, but this was only to live ill, for I was one of those who knew the ninety-nine names of Muhammad. If you know these names, you are free to do any harm you choose during the day: you can steal, sleep with other men's wives, lie, provided only that at night you recite the ninety-nine names. Then you will obtain forgiveness of your sins.[20]

After having heard the word of Jesus I understood that it was a mockery of God to sin as much as you liked during the day and then recite the ninety-nine names of Muhammad at night. I saw clearly that these names could not save, since you only recited them in order to be able to carry on sinning the next day.

Since I received baptism I feel that my soul has received a new life in Jesus. Even if my body protests, I feel that my soul is full of life, as if it were new.[21]

Marcel Assane Boukari was a friend of Daoudou, and at first he was strongly opposed to his conversion. With several other immigrant workers in Ghana, he set out on foot to make a journey of several days to save his friend from this new religion which had turned his head. The effort was unsuccessful, and he tells us the sequel:

Some months later when I was back in my village I used to pass the time playing cards or singing with the lute. I made no further attempt to persuade Jean-Baptiste, but his conversion to Jesus troubled me greatly. I had no luck at cards and lost nearly all the money I had earned in Ghana. I went to a marabout, and then to a diviner, for good luck charms. They did no good. I then heard that Christians had a lucky ring and I went to see Antoine Douramane, the catechist, to see if he could help me. He told me:

'I know what you want, you want to recover the money you have lost. If you found something more important than money, would you abandon card playing?'

I said I would, and he then recounted the history of the people of God, from Abraham to Jesus. He talked for a long time, and I returned home thinking about what he had said. But soon I went back to him, for I had 'a real hunger in my heart', like a madness. It was as if I could never be satisfied. I kept going back to the catechist, and my hunger only increased. I no longer recognised myself. I thought no more of cards or money but only of what he had shown me.

From then on, when people in the village started talking about Jesus, I would interrupt the conversation and say: 'That is not only the business of Douramane. It concerns me too. Jesus is truly the one sent by God to save men from evil and to give them a new life. Look at what I used to do and what I do now.'

And the people said, 'It is true.'[22]

It is interesting to observe, in these unsophisticated tales, the different stages through which both these young men passed: at first their attention focuses on the Christian whom they meet;

then they become conscious of an interior transformation; and finally they come to the Saviour, Jesus, as the source of the transformation. And the genuineness of the experience is guaranteed for everyone who knows them by the transformation in their lives. It may however take time for other people to acknowledge the transformation which has taken place in the life of the convert.

PATIENCE IN THE FACE OF OPPOSITION

In 1947 *Mehri Khanum*, daughter of Mahmoud Jalily, went to see a missionary in Iran and asked him for baptism. It was eighteen years since her father had been converted to Christianity and she had judged him severely at the time. But then something happened which made her think. She heard her father being insulted to his face and made the object of totally false and malicious accusations. But he listened patiently and made no attempt to retort or to defend himself.

> That was too much for me, for I had never seen so noble a spirit as that. My father is poor, I am wealthy and have all that one could desire, but I don't have my father's patience and forgiveness. I am not happy and I want what he has. So I have come to you to ask you to lead me to Christ, to put my hand in his hand, that I may become like my dear father![23]

Mehri spoke with tears of the burden of sin and guilt she was carrying, asked pardon of God and offered Christ the control of her life. Shortly afterwards she was baptised and served Christ faithfully and joyfully until her death some years later.

THE PEOPLE OF JESUS

Christians who invite, Christians who radiate their faith and make others want to be transformed and be like them, a community which sings and celebrates and in which one feels at home: in all these ways, and many others, the visible Church attracts. Some admit that at first they only came to religious services to be with their friends. Only later do they discover the person of Jesus who beckons them.

There is another striking point. However important the community may have been as the starting point of their conversion, for most converts the irresistible personality of Jesus eventually takes over as incomparably more important than the community. The Church has meaning only as the people of Jesus.

An imperfect Church

Those born into the Christian tradition are usually very critical of the Church and its clergy. They are bound therefore to be struck by all these converts who find the Church so attractive.

'They will be disappointed!'

We may wonder if later on these converts become disenchanted with the Church and even go back on their decision. If the convert is looking for no more than a substitute family, disappointment of this kind is possible and even probable. But the convert who has been truly converted to Jesus does not stop at the Church: he or she goes to Jesus—and Jesus does not disappoint.

We have already looked at *Paul Mehemet Ali Mulla Zade*. When he was a priest he composed a hymn to the Church for the benefit of a confrère who had asked him what had brought him to the Catholic faith. Writing in 1922, seventeen years after his baptism, he says:

> Only the name Catholic keeps me within the Church, said St Augustine. For me too it is the word Catholic, *universal*, which attracted me to the Church and keeps me within her. She is universal in time and space, she is in touch with the origins, she speaks to all peoples.
>
> She combines actions and words, justifying her claims by the best possible proof: by her works—*operibus credite*.[24] The Catholic Church is the only religious society which *takes its role seriously*, which does what it says, which *effectively* operates as an institution with a supernatural mission, a mission which is exercised *in* this world but which is not *of* this world, the mission, that is, of preparing, and inaugurating even here, 'the kingdom of God'.

The Catholic Church seems to me the high point of humanity, a community *penetrated with this thought of a supernatural destiny*, and a community which works seriously and methodically to bring it about. Elsewhere, no one dares to speak of loving God, except perhaps as a meaningless routine formula. Outside the Church, one hears only an echo; but within the Church God is *truly* loved, one has the impression that he is truly present. Here one speaks of things which one lives. Elsewhere, people recognise that they are sinners in a general way and enter into a compromise with it; here there is repentance and tears for actual sins, there is a systematic and collective effort to purify oneself of sin. There is a healthy self-hatred which is inseparable from the hunger and thirst for perfection.

The Church is the society of men united among themselves and with God. 'May they be one, as we are one,' says Our Lord in his priestly prayer. It is in the light of this ideal of final unity ('may they be completely one') that one must explain the external Church with its authority, and hierarchy, and discipline and order. The Church only has meaning in terms of human and divine unity, and one can only make her loved by unbelievers in those same terms. Only thus can we begin to understand and appreciate the Church's discipline in belief, in the practice of life, in worship. Only thus can we make sense of the Church, of the creeds and councils and dogmatic definitions; the Church of spiritual jurisdiction, of the confessional, of Canon Law, of the sacraments. Here authority is the fruit of love. There is order and discipline, but all is ordained to the final consummation in unity.

A thousand pardons, dear friend, for these disconnected thoughts which are all that I can find time for at present in response to your very interesting and important question. Such as they are, they may help you to perceive some of the attraction which this Church had, and still has, for me. I can say with Newman that I love her with love.[25]

The reference to Newman will be clear to anyone acquainted with this Anglican who became a Catholic priest and finally a Cardinal, but who had much to suffer from malicious criticism from within the Church herself. He did not love her any the less on that account. Like him, Father Mulla, seventeen years on, knew very well that the Church is far from perfect, but he loved her for the treasure which she carries in vessels of clay.

Notes

1 His life story can be found in a book written by his nephew: J.M. Rasooli and C.H. Allen, *Dr Sa'eed of Iran, Kurdish Physician to Princes and Peasants, Nobles and Nomads* (W. Carey Library: Pasadena, Ca., USA, 1957, 1983); or: W.McE. Miller, *Ten Muslims Meet Christ* (Eerdmans: Grand Rapids, Mi., USA, 1969, 1980), pp.15–48.

2 J.M. Rasooli, *op. cit.*, p.35.

3 Koran 3:110.

4 J.M. Ducroz, *Les Actes des Premiers Chrétiens du Gorouol* (Nouvelle Cité: Paris, 1977), p.43. The Songhay mentioned here live along the Niger river. Very early on, they converted to Islam and founded a Songhay empire where Islamic learning and culture flourished in the fifteenth and sixteenth centuries.

5 His testimony can be found in N. Lotfi, *Iranian Christian* (Word Books: Waco, Texas, 1980).

6 R. Deniel, *Chemins de Chrétiens Africains* (Inades: Abidjan, Ivory Coast, 1982–1983), No.5, pp.24–31; J.M. Ducroz, *op. cit.*, pp.38–39.

7 W. McE. Miller, *Ten Muslims Meet Christ* (Eerdmans: Grand Rapids, Mi., USA, 1969, 1980), pp.133–147.

8 G. Kepel, *Les Banlieues de l'Islam* (Seuil: Paris, 1987), pp.25–60. In this survey of Islam in France, the author presents an analysis of the four types of answer that a Muslim living in Europe is likely to give to a non-Muslim who invites him to a meal at home. A similar variety may be expected when the invitation concerns a more religious occasion.

9 Maalim Said bin Ahmed, *Kwa Nini Sikuwa Mkristo* (Muslim Youth Cultural Society: Mombasa, Kenya, 1962).

10 The original text is in Swahili. English translation available in J.M. Gaudeul, *Encounters and Clashes—Islam and Christianity in History* (Vol. 1: *A survey*; Vol. 2: *Texts*) (PISAI: Rome, 1984). See Vol. 2, pp.332–337.

11 J. Sallam, *Autobiographie* (SMA-PB Archives: Rome, Doc. 925.2).

12 When the Koran speaks of 'signs' (*âyât*), it is, most of the time, in the context of a dispute between the Prophet and his opponents. The 'sign' aims to prove that God is confirming the Prophet's truthfulness.

13 M.E. McMurray, 'Juramentados and a Moro Convert', *Muslim World*, 32, 1942, pp.324–328.

14   A. Salles, 'De l'Islam au Christianisme, (2) L'intégration difficile',
     La Croix, 5 March 1987, p.14.

15   His witness can be found in a book in Arabic: *Nur-ed-Din
     Ishraqiyya, Al-Dâ'i` yagidu tarîqahu ilâ l-salîb* (Lost, he finds his
     way to the cross), (Centre for young adults: Basle, Switzerland).

16   We should remember that Islam forbids the making of statues. In the
     presence of a statue in a park, Nureddin is reminded of the freedom
     experienced by Christian artists.

17   W. McE. Miller, *A Christian Response to Islam* (Presbyterian and
     Reformed Publishing: Nutley, NJ, USA, 1976), pp.122–125.

18   This idea has already been developed in chapter 2: A Jesus who
     answers prayers, a Saviour who really saves, the power of the name
     of Jesus. The emphasis in the present chapter is on the part played by
     the Church in presenting Jesus.

19   Let us remember the parables of a seed in Matthew 13:31–32 and
     Mark 4:26–29): 'Night and day, whether he sleeps or gets up, the
     seed sprouts and grows although he does not know how.'

20   This has nothing to do with the official teaching of Islam. It is rather
     one of these popular ideas that one can find in all religions. Formerly,
     some Christians made a similar use of devotions such as wearing a
     scapular or attending mass on nine first Fridays of the month.

21   J.M. Ducroz, *Les Actes des Premiers Chrétiens du Gorouol* (Nou-
     velle Cité: Paris, 1977), pp.39–41.

22   *Ibid.*, pp.44–47.

23   For the story of Jalily (1882–1969) and his daughter, read: W. McE.
     Miller, *Ten Muslims Meet Christ* (Eerdmans: Grand Rapids, Mi.,
     USA, 1969, 1980), pp.133–147.

24   Allusion to John 10:38 where Jesus tells his opponents: 'Even
     though you do not believe in me, believe my actions.'

25   C. Molette, *'la VERITE où je la trouve', MULLA ZADE, Une con-
     science d'homme dans la lumière de Maurice Blondel* (Téqui, Paris,
     1988), pp.91–92.

CHAPTER 7

THE NEED FOR FORGIVENESS

Christian mission seeks to ransom and save. Islam holds man to be not in need of salvation. Instead of assuming him to be religiously and ethically fallen, Islamic da'wah *acclaims him as the* khalifah *(viceregent) of Allah, perfect in form, endowed with all that is necessary to fulfill the divine will indeed, even loaded with the grace of revelation! 'Salvation' is hence not in the vocabulary of Islam.*

Isma'il al-Faruqi, at the 1976 Chambésy conference on Mission in Islam and Christianity (*International Review of Mission,* No.260, October 1976, p.399).

The speaker was one of the Muslim delegates taking part in a Christian-Muslim conference. In the same talk, he added that men and women are not objects of salvation, but its subjects. The forcefulness of these statements lead us to understand that there is, on this point, a radical difference between the two religions.

If this presentation of Islam is correct, we should not be surprised to find that there are Muslims who become Christians precisely because Islam does not satisfy their need for a God who saves and who saves them just as they are. Their search is often met with some perplexity by Christians who tell them that they should remain where they are, on the grounds that 'salvation can be found in all religions'.

We certainly believe that God will save members of all religions, but this does not mean that we should paper over real differences of doctrine and regard Islam as nothing more than another version of Christianity. Islam has the right to be recognised in its specificity. Only then will it be possible to understand what some of its adherents find in it and what others find missing.

The message of Islam

It is not possible to do justice to the reality of any religion in a few lines. We shall however make the attempt, while recognising that many things must remain unsaid.

At the heart of Islam is the clear and trenchant affirmation of the existence and grandeur of God. The God presented in the Koran is also the compassionate and merciful one, the one who always forgives, who is patient and generous.[1]

At the same time, the God of Islam is just. He is present everywhere, he sees all things, knows all things, and is the judge before whom we shall all have to appear. He keeps an exact record of all our actions. The God of Islam is also the avenger God.[2]

It is in the name of this strictly just God that Muslim theology rejects the idea of a redeemer or saviour. Each human being is responsible, each will have to account to the judge for the smallest of his actions: 'He who has done an atom of good will see it, and likewise he who has done an atom of evil' (Koran 99:7–8). The outcome of the judgement will be either paradise or hell, each of which the Koran describes in some detail.

The basic message of the Koran is therefore a call to conversion to the virtuous life, with the assurance of a strictly proportionate reward and punishment after death; for the mercy of God cannot interfere with his essential justice. Divine forgiveness can only be given when divine justice has been satisfied and sins have been expiated.

Christianity also uses the terms 'justice' and 'mercy' but in quite different proportions. God offers an unmerited forgiveness which heals and transforms the sinner, pouring into his weakness the strength of the Holy Spirit.

The difference between the Muslim and Christian ideas of

God's forgiveness may be illustrated by a story which may or may not be authentic, but some Muslims accept as historical. It is one of the Islamic traditions.[3] As such, it represents an early Islamic concept of divine forgiveness which requires that justice be done first:

> A certain woman, Ghâmidiyya, one day saw the Prophet and said to him: 'O man of God, I have committed adultery! Purify me!' He repulsed her. The next day she came back and said, 'Why do you reject me? . . . I am with child.' 'In that case,' replied the Prophet, 'go away until you have given birth.' She came back after the birth of the child, and the Prophet said, 'Go away until he has been weaned.' Finally she returned, the child in her arms and eating a piece of bread. The prophet took the child and gave it to a Muslim. He then ordered the woman to be buried in the sand up to the breast and to be stoned by the crowd. Her blood splashed over the face of one of those who was doing the stoning and he cursed her. When the Prophet heard this, he said, 'Do not curse her. Truly this woman was repentant. If the publican had been like her, he would have received forgiveness.' And the Prophet himself presided over the woman's burial.

Whatever the truth about the historical value of that story, there is here a concept of divine forgiveness very different from that in the Gospel story of the woman taken in adultery:

> Jesus bent down and started to write on the ground with his finger. When they kept on questioning him, he straightened up and said to them, 'If any one of you is without sin, let him be the first to throw a stone at her.' Again he stooped down and wrote on the ground. At this, those who heard began to go away one at a time, the older ones first, until only Jesus was left, with the woman still standing there. Jesus straightened up and asked her, 'Woman, where are they? Has no-one condemned you?' 'No-one, sir,' she said. 'Then neither do I condemn you,' Jesus declared. 'Go now and leave your life of sin.'
>
> (John 8:7–11)

To put the matter in formal terms, in Islam forgiveness has to be earned by repentance and acceptance of punishment. Paradise is a reward for a virtuous life.

In Christianity, on the other hand, forgiveness is simply offered to the sinner. Paradise is granted both to the workers of the eleventh hour and to those who had worked since dawn, as well as to the dying criminal.[4] Jesus presents forgiveness as a seed which can either bear fruit or wither, according to the way in which it is received. Once forgiven, man learns to forgive in his turn. As a mother bears within her a new life, so human beings carry within them a seed of forgiveness. They can either abort it or allow it to be born; but it is already given.

Christianity too speaks of a judgement, but this is simply the moment when God's forgiveness will be revealed, provided only that human beings have not themselves rejected mercy, hardened their hearts against it or refused to let it find expression in their own lives.[5]

Let us not forget, however, that Islam also asserts that the generosity of God extends beyond our deserts, and that on his throne are inscribed the words, 'My mercy triumphs over my anger.' Many Muslims are convinced that merely belonging to the Muslim community, itself a gift of God, will suffice to win them paradise, in spite of their sins, although these may have to be expiated by a longer or shorter period in hell.[6] Many Muslim reformers have in fact complained about the complacency which such beliefs can generate in the lukewarm of heart.

The thorn in the flesh

It is this message of undeserved pardon which strikes certain Muslims and may put them on the path which leads to Christ.

The desire for perfection

The promises and threats contained in the Koran inculcate a sense of sin and tend to form a sensitive conscience, aware of the sins of daily life. This in turn can lead to a longing for perfection which nothing can satisfy.

Abdul Haqq was born in 1899 in what is now Pakistan.[7] He was the son of a mosque imam and received a classical Koranic education, studying the text of the Koran, as well as Arabic, Persian and

Urdu, the three languages of the Islamic culture of the Indian sub-continent. During his adolescence he lost his religious faith: 'I questioned the belief that God would send sinners to hell. I was not prepared to acknowledge and to worship such a God. Though I outwardly continued to follow the practices of Islam, I knew that I was a nominal Muslim only. At the time I was seventeen years old.'

Abdul Haqq had to spend some time in a Christian hospital and there he came across a tract containing the following verses: 'God so loved the world that he gave his only Son, that whoever believes in him shall not perish but have eternal life' (John 3:16). 'There is no other name under heaven given to men by which we must be saved' (Acts 4:12). 'Here is a trustworthy saying that deserves full acceptance: Christ Jesus came into the world to save sinners—of whom I am the worst' (1 Timothy 1:15).

These verses caught the interest of the young 'atheist' in search of a God who does not condemn sinners. It was above all the third passage that struck him: a man who confesses his sin must be a man of integrity. Yet this man was the apostle Paul, who Muslims say falsified the message of Jesus and founded Christianity as we know it. A man of this quality could not be an impostor.

Abdul Haqq got himself a New Testament:

> As I read the Holy Injil, I was struck especially by the seventh chapter of the letter to the Romans. It dawned upon me that I too was a sinner in need of a saviour—Hitherto I had heard that God favoured only those who did good works. However the Holy Injil clearly declared that it was impossible to earn God's salvation by doing good works. According to the Holy Injil, God demands not merely good works, but a change of heart.
>
> But how, I asked, can a corrupt heart become pure and undefiled?

He became more and more convinced that Christianity was not as false as he had always been taught. He took a job as a watchman at the mission and tried to understand: 'During this period the Holy Injil was my constant companion. I studied it at night by the light of the lantern. Yet when the thought of becoming a Christian crossed my mind, I dismissed it as an evil thought coming from the devil.'

Several passages in the Koran came back to him which seemed to confirm the message he found in the Bible: 'If Allah were to take mankind to task for their wrongdoing, he would not leave hereon a living creature' (Koran 16:61; 35:45). He also remembered a word addressed to the Prophet which added: 'The Prophet said: "No one of you will enter paradise through his good works." They said, "Not even you, O Apostle of God?" "Not even I," he replied, "unless God cover me with his grace and mercy."'

Abdul Haqq then started to ask himself how God's mercy and justice could be reconciled. Convinced that the Bible spoke the truth, he found in its message the answer to his question: through Jesus, God offers us a transformation which gives us a new heart, something we could never achieve by our own efforts. Enlightened and convinced, Abdul Haqq asked for baptism. The request was coolly received, for Christians felt uncertain about this eighteen-year-old fledgling Muslim scholar who had been fed all the anti-Christian propaganda of his culture. Finally he proved his sincerity by refusing all material assistance and he was baptised when he was nineteen. He was employed by a Christian newspaper and then entered a seminary, becoming finally a professor of theology and a renowned lecturer.

We have in the witness of `Imad-ud-Din Lahiz (died in 1900) a further example of thirst for purification that the Koran created and required but left unquenched. This was not a rapid process, as in the case of Abdul Haqq, but a desperate and persevering search which went on for several years. He opens his story with these words: 'The writer became a Christian on April 29, 1866 simply for the sake of attaining salvation.'[8]

`Imad-ud-Din belonged to a family of mullahs formerly in high standing with the Mogul emperors of Muslim India. He followed the family tradition and engaged in the customary Islamic studies. But he was looking for more than a career as an imam or learned man:

My only object in studying was somehow to find the Lord, for I had heard from Muslim preachers that without knowledge it is impossible to apprehend God. Even during my days as a student, I learned more about religion in the company of the ascetics, the pious and the scholars, as time permitted.

Some contacts with Christians began to raise doubts in his mind about the truth of the teaching of Islam, but he was severely rebuked by his friends and teachers and the doubts disappeared. It was ironic that one of the most fiercely anti-Christian of these, Safdar `Ali, was himself to become a Christian some years later.[9]

The young man had still received no real answer to his doubts, but he placed his trust in his teachers and gave himself totally to the study of Islam:

> Then and there, I set aside the idea of comparing the two religions and commenced to expend all my energy in a systematic study of Islam. Forsaking all other thoughts, I began to study day and night, and continued in this manner for some eight to ten years. Since I understood all knowledge to be a means of apprehending the Lord, I considered all the time spent on study as an act of worshipping God.

`Imad-ud-din was then encouraged to go beyond the usual studies of the Koran, traditions and law, and acquire the 'real learning', reserved for an élite, which was to be found in the mystics. When he looked back on this phase of his life, `Imad-ud-Din saw it as a dangerous trap:

> In short, I also was entrapped in this esoteric science. I chose to speak little, eat little, remain aloof from people, afflict my body and stay awake during the nights. I began to recite the Qur'an throughout the night . . . I performed dhikr [i.e. repeated the name of God] loudly and silently. I sat in seclusion with closed eyes and mentally began to write the word 'Allah' on my heart . . . In short, whatever troubles and pain are within the power of man to bear, I have borne them and suffered them in their fullest intensity. But apart from deception nothing came out of it and I never found peace.

At the time of the great controversy with Christians in 1854, `Imad-ud-Din had been appointed preacher in the principal mosque of Akbarabad. He continued to preach there, but a particular verse in the Koran kept coming back to haunt him:

'[Gehenna:] Not one of you there is, but he shall go down to it; that for thy Lord is a thing decreed, determined' (19:71).

All human beings then, including Muslims, would be thrown into hell, and then God would have mercy on such as he chose. Looking for a way out of this problem, `Imad-ud-Din studied the commentaries on the Koran and examined the theological treatises to see if the intercession of Muhammad could save the believer from this terrible fate. He found that on the question of Muhammad's power of intercession with God, opinions were divided, some accepting it and others regarding it as a heresy. As his unease increased, the young preacher became a wandering monk, covering thousands of miles on foot in pilgrimages and other exercises of extreme asceticism: 'While immersed in such concerns, I comforted myself through excessive worship. In private I wept and prayed for forgiveness.'

On one occasion he made a retreat of twelve days during which he had to fast, recite a certain prayer thirty times a day, and to write the name of God on 125,000 pieces of paper and then throw them into a river. He lived this austere existence for ten years. People from the neighbourhood came to visit him and he was invited to preach in the streets, in mosques, in families.

> But my spirit found no rest. Through such an experience I felt even a contempt for the *shari'ah*, a feeling that daily increased. The shaykhs, the mawlawis, the faqirs and other pious Muslims whom I met, as well as their conduct, inner thoughts, prejudices, deceptions, ignorance and quarrellings which I saw, convinced me that there is no religion in this world which is true . . .
>
> I was no longer following the practices of Islam . . . Yet I still considered Islam to be true, though I did not adhere to the *shari'ah*. But now and again, when I thought about death, the time of departure from this world and the day of the Lord's judgement, my spirit was as if it were standing alone, weak, helpless and needy in a place filled with great dread and horror.

The news then reached him that his friend Safdar `Ali had become a Christian. He was surprised and determined to debate with him. To prepare for the encounter he bought some books of polemics and a Bible. Going through the Gospel of Matthew, he had not finished the first seven chapters when all his old doubts about the truth of Islam rose up again. He studied night and day. One conviction grew within him: the pardon and salvation for which he had been looking for so long was not to be found in the teaching of Islam, but was offered to him by Christianity.

Happy to find at last a way out of his agony, he asked for baptism. Some time later he was followed in this step by his wife and nine children. Imad-ud-Din's experience enabled him to write a number of Christian works for a Muslim public. He became a pastor and told of what happened within him as a result of his decision:

> Ever since I have entered into the grace of the Lord Jesus Christ I have had much spiritual satisfaction. The former agitation and restlessness have completely gone . . . No longer do I experience great anxiety of heart . . . Little remains of that sickness of fear for death and the grave, and I am wonderfully happy in the Lord.

Seven years later Imad-ud-Din added:

> Since becoming a Christian, I have never found this religion to be a source of depression. The joy I experienced at the time of baptism has daily increased . . . Secondly, I have discovered that nothing can deprive me of that joy which I have found in the Messiah and which possesses my spirit. I have been afflicted by difficulties, criticism, temptations . . . But nothing can disturb it. Nor is it that I myself have seized upon this joy and nourished it; rather it has seized me in a way that I cannot depart from it.

He ends by saying that every day he discovers Jesus, his Saviour, more and more, as he also discovers the misery of the world and his own weakness. Instead of continual swings between fear and hope, however, he feels rooted in the sure hope of his salvation.

The experience of sin

For other Muslims, it has been not so much the need for perfection as the experience of their personal sin which has sent them out in search of a Saviour who forgives.

THE TERRORIST AND THE CRUCIFIED

Ghulam Masih Naaman[10] was born in 1923 in Kashmir, in the extreme north of the Indian sub-continent. He came from a comfortably-off family, and studied in the usual middle-class secondary school. At the outbreak of war, weary of study, he joined the RAF and served there for eight years, seeing much active service in Burma. This experience in the British armed forces provided him with his first contact with Christians. It was an ambiguous experience. On the one hand, he encountered racial prejudice, but he also met real Christians, including his own superior officer, who prayed to Jesus with an assurance and an intimacy which the young Muslim found novel: 'Who is this Lord Jesus?' I wondered. As far as I knew from the Qur'an he was simply a prophet, like all other prophets. Yet people do not pray to prophets after they are dead to ask for deliverance! I had never heard of prayer in this fashion.'

Demobilised in 1947, Ghulam found himself caught up in the dramatic events which accompanied Indian independence. The sub-continent was divided into Muslim Pakistan and Hindu India. Kashmir was claimed by both states, and Muslim leaders called for a Holy War. Ghulam became an underground fighter, spending two years in raids and killings and reprisals. Non-Muslims had to be eliminated from the territory.

> It was our general practice to enter a village, send everyone at the point of a gun to their houses, shut the doors securely from the outside and set the whole village alight. Somehow the inhumanity of this kind of act did not penetrate into my consciousness. I was merely doing a job and the job had to be done well. If Allah was pleased, why should I question it?
>
> This freedom fighting went on for two whole years. At the end of these two years certain events occurred which helped to bring to the surface of my mind all those values I had learnt as a child. I could not dismiss them. The sacredness of life my mother had taught me; the desire to live for others. They had been submerged but were destined to come to the surface and to assume priority in my life again.

What caused this revival of conscience was his discovery, while meeting with other guerilla leaders, of a young girl prisoner who was a friend of his family. She had been taken by a band of guerillas and raped twelve times.

> I became speechless. What was I witnessing? Is this the outcome of religious zeal? Does Islam produce this kind of behaviour? For the first time in my self-chosen career a big question mark was raised against my activities. When I saw what had happened to a family close to me, doubts began to awaken within me.

Having freed the girl and restored her to her mother, he resumed his raids on the neighbouring villages, looking for non-Muslims to kill. One night, as he was preparing to butcher a Christian couple and their ten-year-old daughter, the latter asked permission to pray with her parents. As they finished with the words, 'In the name of Jesus Christ, Amen', Ghulam saw a wall of light rise up between him and his victims. Terrified, he murmured, 'Forgive me,' and the family replied, 'We forgive you in the name of Jesus Christ.' The light vanished, but Ghulam and his men left without carrying out the killing. 'We felt as if we owed them something for the suffering we had caused.'

Ghulam's doubts and questions increased:

> I had given up my chance for personal happiness because of my desire to please Allah when I responded to the call to join in the Holy War. But I did not feel a personal relationship with Allah nor believed that he gave me courage to do anything. I relied upon my own resources and ingenuity.
>
> But who was the little girl's 'Jesus Christ' who came and saved her at precisely the right moment? He was someone who kept his promises . . . This Lord Jesus seemed to be pursuing me wherever I went. The amazing thing is that I had asked the family to forgive me. I had never done such a thing before. Had I recognised that I was wrong to even think of murdering them? Was my whole life a sinful and wilful disobedience of doing what I innately knew to be wrong?

Ghulam began to perceive a certain continuity in the various experiences he had undergone. They seemed like separate pearls strung on a necklace. A final experience proved decisive. One night he and his men had encircled a village. He sent some of the party to burn the houses with their inhabitants, while he waited in ambush to kill anyone trying to escape. He intercepted an old woman carrying a child. She threw the child at his feet and exclaimed, 'Kill ! Go on, kill it! This is a Hindu child. Your God likes killing people, so kill it!'

Ghulam was paralysed. The hand raised to strike was stopped. Like one in a daze he heard the old woman reminding him of how fond he was of his toys when he was a child. She continued:

Well then, my son. Just imagine that this little soul is a God-made body or sort of toy which his hands have made and which expresses his goodness. If you were disgusted when anyone ruined anything you had made then how can you think that God likes all these things that you are doing? Is God so weak that he asks your help in killing infidels? If God does not like any person or thing then he is well able to put an end to it himself. Why does he tell you to kill infidels or his people?

Ghulam was thunderstruck. He told his men to withdraw. He left the guerrillas and returned to his family, looking for work, but above all for peace. He was sick at heart when he considered all the horrors he had perpetrated. He also felt cheated by an Islam which had ordered him to commit them, deceived by the Muslim 'learned men' who had launched him on such an adventure, by the mystics who seemed to him to be living hypocrites, by the mullahs who enriched themselves at the expense of the poor.

From a period of questioning he proceeded to a period of prayer. He would often rise during the night and ask God to guide him:

'My evil deeds convince me that hell is my portion, for you, O master, will judge sinners. I do not trust any religions and creeds in this world. O my Lord, show me the straight path. I do not want to go to hell. If you exist, show me the right path so that I may behold you. I am suffering, O master. I desire peace of mind and cannot find it. Help

me, Lord. My consciousness of my sin pierces me like a lancet. Have
mercy on me, O God, have mercy, Amen.'

I do not remember the date but it was three or four o'clock in the
morning and I was making my usual supplications. I was weeping bit-
terly and was more than usually despondent. I was in the waiting
room of a railway station when this particular prayer was uttered.
Suddenly I was conscious that someone had come up behind me, put
a loving hand on my shoulder and said, 'My grace is sufficient for
you!' This sentence was repeated three times and when it was
repeated the third time, I felt as if an electric charge had gone through
my body and the weight on my mind was immediately lifted. It was
as if an invigorating and exhilarating ecstasy had unexpectedly over-
taken me. I felt lifted up and experienced what I can only describe as
a union with God. Nothing seemed to separate us. The sense of forgiveness and reconciliation was so real.

Coming out of the waiting-room, Ghulam kept repeating beneath
his breath this phrase which he did not understand, 'My grace is
sufficient for you!' A sweeper heard him and said, 'Son, are you
a Christian?' It was this same humble sweeper who told Ghulam
that the phrase occurred in the Christian Scriptures and was
spoken by Jesus to his servant Paul (2 Corinthians 12:9). The
sweeper suggested that Jesus was calling him, Ghulam, to
become his disciple and to be baptised. He gave him the address
of a pastor.

In 1949, after two years spent in instruction, humble progress
and effort, Ghulam was baptised. He was roughly handled by his
family and locked up. Eventually he escaped and became first an
evangelist and then, in 1960, an Anglican minister.

One cannot fail to be struck by the parallels between the career
of the Apostle Paul and that of Ghulam Masih. Paul too had practised violence in the name of his religion until he was laid low by
Christ.

FROM PRISON CELLS
Prisoners occupied a privileged place among those to whom Jesus
proposed to preach the good news: 'The Spirit of the Lord is on

me, because he has anointed me to preach the good news to the poor. He has sent me to proclaim freedom for the prisoners, the recovering of sight for the blind, to release the oppressed, to proclaim the year of the Lord's favour' (Luke 4:18–19).

It was with these words, taken from the book of Isaiah, that Jesus began his preaching, adding: 'Today this scripture is fulfilled in your hearing.' It is therefore not surprising that people in prison, Christians, Muslims or unbelievers, quite often meet Jesus.

Even before they have been tried, the act of arrest makes a person the object of social disapproval, rejection and condemnation. Muslim societies have always stressed this penal aspect of their institutions, and modern movements which aim at establishing a strict Islam include in their programme the restoration of Koranic punishments: mutilation, stoning, flogging. Other societies have their own methods of excluding and punishing the delinquent. Muslims feel this social exclusion particularly keenly when they perceive that they are being rejected in the name of God and of faith.

A sizable proportion of people in prison in France give their religion as 'Muslim'. However, many of them have received no Islamic formation and their faith may be either dying or dead. But many retain an awareness of religious things acquired in their childhood.

If the family of a Muslim prisoner lives in France, his people may maintain contact with him if he has been guilty of some minor offence. If however he is in prison for a serious crime, or if he is a habitual offender, the head of the family may well forbid anyone to visit him. He is rejected by the family on which he has brought dishonour. Some French newspapers like to present the Muslim community as a breeding ground for criminals. This may induce the community to distance itself from any of its members who have tarnished its good name in the eyes of the population at large. Muslim religious leaders have the same rights as Christian and Jewish prison chaplains, but it seems they rarely make use of them.

The message received by many Muslim prisoners is that God condemns them and demands their rejection:

I lived in a milieu where faith was non existent. When I was young, I was taught religion through violence. I learned the Islamic religion through a thousand blows on every part of my body. During the day I was beaten, and in the evening I wept and insulted God. People cannot be brought to love by violence and suffering. Love must come by itself . . .

I do not criticise the Muslim religion, far from it, but that is how things are with us. There is no forgiveness. If you have committed a fault, you must pay.[11]

Some Muslim prisoners, either out of curiosity, or on the invitation of a fellow-prisoner, may go to mass or start reading the Bible. In this way their need to be loved may be met by the God offered to them by Jesus. One of them wrote on returning to his cell: 'Whenever I go to a religious service, I return to my cell marvelling. The question I put to myself is this: Why am I so happy in spite of the fact that I am in prison? . . . It can only be that this man is making me so. O my God, he is marvellous.'

What was the message which so struck this prisoner, who knew who he was and what he had done? He quotes the words of the sermon which impressed him so much that he keeps repeating them: 'You are a man, you are beautiful, Jesus loves you. Trust in him and you will be happy.' He could not get them out of his head.

Another read the story of Nicky Cruz[12] and was struck by these words: 'Go to God, tell him of your pain and anger. Just tell him, as simply and directly as possible, what it is that you are feeling. He will not be surprised or shocked.'

Another speaks of his joy at having discovered 'one who loves us in spite of our often unclean hearts. We have to learn to receive this marvellous heritage, we all need to be washed from the faults we have committed.'

This discovery of God's unconditional love for everyone, and of his forgiveness, is such a shock for some prisoners that they start reading and meditating on the Bible for several hours every day:

I love the God whom I find in the Bible. I really feel that God is as you have said. Yes, truth, freedom, that is God, that is the Bible . . .

From the day that I first opened the Bible, a voice has been summoning me ever more strongly . . .

I have been interested in the word of Jesus for months. Where and who am I? What am I looking for? For months and months, even in my darkest days in prison; during all the months I spent in solitary confinement, I hardly felt it, for I had a Bible! What is it, this Bible? Yes, my eyes were opened in a flash. 'Love follows me even into the solitary cell.' A conclusion impressed itself upon my mind. On every page of the Bible, one meets love, goodness, fraternity. At the risk of atrocious sufferings, men and women have given their love, their friendship, to their brethren. The Lord himself cried, 'Father, forgive them!'

The great discovery is that Jesus is the forgiveness of God offered to everybody and that he came not to condemn but to heal:

All began when I had lost everything: my house, my children, my wife . . . I found myself locked up here, full of pain and remorse. Despair took hold of me . . . and then one day I met a man who came to visit me in my cell, who prayed for me, who brought me to know and love Jesus so that he might help me. I opened my heart to Jesus. He put his love in the place of my despair. He came into me, not all at once, but little by little, without frightening me, to cure me, to comfort me in my sorrow, to bring back my smile and my joys. He came into me like a seed which, day after day, grew peacefully into love and joy. That is why I had myself baptised, to listen to him better and to serve him.

At a stroke, the excuses and evasions fade away, one can be accepted by Jesus just as one really is. It is a transformation:

With us religion is national, it is obligatory . . . I was not a practising Muslim, I was only called a Muslim . . . It is thanks to a priest and to the Bible that I have become a man, for I realise that until I met the Lord I was only a lost animal, without belief, without anything.

Today I am a practising Christian and I live happily in the presence of the Lord who never leaves me, in my prayers, in my work, in my sleep, in every moment of the day. I am almost glad that I came to prison, for if I had not committed the crime which brought me here I would never have met the Lord nor recognised my fault. For Jesus said that he would not abandon without forgiveness those who acknowledge their fault. Of course I regret infinitely what I did, but it is too late now for regrets, and I am happy that the Lord has forgiven me.

These prisoners recognise that Christ offers them what they need above all things: a love which forgives; and this discovery leads them into the very heart of the message of Jesus Christ.

God's forgiveness: tangibly experienced

A longing for an unattainable perfection.
A need for a love which forgives sins.

These are the two main reasons why some of those brought up in Islam feel the need to search for salvation. The longing and the need persist like a thorn in the flesh.

At the same time, all these testimonies make us understand how people need a tangible experience of salvation.

The story of *K.K. Alavi*, a Muslim born in 1951 in Kerala, India, and now a Christian missionary, is particularly instructive in this regard.[13] This Muslim family was deeply mortified to discover that one of its children seemed compelled to make contact with the Christians of the neighbourhood. In spite of all the physical punishment, he persisted in reading the Gospels, in following catechism lessons, in writing away for correspondence courses. Finally his parents bound him and locked him up for three weeks while deciding what they should do with him. But he got away.

How can we possibly explain this compulsion and this perseverance on the part of a mere boy, extending over several years? The explanation was that one day Alavi had found on a market-stall a little book which described the experience of a young Christian when he allowed himself to be taken over by the forgiveness of Christ.

Alavi knew well enough the teaching of Islam to be made uncomfortable by the idea that a prophet like Jesus could forgive sins. The book however did not defend any theory but presented an experience: an experience of peace and joy, and especially the experience of feeling transformed by a love coming into oneself from without. The desire of having such an experience himself took root in Alavi's heart and allowed him no peace.

It was this gnawing desire which enabled him to endure blows and mockery and the separation from his family. Through careful study of the Bible and the Koran, he managed more or less to soothe his principal doubts. But he would only reach his goal on 19 June 1970, the day of his baptism:

> It was on July 19, 1970, that I surrendered to Jesus the Messiah. I confessed all my sins and all my doubts, and by holy baptism I was joined to him and his forgiving love. My whole body trembled, I could feel divine power entering into me, I rose from my knees as a changed man, with peace in my soul, joy in my heart and assurance in my mind. (Even today I testify to the same peace, joy, hope and assurance.) Though I could not explain it, in my heart I believed that all my sins were washed away through the precious blood of Jesus Christ, that I had received power for a new life of love, and that the Lord Jesus himself was reigning in my heart.

Many 'traditional' Christians are so accustomed to speaking of Christianity in terms of theological beliefs and ritual practices, that it may come as a surprise to observe that all these pilgrimages culminate in a 'palpable' entry of Jesus into people's lives, and in a real experience of a transforming forgiveness. This phenomenon may enable 'traditional' Christians to perceive a new meaning in the words of Zechariah, John the Baptist's father, when he sang of the coming of a salvation which one could truly know, by personal experience and not simply at second hand: 'You will go before the Lord . . . to give . . . *knowledge* of salvation through the forgiveness of their sins' (Luke 1:76–77).

Beyond all alibis

Sometimes converts can get side-tracked, or they may resist the appeal of which they are conscious.

Beyond polemics

A not uncommon tactic to avoid God's call is to engage in some kind of 'diversionary attack'. One may manifest a zeal for perfection, but it is a perfection for others: one never genuinely questions oneself. This was the case with those who brought to Jesus the woman taken in adultery. They avoided confronting their own sin by projecting their accusations and condemnation onto another. Jesus saw through this tactic: 'If any one of you is without sin, let him be the first to throw a stone at her' (John 8:7).

A further advantage of engaging in a polemic against others is that it gives one the illusion of power. To unmask the weakness of others gives one an agreeable sensation of one's own superiority. Such was the case with *Sultan Muhammad Paul*.[14]

He was born in 1881 in Kabul, Afghanistan, where his father was a colonel, but went to India for his Islamic studies, first in Delhi and then in Bombay. One day he came across a Christian who was explaining his religion to a group of loungers. He was using passages from the Koran in which God speaks of himself in the plural to explain the doctrine of the Trinity. The young student intervened to explain that this was merely the 'royal plural'.

He was so proud of having got the better of the argument that he became an energetic anti-Christian polemicist. Eventually this became a veritable passion with him. He started reading the Bible, but only to find ammunition which he could use in arguments against Christians. While continuing his own studies, he founded an association dedicated to controversy against all religions other than Islam. The trap snapped shut. Sultan could think of nothing except his disputes.

It was during a pilgrimage to Mecca that he felt the first touch of grace. Far from any adversary, he was able to devote himself to prayer. Suddenly the thought came to him: 'If Islam is not the true religion, what will my condition be on the day of resurrection?' He was given there the opportunity to desire the truth, and not simply the triumph of Islam. He prayed: 'God, show me the true religion and thy true way. If Islam is the true religion, keep me steadfast in it, and grant me grace to silence the opponents of

Islam. If Christianity is the true religion, then reveal its truth to me. Amen.'

Some time later Sultan returned to Bombay and organised a debate with a Christian on the theme of salvation. He offered a brilliant defence of Islam, and everyone congratulated him. But he knew himself that his arguments were weak and he was not convinced of what he was saying: 'Though I was making much more noise than my antagonist, his voice was thundering in my soul with an indescribable power.'

What struck him most was the undoubted fact that human beings are weak and sinful. The great question was to know how he could obtain salvation. He hoped that it was in Islam. But suppose it was in Christianity? One needed to be clear about it. He fell on his knees, wept and prayed, and decided never again to read the Bible merely to mock but to find out how a sinner like himself could find salvation.

Then began a period of study during which he examined Islam, Christianity and Hinduism, and compared their teaching on the salvation of the sinner. He soon discovered in Islam the themes we have mentioned above. He was struck by the verses in the Koran (19:71–72) which said that everyone was destined for hell, and even more by another verse: 'I will certainly fill Gehenna with demons and human beings together' (11:19). He was deeply troubled and began to fear that he might have to leave Islam. He looked for comfort in passages in the traditions about Muhammad. He found there the two opinions we have already met: some words promised paradise to the Muslim, even if he were a sinner; but other words plunged him afresh into fear and despair:

Abu Huraira reported that the Prophet of Islam said: 'No one of you will enter paradise through his good works.' They said: 'Not even you, O Apostle of God?' 'Not even I,' he replied, 'unless God cover me with his grace and mercy. Therefore be strong, and morning and evening, nay, every moment, try to do good.'

Abu Huraira related as well that the Prophet arose and began to proclaim: '. . . I cannot save you from the punishment of the day of resurrection. Take care of yourself, O my daughter Fatimah; you may use my property, but I cannot save you from God. Take care of yourself.'

Sultan could come to no firm conclusion and his distress remained. He then turned to the Gospels to complete his research, and came across the passage where Jesus says, 'Come to me, all you who are weary and burdened, and I will give you rest' (Matthew 11:28).

This verse had an extraordinary effect on him:

> It was the God-given answer to my hard labour and sincere investigation. For a sinner like me it was indeed the supreme proclamation of good news. This life-giving verse had a tremendous effect upon me. It brought me peace, comfort and joy and immediately banished all uneasiness and uncertainty from my heart.

Thus encouraged, Sultan Muhammad set about reading the New Testament. He found illumination in innumerable passages which brought him to the conviction that forgiveness is offered to humanity in Jesus. He explained to the members of his association the outcome of the debate which he had been conducting with himself for several months. He then asked for baptism in 1903 and became an Anglican priest.[15]

Deeper than theories

One may dimly perceive within one's heart a call to personal repentance and try to avoid it by taking refuge in beautiful ideas and theories.

Rajab Ali Nozad (1889–1944), an Iranian who was converted in 1905, provides us with an example.[16] Orphaned while still a child, Rajab Ali found work as a domestic servant. He writes of the life he lived during this period:

> Since the sins of this young man were beyond description and narration, I will forego setting them down. By way of introduction I will say that I was that young man.
>
> In observing the tenets of the religion of my fathers, I was fanatically zealous—my prayers were said without neglecting the

appointed times, the fast I kept, I remembered the martyrs and I went on pilgrimages. My fanaticism went beyond those of my own age, yet sin had dominion over me and I fulfilled all of its desires. Although my heart was unsatisfied and my conscience rebuked me, I was a slave of sin.'

After some time he made the acquaintance of an old scholar who lived in solitude amid his books, while giving occasional private lessons in science and medicine. This man was well versed in the religious learning of Islam, but, curiously, he never spoke of it. Rajab was intrigued and one day summoned up the courage to ask him the reason for his reticence. 'I believe in God ... But I have no belief in any of the persons who have made pretensions to being prophets except Jesus. He withstands me most disconcertingly! For a long time I have tried to resist him, but I cannot prevail.'

The explanation he offered for this curious attitude constituted a devastating criticism of Islam, the Koran, the Prophet, Muslims and especially the mullahs. For a moment Rajab thought of killing him for such blasphemy, but then he decided to examine his elderly friend's accusations. For two years he read, consulted, listened to learned men. What he learned seemed only to confirm the old scholar's objections. Rajab lost his faith and was in despair. The universe seemed to have no meaning, religions were false, the scriptures mere fables.

Finally he had the idea of going to see a Christian priest to find out more.

Three times I went to his house, and every time for several hours I conversed and debated with him, but did not get the real meaning of a thing he said.

The fourth time, which was to be the last call I made upon him, I heard these words [from him]: 'Just as malaria is widespread in the world, and its cure is effected only with quinine, even though it is bitter, in the same way all mankind is sick with sin, and the sole medicine for that is the gospel. Everyone has the choice of accepting it or rejecting it.'

Rajab left the priest and wandered about in despair. Hardly know-ing what he did, he lifted his arms and said:

'O God, if thou dost exist and Jesus is from thee and the gospel is the remedy for the sickness of the world, guide thou me, for I am in great perplexity! If thou art not, then I have spoken to the wind.'

Suddenly I saw above my head two spiritual forms whose coun-tenances and clothing were like the colour of the sky who said in loud tones, 'God is, and Jesus is true. Of that rest assured, and come!' Immediately they disappeared.

Terrified, Rajab ran towards the town. As he saw the people coming and going, his fear subsided, and he also discovered to his surprise that his depression and despair had also lifted, leav-ing him in a quite novel condition of joy and peace. Opening the New Testament, he discovered that the words were now clear and transparent and full of meaning, adapted to his needs and thoughts. He spent four days and four nights reading the Gospels, and then began to study the rest of the Bible.

As long as he was only looking for information, the words which people spoke to Rajab seemed incomprehensible. But as soon as he admitted his misery and committed himself to live according to the response which God might offer, the Bible began to speak to him. He was eventually baptised Nozad, which means 'new-born'. He found various kinds of work, as a craftsman, a watchman, a detective, and became known to all for his Christian faith.

Study and beautiful thoughts were not a flight from God's call for *Dr Ibrahim Deshmukh*, the Indian doctor born in 1934 into a somewhat lukewarm Muslim family.[17] He was a methodical per-son, and he progressed towards faith by first seeking answers to his objections. But he too had to go beyond ideas. He felt a vague sympathy for Christians as a result of biblical films he had seen during his student days. He also had Christian colleagues, and even found among them his future wife. But he felt no urge to go further.

Things changed for him when his fiancée, Milly, gave him a

Bible and asked him to read it. Muslim leaders in general forbid their flock to read the Bible lest it contaminate their faith, and Ibrahim decided therefore to put off reading the Bible until he had seen what the Koran had to say about it. He drew up a list of nine sorts of statements. In eight of them the Koran praises and approves the Bible, and recommends its reading; in one, the people of the book are accused of falsifying the Bible. Ibrahim tried to reconcile the contradiction by arguing that the latter accusation was only addressed to the Jews and Christians of Muhammad's own time. In this he followed the opinion of a number of Koran commentators.

He was then ready to open the Bible and see if Muslim objections were well founded. He compared the message of the Koran with that of the Bible. He had the feeling that in the Koran the stress was on war, while the Bible offered rather a message of peace. All these studies did not lead to any practical conclusion as long as Ibrahim restricted himself to a detached kind of reading.

The change came when he consented to become personally involved. He began to be conscious of his sin: 'I sensed I needed even to be saved from myself, to be changed from within'. He then found himself described in the Bible—he was the prodigal son of Luke 15:

> My decision to follow Jesus and to be baptised was no light decision. Indeed, it was the result of much intellectual and spiritual travail. I did not make the decision blindly unaware of and callously unconcerned with its consequences within my family and community. Despite the heavy cost, I knew the 'joy in heaven over one sinner who repents'. It was as if I had returned, where I belonged, to my heavenly Father and had thrown myself into his open arms of mercy (Luke 15). This chapter's story of the coin, the sheep and the son, spoken by Jesus and inscribed upon the pages of the Holy Injil almost two thousand years ago, was my own biography, a transcript of my relation with God. How could I dismiss this portrait of my life as irrelevant, superseded, abrogated!

In the same way, he found it unthinkable to state that the Koran has no need of the Bible when essential texts such as the parable of the good Samaritan, the sermon on the mount, and the hymn to love in the first epistle to the Corinthians, do not figure in it.

Once Ibrahim became personally involved in his search, he began to understand things that had remained sealed to him when he simply looked into them as a student. This is why he could only conceive of his new Christian life as a total commitment. He resigned as a public service doctor and opened a dispensary in an area where the poor had no medical facilities. He suffered from cancer for three years, but after recovering he returned to his patients 'so that they might know that God cares for *them*, that ultimately he is the source of all healing, that medical staff, scalpel and drugs are simply his gifts, and finally that the stance of both patients and staff is simply to say, "Thank you, dear God!"'

Selfless love rediscovered

On judgement day, each will receive his deserts. This message of Islam, as it is commonly understood, seems clear. But, as we have seen, there are other elements in the message which correct this simplistic idea that believers can just present themselves before God and demand what is due to them. It is part of the message as well that each person has to be 'covered by the divine mercy'.

Even this however does not satisfy some fervent believers. It is clear that an insistence on heaven and hell as sanctions for our earthly actions could stifle disinterested love and selflessness in the heart of the believers. Muslim mystics have felt this objection, and a pious woman, Râbi'a (713-801), wanted to 'extinguish the fire of hell so that we might no longer serve God out of fear, and to put fire in paradise, so that we may no longer serve God either simply in order to gain heaven. Then we would love God for his own sake and not for ours.'

The Muslim mystics spoke of an ideal of disinterested love, a love beyond any law; and some have found this ideal, magnified, in Christ.

We find it in the case of *Joseph Issifi Bosso*, the Peul from Niger, who 'had a taste for Islam' and served as a Muslim marabout for several years:[18]

One day, during the Ramadan, while I was on a journey, I lay down tired in the shade of a tree, my gourd full of water at my side, waiting for sunset before breaking my fast. I fell asleep, and in a dream I heard a voice saying to me: 'Take the water and drink. It is not that which God wants from you.' I woke up and drank. From that day, I have asked what God wants of me. I have asked him to show me his way.

Evidently Issifi observed the fast with more than ordinary zeal, since he would not even break it on a journey. The voice told him to abandon this minute observance of the law, to break it as one would break an idol, and allow God to lead him to some as yet unknown destiny beyond any law.

The Pakistani mystic *John Parwez* had a not dissimilar experience.[19] He observed minutely all the prescriptions of the law, and added the many Sufi devotional practices: prayers, litanies, vigils . . .

Though I tried with all my might to do good actions, every day I committed some sin or other against God. The worst sin that I was guilty of was pride and conceit; for after worshipping God I thought that I was holy while everyone else was a sinner. I began to be very troubled, wondering how I could be set free from sin and thinking that without good actions I should surely go to hell. This fear was with me continually; I felt that I could not fulfil the law, which had become a heavy burden to me.

It was then that he heard the verse of the Gospel, 'Come to me all you who are weary and burdened, and I will give you rest' (Matthew 11:28).

For him the meaning was clear: Jesus was calling him and wished to liberate him from the burden of the law. In spite of opposition from his family and friends, by whom he was regarded as a saint, he asked for baptism and experienced a radical change: for the cult of the law there was substituted a spirit of service to others:

My life has completely changed. A spirit of service has taken the place of pride and conceit. After my conversion I have had to do very ordinary jobs: sweeping floors, washing dishes, acting as night-watchman, and so on, and that without any distaste. This blessing has come to me through trusting Christ, who said, 'Among you, whoever wants to be great must be your servant.' (Mark 10:43–44)

We see from these testimonies what can happen in the life of a man or woman when the undeserved forgiveness of God enters the soul and stamps it with its distinctive mark. 'Undeservedness' becomes a way of life, a new way of entering into relationship with God and other people. This way of life becomes possible, but this does not mean, as we shall shortly have occasion to see, that it is always easy.

We may note in passing that most of these converts in search of forgiveness find their way into Protestant churches. These are the Christian churches which lay the greatest stress on the unmerited forgiveness which God offers us in Christ. It is a dimension which is often less visible in the Catholic Church which, often in opposition to Protestantism, tends to place greater emphasis on works. To outsiders, the result can easily appear to be a religious system very like Islam. The dream of a Church of pure souls, a pastoral approach based on commitment, and the activism which can result, can easily appear to the prospective convert as a return to a cult of the law.

Notes

1 Here, we only translate some of the names used to describe God in Islam: *rahmân, rahîm, ghafûr, ghaffâr, 'afûw, halîm, karîm.*

2 Here again we use the same list of divine names, in particular: *'adl, wâsi', basîr, samî', 'alîm, hakam, muhsî, muntaqim.*

3 Quoted by Abâ Hamid al-Ghazâlî, *Ihyâ' 'ulâm al-dîn* (Reviving the sciences of religion), (Matb. M. al-Bâbî al-Halabî: Cairo, 1939), Vol.4, p.37, in the Book of Repentance.

4 We could read the parable of the vineyard labourers (Matthew 20:1–16), that of the prodigal son (Luke 15:11–32), or the promise made by Jesus to the criminal who was crucified with him (Luke 23:39–43). We may remember as well so many other texts of the New Testament: 'Therefore, there is now no condemnation for those who

are in Christ Jesus' (Romans 8:1) or 'God has bound all men over to disobedience so that   he may have mercy on them all' (Romans 11:32).

5 The Gospel teaching about the last judgement is clear: in Matthew 25:31–46 only those who have never given food to the hungry are condemned: forgiveness has been killed in those persons' hearts. On the contrary, whoever is found as having, only once, given a glass of water is saved (Matthew 10:42): there is still life in that heart. There is no question of drawing up a balance-sheet between good and evil. This would appear like a medical examination looking for the least sign of life in a human body. How soothing this is for anxious and troubled people!

6 A saying ascribed to Muhammad has the Prophet stating: '"A messenger coming from God told me that any member of my community who dies without having worshipped any one but God will enter paradise." I asked him: "Even though he is a thief or commits adultery?" "Yes," he replied, "Even though he is a thief or commits adultery!"'

7 Abdul Haqq, *How I Came to Jesus-Christ* (Chandigarh, India, 1960).

8 Imad-ud-Din Lahiz, *The Life of the Rev. Mawlawi Dr Imad-ud-din Lahiz* (Henry Martyn Institute: Hyderabad, India, 1978).

9 The story of his conversion has been told in chapter 3.

10 Ghulam Masih Naaman and V. Toon, *The Unexpected Enemy, A Muslim Freedom Fighter Encounters Christ* (Marshalls: Basingstoke, UK, 1985).

11 All the testimonies given here come from confidential sources and the authors must remain anonymous.

12 For the story of this young gangster who found his way to God, read D. Wilkerson, *The Cross and the Switchblade* (Pyramid Books, New York, 1962) or N. Cruz and J. Buckingham, *Run Baby Run* (Pyramid Books).

13 K. K. Alavi, *In Search of Assurance* (Gospel Literature Service: Bombay, India, 1977).

14 Md. P. Sultan, *Why I Became a Christian* (Gospel Literature Service, Bombay, India, 1978).

15 One finds a similar evolution in J. Ali Bakhsh, 'The Story of My Conversion', *Muslim World*, 16, 1926, pp.79–84.

16 W. McE. Miller, *Ten Muslims Meet Christ* (Eerdmans: Grand Rapids, Mi., USA, 1969, 1980), pp.55–67.

17 His conversion has been described in chapter 2. All details can be

found in his book: I.O. Deshmukh, *In Quest of Truth* (FFM: Toronto, Canada).

18 R. Deniel, *Chemins de Chrétiens Africains* (Inades: Abidjan, Ivory Coast, 1982–1983), No.5, pp.24–31; J.M. Ducroz, *Les Actes des Premiers Chrétiens du Gorouol*, (Nouvelle Cité: Paris, 1977), pp.38–39.

19 R.W.F. Wootton, *Jesus More than a Prophet, Fifteen Muslims find forgiveness, release and new life* (Inter-Varsity Press, Leicester, UK, 1982), pp.30–33.

CHAPTER 8

THE THIRST FOR GOD

I was astounded by the declaration of the great writer that he did not address God with the deference due to his grandeur but as one friend speaks to another. Should the love of God make us forget his power and his glory, should we be raising ourselves up to his level, or dragging him down to ours? . . . I am no less astonished to hear the author further assert that he had heard, or thought he had heard, a response from God himself, addressed to him, allowing a conversation between them.

Dr M. al-Tayyib al-Najjâr, Rector of the University of Al-Azhar, in Al-Ahrâm, 8 March 1983.

The writer in question was Tawfîq al-Hakîm (1898-1987), one of the best known of contemporary Egyptian writers. Born at the turn of the century, he studied law in Cairo and Paris and became a magistrate before turning to writing plays for the theatre. After a brilliant career, he lived in peaceful retirement until, in 1983, he published five articles which aroused a storm of protest in Egypt. He was called a heretic and an apostate, and was obliged to retract.[1]

What caused such scandal was that the author published a series of informal prayers in which he conversed with God in a familiar manner and received imaginary replies. Christian readers may be acquainted with this sort of literature, for example the 'Prayers' of Michel Quoist and *The Imitation of Christ*. They may ask why such prayers were considered so offensive to Islam by religious authorities such as the Rector of the University of Al-Azhar. Are there certain kinds of prayers which are familiar to Christians but forbidden to Muslims?

An Islam beyond Islam

A brief outline of the essential features of Islamic teaching will help us to appreciate better the spirituality of those who live their faith within the framework of Islam.

At the same time, we will understand a little better the motivations of those Muslims who come to Christianity in order to find a certain type of prayer life for which they thirst.

The initial experience: the discovery of God

It cannot be repeated too often that at the heart of Islam is the religious experience of the Prophet Muhammad, the founder of the Muslim community. Born and brought up in the paganism of sixth-century Arabia, he sought and found a truth obscured by the pagan cults of his time. Beyond all the tumult of the world, infinitely above the illusory goals of ambition, profit and idols, there is God, the unique, the true, the creator of all things.

AN OVERWHELMING TRANSCENDENCE

This discovery affected Muhammad like a stroke of lightning. It was a blazing light which left everything else in darkness. Revelation stood out against a background of ignorance: faith was defined by its opposite, unbelief, now destroyed by the clearest evidence.

The Koran formulated this discovery of God by Muhammad in negative terms. All else had to be rejected: false gods, idols, man-made divinities. God, the all-highest, has no equal or rival or associate, nothing in heaven or on earth can compare with him. Both the Old and New Testaments of the Christian Bible are full of similar expressions. To emphasise the greatness of God, the writers contrast the littleness of the creature. To express his majesty and transcendence, they declare that he cannot be contained within the limits of our finite and contingent condition.

TRANSCENDENCE IN PRACTICE

After the generation of the Prophet had passed away, Muslim thinkers began to examine in the first place how Muhammad himself had behaved. In this way they came to draw up the Muslim programme of daily prayer of which the Koran itself gives no details.

Using the vocabulary of Greek philosophy, the thinkers then started to examine and comment on the text of the Koran. The insights of this book were given more precise and technical formulation.

These 'Fathers' of Islam declared that since God is the wholly other, he must be radically unknowable. He does not reveal himself, but only manifests his will and his commandments in the Koran. Since he is the most high, he is infinitely above his creatures, and any attempt at intimacy with him would be an act of disrespect towards his majesty. There can therefore be no question of union with God, either in prayer or in life.

In the Koran, Muhammad is presented as the 'seal of the prophets'. Theologians concluded from this image, not only that the teaching of Muhammad confirmed that of his prophetic predecessors, but also that he was the end of the series, the last Prophet. It was not to be thought that any later believer could have an experience of divine revelation, since this would make him a prophet later than the last Prophet.

The prayer of the Muslim believer thus remains within strict limits. It is expressed in certain rites whose words and gestures are carefully fixed. It excludes all familiarity with God. It may not admit the illusion that God can communicate himself or reveal himself to the believer. His voice cannot be heard except through the Koran.[2] This religious climate explains why Tawfiq al-Hakîm's 'conversations with God' gave such scandal in official Muslim quarters.

To sum up: Islam admits *no union with God*, in life or in prayer, and no possibility of a *personal knowledge of God*.

MYSTICISM UNDER SUSPICION

Islamic orthodoxy, as defined in the eighth and ninth centuries, is marked by the cult both of the law and of the strict letter of the

Koran. It came into collision with another category of believers, the Sufi, pious Muslims who were more sensitive to the call of God than to the warnings of learned men about the limits of devotion. They too had scrutinised the tradition concerning the words and deeds of the Prophet, and they had found there invitations to get to know this unknowable God, from whom, it was said, Muhammad had received these words: 'I was a hidden treasure, but I wanted to be known, and so I created the world.'

Searching for the knowledge of God, these prudent and closed Sufi groups developed a spirituality which led to a certain experience of union with God. When this ideal was made public, it led to persecution, and some of the Sufi were executed, among them Mansûr al-Hallâj, in 922. During the following centuries, books were written in an attempt to contain the Sufi mystics within the limits of orthodoxy. They were obliged to bridle their burning desire to meet God directly and content themselves with formal prayer. To this day the conflict between Islamic orthodoxy and mysticism has not been resolved, and there are numerous local confrontations between them.

This conflict is in fact mirrored in the heart of every believer. It may be no more than a fruitful dialectic, a tension between love for God and the respect which is due to him. At the same time, a too narrow religious training, or particular circumstances, can bring certain Muslims to feel that they are in an impossible situation, torn between an irresistible desire for a personal encounter with God and a loyal desire to respect the official veto on any such encounter.

It is not therefore surprising that some Muslims find in Christianity the reconciliation between these two aspirations. They find that Christianity fulfils the aspirations which Islam had aroused.

The ultimate experience: Lamin Sanneh

Such was the case with *Lamin Ousmane Sanneh.*[3] He was born in 1942 in the Gambia, and brought up as a strict Muslim, with a particular bias against the traditional African religions. Very early in life he was exposed, not only to traditional African culture, but also to what he calls the official system—the religious code established by Muslim theologians. Islam in sub-Saharan Africa is deeply marked by the cult of the saints: they are invoked, and often, it is believed, people are in fact helped by them. The saints communicate *baraka*, the power which comes from God.

From his adolescence Lamin had certain problems concerning the transcendence of God. This eventually led him to discover Christ. His spiritual odyssey had three stages.

A GOD WHO INTERVENES IN HISTORY

The Koran itself shows that God spoke to Muhammad and thus showed an interest in human history. How then could we believe in a God who had no interest in our activities? Lamin began to examine how the Koran speaks of the Prophet, and was struck by several passages:

> God said, concerning his pact with the prophets: I have really given you a Book and a Wisdom. Then a Prophet came to you, confirming you in your possession of these things. Believe him and help him. Are you resolved, and do you accept my alliance on this condition? They replied: We agree! He said: Be then my witnesses. As for me, *here am I with you, among the witnesses*. (Koran 3:81)
>
> Yes, God and his angels bless the Prophet. Oh you believers, bless him and call salvation down upon him. (33:56)

These verses, and many others, show how God took a personal interest in Muhammad. Further, they show God acting just as we do and as present among us as a witness to the mission of his Prophet. God invites us to bless the Prophet as he himself blesses him. Later theologians tried to gloss over this proximity of God and this resemblance he creates between humankind and himself; but the text remains. In describing God as one who is grateful and who thanks believers for their faith and fidelity (35:34–36; 76:22), the Koran reveals a God who establishes a real reciprocity between himself and humanity. This means much more than an impersonal retribution.

Lamin felt the contradiction between two approaches to God's mystery: the official Islamic position; these verses from the Koran, which found an echo in his own heart.

He decided to follow his heart, encouraged by two traditions according to which the Prophet said: 'God proclaims: My heaven and my earth do not contain me, but the heart of my faithful Servant contains me.' And: 'Search your heart and you will find the secret plan of God proclaimed by the interior knowledge of the heart, which is true faith and divinity.'

GOD WHO REVEALS HIMSELF IN HIS MESSENGER

The vast majority of Muslims accept two sources of faith: the Koran and the Prophet himself, all of whose words and deeds were guided by God. He is the Messenger par excellence, and those who would know how to honour God must imitate him. The theologians explained that Muhammad enjoyed permanent inspiration.

Like all devout Muslims, in Africa and everywhere else, Lamin Sanneh had received from his parents a strong devotion to Muhammad. He prayed to him, asked for his intercession, and looked to him for guidance in the decisions of daily life. The Prophet is a sign of the interest which God takes in our slightest actions and in all our difficulties.

The God of the theologians lived beyond time and space. But the God of Muhammad is present in the history of every human being, and the heart of the believer is moved for there can be found the true God. One can experience his nearness, his favour, his mercy.

In fact the Koran goes even further, for in that book God says to Muhammad: 'We have only sent you as an act of mercy for the worlds' (21:107).

The Prophet is therefore not only a messenger but also the message itself, a living expression of the mercy of God *within* the history of the world. The young Gambian thus developed a sense of God's plan: God wishes to manifest *himself* in his mercy by coming into this world.[4] In Muhammad, he came to believe, God was offering a message to humankind which it was free either to accept or reject; moreover, God was offering himself to our love and making himself vulnerable to our refusal of belief in him.

GOD RECONCILED THE WORLD TO HIMSELF IN JESUS

The Koran was the only book to which Lamin Sanneh had access. He was further struck by the revelation of God in the story of Jesus, as recounted in the Koran.

He found there the tradition which recounts that God could not permit his prophet Jesus to die on the cross, and therefore put a double in his place.[5] Here was further confirmation that God intervenes in human history to save men and women from suffering.

But can't God be moved also by the sufferings of Jesus' double, and by those of other people? And what about Jesus himself? He was the great manifestation of the mercy of God, how could he do other than offer to suffer himself in place of his double? In the divine logic, Jesus could only be this substitute who suffers for the other:

> Jesus proves ... that at least in one case ... God did breach transcendence ... to come across and take part in the drama centered on suffering ... If anyone knew about the heart of God concerning the issue of suffering, it was Jesus ... Through Jesus, God had arrived at a rendez-vous with humanity.
>
> God who normally delegates his authority to the prophets, is committed to the logic of that delegation by being willing to express himself in one such prophet who, by virtue of that special relationship, must henceforth be described by the strong language of filiation. Rather than rendering him immune to the tragedy of human disobedience, such a prophet is in fact the supreme subject and victim of its consequences ...
>
> Jesus is the definitive measure of God's 'numbing' capacity to take on our suffering.

EPILOGUE

Lamin Sanneh was just fifteen when he arrived at this point in his reasoning. He was seized with panic at his discovery, for he despised Christians and wanted to remain a Muslim. Yet he realised that in following the intuitions of his heart to the end he had arrived at Christianity's most powerful symbol: the cross.

For some months he resisted and plunged himself into a frenzy of Islamic devotions. It was in vain. Indeed Jesus began to assume in his eyes a cosmic importance: Jesus is the presence of God at the heart of our world. This was at a time when Lamin had still read nothing of the Bible. To find peace, he finally decided to enter into the mystery of Jesus.

The first consequence of this decision was that he overcame his contempt for Christians and tried to see them with the eyes of love with which Jesus saw them and all men and women. He felt called to enter the Church and submitted himself to the call.

Like many other converts, he encountered suspicion and indifference. The Protestants sulked, the Catholics showed no interest. Finally he was accepted by the Protestants. He undertook advanced studies in Islam and Christianity, became a university teacher, and is now Professor of World Christianity at Yale in the United States.

A pilgrimage such as his is rare. However, other people, from the depths of their simple faith, may share the same religious insights even though they cannot express these as articulately as Lamin Sanneh.

The pedagogy of Tahar

Tahar is a pseudonym for a Muslim who came to Christian faith in Paris after a spiritual journey which lasted for twenty-five years, and which, he tells us, he often speaks about with other searching Muslims.

- He first meditated on the absolute *transcendence* of God, ineffable and unknowable.
- He then thought about God as *immanent*, the present God of whom the Koran speaks: 'He is there between man and his heart . . . He is nearer to a man than his jugular vein' (8:24; 50:16).
- He then tried to penetrate the meaning of the verses in the Koran which speak of the mutual *love* between God and men (3:31; 5:54), and suggest the mystery of a certain mode of divine presence.
- Leaving aside the verses of the Koran which speak of Jesus, and which can too easily lead to polemics between Muslims and Christians, Tahar dwelt on those which speak of the *Virgin Mary*, preserved from all evil at her birth, and of the child given to her, a word

of God become man. He wondered about the reason for these privileges and this miraculous birth.

The spontaneous response which rose from the depths of his heart when he considered the mystery of the divine will was that of every believing Muslim: 'There is no power save in God, the most high.' What was there to prevent God from rendering present his word in Jesus, under the form of man, as he rendered it present in the Koran in the form of a book?

Tahar has now been a Christian for many years, and he uses his own experience to help Muslims who consult him. He makes no effort to persuade them to take the same decision as himself. He only leads them to the threshold of the mystery, according to each one's rhythm. "He seeks only to show them that there is another way of reading the Koran, one which leads them morally and psychologically to accept and respect another possible faith. Respect is indispensable and it is an extraordinarily potent instrument. In this way he brings his friends to reflect, while excluding any suggestion of polemics." They are left to take their own decision, whatever it may turn out to be, under the influence of God. "One should add nothing further, respect the other's decision and pray to the Holy Spirit."

Meeting God

Tahar's last sentence reflects one of the most fundamental principles of the Christian apostolate. Christians do not aim at teaching a doctrine, nor at recruiting followers. Their task is simply to bear witness to the experience which has been granted to them. They have met the living God, they feel themselves loved by the Father, they live in continual intimacy with the living Christ, they pray and act with a new strength—that of the Spirit of God.

This experience cannot be manufactured or produced by any kind of trick. It is a completely unmerited gift of God. Christians only make known that this encounter is possible since they themselves live in it, and that it can be asked for. The rest is in God's hands alone: he disarms fears and objections, encourages the heart to be bold and to ask.

A God loved personally: Iba Zizen

A personal experience of God is central to Christianity. Jesus said: 'He who loves me will be loved by my Father, and I too will love him and show myself to him . . . If anyone loves me, he will obey my teaching. My Father will love him and we will come to him and make our home with him' (John 14:21, 23).

It was to this kind of encounter that the young Iba Zizen, whom we met in chapter 5, aspired. We traced his cultural pilgrimage from Kabylia to Christian France, and noted that his legal career culminated in the Council of State.[6] It is now time to hear the second half of his story, the spiritual pilgrimage.

Iba Zizen was only a small child when he first became aware of a desire to encounter God. He explains how he had received from his family a sense of the sacred, mingled with dissatisfaction:

> The context within which I passed my childhood implanted in me a feeling both of fear and of curiosity. I could not grasp the real meaning of these invocations and gestures, and none of it really took root within my spirit. I did not argue, but I did not really accept it.

Speaking of family pilgrimages to local saints, in which he loyally took part on his little legs, he notes:

> What in truth did these pilgrimages mean to me as a child? At first they were little more than an opportunity to escape from the monotony of family life, to make new discoveries, to have different experiences. At the unconscious level, there was no doubt the search for a hidden reality which was beckoning. I set out in the hope of a pleasant surprise, of a revelation which would effect a change within me. But I came home dry, without any other feeling than the satisfaction of having seen new places and a sense of being no longer a child. I was in fact beginning to be treated as a 'grown up'.

We might be tempted to see in this account no more than an old man's version of his memories, a projection onto his childhood of what were in fact the discoveries of maturity. There is however more to it than that. He speaks of a visit which he made on his own to the tomb of Sidi Moussa where he scrupulously observed the rites:

> On one occasion however I discovered more. I made the round of the tomb seven times, as I had been taught, for seven was the magic number. Then I waited . . . For what? Not for anything precise certainly. Perhaps I hoped to hear a voice, or the revelation of something hidden. But nothing spoke to me.
>
> When later on I would consider the meaning of these excursions, I would recognise a thirst which was destined to remain for a long time unsatisfied. My young mind, following a dark road, had not yet found a secure reference-point, nor even a starting-point. I was unfulfilled, and, while being unable to formulate my need, I was *waiting for another encounter*, an encounter with the God who, in the words of the immortal Pascal, 'is capable of satisfying all our needs'.

Iba Zizen was still only eleven when he was struck by an experience which convinced him that such an encounter with God was not only thinkable but possible. He had occasion to visit a missionary in his office, and he was struck by a picture in a wooden frame on his desk. It was the picture of a woman's face surrounded by a veil. He enquired about it, and the priest simply said to him:

> 'It is the little Sister Theresa of Lisieux, who died a dozen years ago—as a saint.'
>
> The words meant nothing to me, but they took root in my heart because of their connection with the fascinating picture which I kept looking at. The Father, struck by my attention, felt moved to add more words. I can in fact only remember a few scraps of what he said:
>
> 'A Christian girl so full of the love of God that she offered him her youth and dedicated to him her life. She died in a convent at the age of twenty-four, after a burning quest for the virtues which God wishes to find in his creatures.'
>
> I could not grasp the meaning of everything that was said, but the words echoed in my heart. They seemed to justify and even to round off my fascination with the picture. They gave it a dimension which caused my childish heart to swell: so to love God as to live only for him! What I had sought while going round the tomb of Sidi Ali

Moussa, and in stroking the stiff brocade, was now shining out at me from a young face and a young life. The features framed in white, the brown Carmelite veil falling over the shoulders, the ineffable gaze which seemed to be looking into the world beyond and pointing me in the same direction, the slight pursing of the lower lip: all the details of the picture sunk into my soul with an irresistible appeal. I had the impression that I had found someone who had been waiting for me and was now ready to show me the way I was looking for in my childish manner. A window onto Christianity opened for me, with the realisation of the possibility of a life transformed.

Seventy years now separate me from this encounter with Theresa of Lisieux, but her picture remains engraved on my soul. She will come before me again in all the emotional shocks of my existence, and will be, along with others, a beacon lighting the whole of my spiritual journey.[7]

Still under the influence of his encounter with Theresa of Lisieux, Iba Zizen accepted an invitation from Louis Rouani, a Kabyl from his village who had converted to Christianity. Rouani said that his Christian prayers had in fact a universal value, and could be said by Muslims and Christians alike. He wanted his friends to pray with him. One evening therefore Iba Zizen set out with three companions. They were half-expecting to have a joke at Louis' expense, but in the event they could not but be impressed by the seriousness and recollection of their host. When Louis began to say the Our Father, Iba Zizen saw again that face in the picture and it seemed to be saying to him: These words which you are saying, I have said them many thousands of times before you! The whole experience of kneeling in prayer constituted for the young visitor a real faith-experience.

Rumours began to circulate in the village about this little prayer group. Anxiety was aroused, and the young people had to double their efforts to safeguard their secret, which only had the effect of strengthening their faith:

We felt rather more united, now that we were accomplices in refusing a religious ban which was an offence to our freedom. For myself, my rejection of the ban was connected with a need to go further and to try and reach truths vaguely sensed but still inaccessible. Little by little, in this catacomb existence, there came to us a joyful sense of secretly possessing a treasure unknown to our neighbours, who would certainly have insulted us had they seen us at prayer . . .

I sometimes live again the circumstances of my first spiritual steps, both trembling and trustful. I could not help feeling, humbly but profoundly, the sense of having been chosen: this was a favour implying as its converse an obligation and a responsibility, the responsibility of becoming somewhat more a man.

Iba Zizen was to be marked by another shock some time later. Visiting the mission chapel, he saw a statue of Christ. 'The heart was visible on the breast and above was a scroll with the words, "See the heart which has so loved men." '

The picture of Theresa had spoken to him of humanity's love for God; now this statue of the Sacred Heart of Jesus, and these words, were telling him of God's love for humanity.

How could men respond to this ardent love except in kind? Was this then Christianity: a hidden but fervent relationship to the present God, a relationship both living and personal? My adolescent mind was not able to give a clear answer to such questions, but I felt that I was 'hooked', that I was on the way to finding what I lacked.

Something similar no doubt happened to the apostles on the Lake of Tiberias and led them to follow the Galilean. All that was required was good will. They heard a call, nothing more. There was no need for profound reflection.

Since that time, I knew what I was looking for, and I also discovered the path of personal freedom: I yearned for a 'beyond' which bore the stamp of love, and I knew where to find it.

Iba Zizen was at this time still a youth and could not think of separating from his family. For more than ten years his spiritual life was a gradual percolation of this call, nourished by the prayers learned in Rouani's 'secret garden', into his mind and heart. There were the studies, the 1914–1918 War, during which he became an officer: throughout all these years he ruminated on the early experiences which were settling into his heart and pushing him to go deeper into the moral and spiritual treasures of Christianity.

It was only in Paris in 1920, when he was twenty-two, that he ventured to reveal his secret to an older woman who worked with him in an office. He told her that he was convinced of the truth of Christianity and that he had for years been praying as a Christian. She invited him to come with her to church and introduced him to a priest who prepared him for baptism. It was an austere preparation, for the priest wanted to be sure that the young catechumen was looking for Jesus Christ and for him alone.

After baptism, his spiritual pilgrimage took the form of an energetic spiritual combat in which he sought to allow Christ to reign in him: over his emotions, his sexuality, his whole life. He was greatly helped by all the distinguished friends who surrounded him at this time. He devoured the works of Léon Bloy and Bernanos, and knew personally Jacques Maritain and Louis Massignon. These contacts, both personal and academic, affected him profoundly. He was immersed in a climate of Christian spirituality, something he had been deprived of in his youth in Kabylia, where he could not join a Christian community.

When we read Iba Zizen's witness, we realise how much he needed, not only religious knowledge and practice, but also a mental and emotional atmosphere in which his new identity could flourish. The Catholic writers and intellectuals of his time provided this young student and lawyer with this atmosphere which he needed over and above his link with any local group of Christians.

The following passage allows us to see that his immersion in this Christian world had nothing to do with his political choices:

Massignon was the means through whom I made a number of contacts which proved both strengthening and enriching. He introduced me to his friend Claudel, and one day took me to see the historian Georges Goyau, of the Académie Française. We had a long conversation with Goyau, who wanted to know whether my option for France had facilitated my conversion to Catholicism, or whether it was the latter which had strengthened the former.

Searching my past, I came to the conclusion that the two 'conversions' were independent of each other. I owed my option for France to my father, as well as to a number of my primary school teachers, who were all free-thinking, liberal, anti-clericals, and never for one moment recommended the Christian religion. My spiritual pilgrimage was a process and it was quite separate from my 'Frenchness'. The two domains were distinct, even if the culture of France was so deeply impregnated with Christianity. One can be a Christian and pray to God in any national costume, in any language, and under any flag.[8]

Now Augustin Iba Zizen, he returned to practise law in Algeria. Of this return and his subsequent life he writes as follows:

I felt free to practise my faith like any other Christian. My life, no doubt like theirs also, knew ups and downs, periods of fervour and of slackness, fidelity mixed with carelessness, falling and rising again. In all these experiences, the last word remained always with God.

He concludes thus:

Unlike those children of whom St Luke speaks, who remained deaf to the call of Christ, I aspire today to be able always to respond to the Lord: 'You have played on your pipe, and I have danced for you; you have sung to me a funeral song, and I have wept.'

And now I have only to wait, in peace and hope, until the day comes for me to glide towards you, for ever.

In fact Iba Zizen left for the meeting with God to which he had for so long aspired before the appearance of his book in 1984.

A Father

The meeting with God can take the particular form of an encounter with the tenderness of the Father. Such was the experience of *Bilquis Sheikh*, an aristocratic lady belonging to the high society of Pakistan.[9]

Bilquis was born in 1919 and brought up as a strict Muslim. Between the ages of four and eleven she learned the Koran, while also receiving the European-type of education usual for persons of her class. She married General Khalid Sheikh, Pakistan's Minister of the Interior, and mixed in international political circles, visiting the capital cities of the world.

BACK TO THE QUR'AN

Her divorce in 1961 plunged her into profound disarray. She returned to her childhood home in the countryside, and, surrounded by devoted servants, dedicated herself to bringing up her four-year-old grandson, Mahmoud. During 1966, the child fell sick, and Bilquis called a holy man to come and recite verses from the Koran for the child's recovery. She herself felt estranged from these prayers, and confessed: 'God has forgotten about me, and I have forgotten about God.' At the same time she was conscious of a certain inner uneasiness which she attributed to an evil spirit, or perhaps to a recent murder in the neighbourhood: a young girl of the village had been killed by her family after her conversion to Christianity.

Her condition however persisted, and she determined to take active steps to put right whatever was wrong within her:

After these experiences I found myself drawn to the Koran. Perhaps it would help explain the events and at the same time fill the emptiness within me. Certainly its curved Arabic script held answers which had often sustained my family.

Always before, I had read the Koran as an obligation. This time, I felt I should really search its pages . . . At first I was lost in the beauty of the words. But later on in the book there were words that did not comfort me at all: 'When ye have divorced women, and they have reached their term, then retain them in kindness or release them in kindness' (2:231).

My husband's eyes had been like hard steel when he told me that he did not love me any more. I shrivelled inside as he spoke. What had happened to all our years together! Could they be dismissed just like that? Had I, as the Koran said, 'reached my term'?

The next morning I picked up the Koran again, hoping to find in the curling script the assurance I needed so desperately. But the assurance never came. I found only directives for how to live and warnings against other beliefs.

After several days of applying myself to the holy book, I put it down one afternoon with a sigh, got up and walked down to my garden where I hoped to find some peace in nature and in old memories . . .

Softly in the distance I could hear the muezzin's sunset prayer call;

its haunting strains only deepened the loneliness within me. 'Where? Oh Allah,' I whispered to the prayer rhythms, 'where is the comfort you promise?'

Back in my bedroom that evening I again picked up my mother's copy of the Koran. And as I read was again impressed by its many references to Jewish and Christian writings which preceded it. Perhaps, I wondered, I should continue my search among those earlier books? But that would mean reading the Bible.

Not without difficulty, Bilquis obtained a Bible, leafed through it, and then forgot it. On the same day she received a visit from her daughter Tooni, who was a doctor in a hospital in the town.

It was then that Tooni noticed the Bible resting on the table near me.

'Oh, a Bible!' she said. 'Do open it and see what it has to say.'

Our family views any religious book as significant. It was a common pastime to allow a holy book to fall open, point blindly at a passage to see what it said, almost like having a prophecy.[10]

Lightheartedly, I opened the little Bible and looked down at the pages. Then a mysterious thing happened. It was as if my attention were being drawn to a verse on the lower right hand corner of the right page. I bent close to read it:

> I will call that my people, which was not my people; and her beloved, which was not beloved. And it shall be, that in the place where it was said unto them, Ye are not my people, there shall they be called sons of the living God.
>
> (Romans 9:25–26)

I caught my breath and and a tremor passed through me. Why was this verse affecting me so? . . . The words burned in my heart like glowing embers.

The epistle to the Romans which contains this passage is one of the key texts of the New Testament. With remarkable clarity Paul gives there the essence of the Christian message: the drama of sin, the intervention of Christ, dead and risen, who gives us a new life, the life of the Spirit of Christ within us. Taking up the Bible again, Bilquis discovered all this. She felt that there was here a teaching very different from that of the Koran. She was profoundly disturbed: where indeed is then the truth?

BETWEEN THE BIBLE AND THE KORAN

A series of unusually clear dreams sent Bilquis back to read the Bible. She saw herself eating and drinking with Jesus in peace and joy. Then she encountered a man whose name she knew without ever having read it: John the Baptist. She asked him: 'Will you lead me to Jesus?'

Another night, the dream was about a pedlar who brought her a perfume whose odour, he said, would spread throughout the world. She put the flask on the table at her bedside. When she awoke, she found the Bible in the exact spot where she had seen the flask in her dream.

All these dreams seemed to be encouraging Bilquis to read the Bible.

> I continued reading both the Bible and the Koran side by side, turning from one to the other. I found myself picking up the Koran out of a sense of duty, and then eagerly turning to the Christian book . . . Each time I opened the Bible a sense of guilt filled me. Perhaps this stemmed from my strict upbringing.

She was aware of the gossip which she might be causing, but she was filled with a new courage and went to visit some Christian missionaries in the neighbourhood to ask them for enlightenment.

> Again for several days, I found myself alone with two books—the Koran and the Bible. I continued to read them both, studying the Koran because of the loyalty of a life-time, delving into the Bible because of a strange inner hunger.
>
> Yet, sometimes I'd draw back from picking up the Bible. God couldn't be in both books, I knew, because their messages were so different. But when my hand hesitated at picking up the Bible, I felt a strange let-down.

In a confused way, Bilquis felt that her dreams and spiritual experiences were offering her an entry into a beautiful world to which the Bible was the key. But she could not explain why.

THE ENCOUNTER

At this point she was moved to visit the hospital where her doctor daughter was working with Christian sisters. In the waiting room, she met briefly one of these sisters and spoke to her of her dreams, her readings and her doubts. She concludes:

'Whatever happens, I must find God. But I'm confused about your faith. (I realised that even as I spoke I was putting my finger on something important.) You seem to make God so . . . I don't know . . . *personal*!'

The little nun's eyes filled with compassion and she leaned forward:

'Madame Sheikh, she said, her voice full of emotion, there is only one way to find out why we feel this way. And that is to find out for yourself, strange as it may seem. Why don't you pray *to* the God you are searching for? Ask him to show you his way. Talk to him as if he were your friend.'

I smiled. She might as well suggest that I talk to the Taj Mahal. But then she said something that shot through my being like electricity. She leaned closer and took my hand in hers, tears streaming down her cheeks: 'Talk to him,' she said very quietly, 'as if he were your father.'

I sat back quickly. A dead silence filled the room . . . I stared at the nun with the candlelight glinting off her glasses. Talk to God as if he were my father! The thought shook my soul in the peculiar way truth has of being at once startling and comforting.

Bilquis returned home with the strange feeling that something decisive had happened.

My mind was on this new way to find God. I went up to my bedroom to consider all that had been happening. No Muslim, I felt certain, ever thought of Allah as his father. Since childhood, I had been told that the surest way to know about Allah was to pray five times a day and study and think on the Koran. Yet the nun's words came to me again. 'Talk *to* God. Talk to him as if he were your father.'

Alone in my room I got on my knees and tried to call him 'Father'. But it was a useless effort and I straightened in dismay. It was ridiculous. Wouldn't it be sinful to try to bring the Great One down to our own level? I fell asleep that night more confused than ever. Hours later I awoke. It was after midnight, my birthday, December 12th. I was forty-seven years old.

Childhood memories rose into her mind . . . other birthdays . . . her parents . . . the tenderness of her father whom she could always disturb in his office without his ever becoming cross with her. On the contrary, he would take her in his arms and ask, 'Now, what can I do for you?'

It was well past midnight as I lay in bed savouring this wonderful memory.

'Oh thank you . . .' I murmured to God.

Was I really talking *to* him? Suddenly, a breakthrough of hope flooded me. Suppose, just suppose God were like a father. If my earthly father would put aside everything to listen to me, wouldn't my heavenly Father . . .?

Shaking with excitement, I got out of bed, sank to my knees on the rug, looked up to heaven and in rich new understanding called God 'My Father'.

I was not prepared for what happened.

'O Father, my Father . . . Father God.'

Hesitantly, I spoke his name aloud. I tried different ways of speaking to him. And then, as if something broke through for me I found myself trusting that he was indeed hearing me, just as my earthly father had always done.

'Father, my Father God,' I cried, with growing confidence. My voice seemed unusually loud in the large bedroom as I knelt on the rug beside my bed. But suddenly that room wasn't empty any more. *He* was there! I could sense his presence. I could feel his hand laid gently on my head. It was as if I could *see* his eyes, filled with love and compassion. He was so close that I found myself laying my head on his knees like a little girl sitting at her father's feet. For a long time I knelt there, sobbing quietly, floating in his love. I found myself talking with him, apologising for not having known him before. And again, came his loving compassion, like a warm blanket settling around me.

Bilquis then remembered her hesitations about the Koran and the Bible. She took the books, one in each hand, and asked God: 'Which, Father? Which one is your book?'

Then a remarkable thing happened. Nothing like it had ever occurred in my life in quite this way. For I heard a voice inside my being, a voice that spoke to me as clearly as if I were repeating words in my inner mind. They were fresh, full of kindness, yet at the same time full of authority:

'In which book do you meet me as your Father?'

I found myself answering:

'In the Bible.'

That's all it took. Now there was no question in my mind which one was his book. I looked at my watch and was astonished to discover that three hours had passed. Yet I was not tired.[11]

SOME REFLECTIONS

We had first to allow Bilquis to tell us of her meeting with God in her own words. We will now attempt to pick out certain aspects of her story which seem to be particularly significant.

We are clearly here in another world than that of religious controversy. As in the time of the apostles, as indeed during the time of Jesus, *what has precedence over everything else is the experience* of an encounter with God, with the Father. Doctrines only carry conviction in so far as they reflect this experience. It was because she had met God as her Father that Bilquis was able to accept the explanations of the Christian Bible.

We should not too quickly dismiss experiences like those of Bilquis as abnormal. The Gospels themselves seem to regard them as perfectly normal: 'The sheep listen to [the voice of the shepherd] . . . they know his voice . . . I have other sheep . . . They too will listen to my voice' (John 10). 'When you pray, go into your room, close the door and pray to your Father who is unseen. Then your Father, who sees what is done in secret, will reward you' (Matthew 6:6).

Many who have not themselves gone through the experience of a meeting with the Father may understand these last words as referring to the future world. It seems more likely that they mean what they say, namely, that the Father will reply to the one who calls upon him, that this prayer will bring results: 'And your Father, who sees what is done in secret, will reply to you.'

If we take the Gospels literally, a meeting with the Father is to be regarded as something normal, even as something promised by Christ. We shall return later to this, as also to the dreams and voices which made such an impression on Bilquis Sheikh and which are very common in the life of Christian mystics.

We may also note the complete *absence of any negative judgement* on Islam. It is true that Bilquis' experience of Islam was not happy. She was deeply hurt when she read what the Koran had to say about divorce, and she shuddered when she thought of the punishment inflicted by Muslim families on apostates and adulterers. But she remained loyally attached to Islam. What attracted her to Christianity was not any disgust with Islam but *an experience of God*—one which Islam did not offer but which Christianity both promised and offered.

Finally one may note the important part played by the *Christian witnesses* in her story. They made no effort to persuade or convince, but simply allowed her to see the experience of intimacy with God by which they lived themselves, while showing her the way to such experience for herself. They could not give her that experience; it can only be given by God in an intimate and personal dialogue with himself.

BEGINNING A NEW LIFE

We return to Bilquis Sheikh and to the sequel of her night in prayer.

Instantly after this encounter with the Father she knew that she had to take a radical step: 'I found myself standing at a great crossroads. So far I had met, personally, the Father God. In my heart I knew I had to give myself totally to his Son, Jesus, or else to turn my back on him completely. And I knew for certain that everyone I loved would advise me to turn my back on Jesus.'

There is such a thing as mystical evidence which is beyond all reason, as that implied in the words of Jesus: 'If God were your Father, you would love me' (John 8:42). For some days Bilquis hesitated, thinking of the pain she was bound to inflict on her family. But then she recalled passages in the Gospels, such as Matthew 10:37, in which Jesus required his disciples to choose between their family and him. Finally she turned to the last book in the Bible and found these words of Jesus: 'Here I am! I stand at the door and knock. If anyone hears my voice and opens the door, I will come in and eat with him, and he with me' (Revelation 3:20).

Here was confirmation of the dream in which Jesus had eaten with her. There could be no more hesitation. She knelt down and made an immediate and final decision to give her life to Jesus:

> 'Oh God, don't wait a moment. Please come into my life. Every bit of me is open to you.'
>
> I did not have to struggle or worry about what would happen. I had said yes. Christ was in my life now, and I knew it. How unbearably beautiful. Within a few days I had met God the Father and God the Son . . . I got up, my mind whirling. Did I dare take one more step? I remembered that, in the book of Acts, at Pentecost, Jesus had baptised his followers with the Holy Spirit. Was I supposed to follow this same pattern?

On that night, 24 December 1966, she fell asleep while asking to be baptised in the Holy Spirit. Waking in the middle of the night, she got out of bed, knelt on the carpet and prayed, again asking the Father that she might be plunged into the Holy Spirit:

> Suddenly I was filled with wonder and awe. For in that silent pre-dawn room I saw his face. Something surged through me, wave after wave of purifying ocean breakers, flooding me to the tips of my fingers and toes, washing my soul.
>
> Then the powerful surges subsided, the heavenly ocean quieted. I was completely cleansed. Joy exploded within me and I cried out praising him, thanking him. Hours later, I felt the Lord lift me to my feet.

On that very day, Christmas Eve, Bilquis hastened to the Christian missionaries: 'David! I cried, using his first name without thinking, I am a Christian now! I have been baptised in the Holy Spirit.'

Stupefaction among the missionaries! Within the space of a few days, this Muslim woman, who had received no Christian instruction, had penetrated into the heart of the most profound of the Christian mysteries, the blessed Trinity. In a way which reminds us irresistibly of the route followed by the first Christians, she was led from experience to doctrine.

The New Testament contains no theory about the Holy Trinity as a dogma. What we do find, on nearly every page, are allusions to the tenderness of the Father, the presence of the risen Christ, and the power of the Spirit of God manifesting itself in the life of believers. Dogma was only articulated later to make sense of this experience.

So Bilquis began a new stage in her life. 'God was making preparations to begin my education,' she says.

She had to insist before the missionaries would admit her to baptism. They, and the local Christians, were afraid of Muslim reprisals against their community. Moreover things had moved too quickly, time would be needed to guarantee solidity.

Meanwhile, after the phase of spiritual discovery, Bilquis experienced a conversion at the level of her relationships with others. No one had taught her this change, but she felt it as an interior call from the Father, source of peace, love and joy, to which she had to yield. She learned to control her moods, to forgive her husband, to be attentive to others, especially the poorest. Grand lady that she was, she felt the call to join the despised community of Christian sweepers—now *her* community.

Her spiritual life developed and she began to search for the Lord's will, discovering how to sift it from her own ideas and intuitions.

Apart from her children, who respected and trusted her, the members of her family at first avoided her, although she continued to remain as friendly as possible towards them. She received threatening letters from neighbours, and there was an attempt to set her house on fire. One of her maids, on the other hand, a Muslim, followed the example of her mistress and asked Jesus to come into her heart:

'Begum Sahib,' she said, her plump face full of emotion, 'I have something to tell you. Do you remember how you have so often told us that if we want to know this Jesus, all we have to do is ask him to come into our heart.' At this she broke into tears. 'Well I did, Begum Sahib. And he did come in. I have never felt such love, ever, in my whole life.'

Things got worse, the threats became more and more dangerous, and in 1972 Bilquis had to leave her country. She settled in the United States where she gives conferences in churches and to Christian groups.

The prayer of the heart

What came as a surprise both to Iba Zizen and his friends, praying secretly in the dark, and to Bilquis Sheikh, hesitating to address God as a father, was the character of Christian prayer. They speak of it as something new, something foreign to the Muslim style of prayer.

Prayer? What are we talking about?

We can only understand the reaction of these converts when we recall the meaning of 'prayer' in the Muslim vocabulary. Prayer is one of the five 'pillars' of Islam, the others being witness, fasting, the payment of the religious tax, and the pilgrimage.

Islamic prayer, or *salât*, consists of a fairly simple ritual, all the details of which are fixed by law. There is a cycle of bows and prostrations accompanied by the recitation of obligatory formulas. It is preceded by a ritual washing, of which likewise all the details are prescribed. Prayer takes place at fixed times: morning, noon, early afternoon, sunset and night. There are also rules for the place of prayer: it must be clean, there must be a prayer-mat, one must turn towards Mecca.

One way of putting it would be to say that prayer, in Islam, means essentially a liturgy. The word therefore covers a much narrower range than the same word in the Christian sense. There are also personal Islamic devotions, but these are not called *salât*.

Furthermore, this liturgical prayer must be recited in Arabic. The Arab peoples now constitute only twenty per cent of the total Muslim world population, and even in Arab countries there is a big difference between the ordinary language and the classical Arabic of the Koran. This means that people do not pray in the language in which they think and speak.

It is of course perfectly possible for a fervent believer to pray to God in a language he or she does not understand. One can lift up the mind and heart to God beyond all words and ideas. A 'sacred language' may act as a kind of spiritual spring-board. Christian charismatics may 'pray in tongues', and there is such a thing as 'wordless prayer' in which devotion to God can be expressed in a variety of bodily gestures. All that is required is that the ritual should be genuinely expressive of personal dispositions.

Beyond rites

It is true that in Islam a certain number of devotions are left to the piety of the individual. Even then however the hundreds of con-fraternities, which developed round saintly individuals, and which in some respects resemble Catholic religious congregations, have each created their own traditional rituals, which still consist in the repetition of litanies, ready-made formulas and verses from the Koran.

All these more personal prayer-formulas are also in Arabic. It is understandable that many Muslims, especially those from non-Arabic-speaking countries, prefer the litany form in their personal devotions, a short formula, that is, whose meaning is known even though the words themselves are not, repeated hundreds or even thousands of times.

Both Christianity and Islam have official rites and stylised prayers which one has only to learn and recite. But Christians are also invited to pray informally, either privately or in groups. Indeed the word 'prayer' in Christian circles means in the very first place a personal and informal dialogue between the believer and his or her God;[12] only secondarily does it designate liturgy in its official and collective dimension. It is precisely the discovery of informal prayer which strikes a number of Muslim believers when they first make contact with the Christian tradition.

At last I understand when I pray!

Not only have they accepted the possibility of praying individu-ally and directly to God, but people experience as well the joy of finally understanding the words of the official liturgy. They feel at home in their spiritual life. God can be encountered, heart to heart, without passing through the intermediary of a rite or of a mystery language.

FELIX ALI TONDI

Ali Tondi runs a co-operative in Niger. He tells us of his joy of speaking to God in his own language. Born in a Muslim family, he had heard Jesus spoken of while he was a child in a primary school, but had somehow got the idea that to be a Christian one had to be a student while he himself left school early and returned to his native village. Putting aside his idea of becoming a Christian, he tried to live as a good Muslim.

> As those about me all prayed in the Muslim fashion, and said that a man should not neglect prayer, I got into the habit of praying in the mosque every evening. But I had never been to a Koranic school and I could not understand a word of the prayers. All I could do was to perform the gestures. One day a man said to me, 'Is that the way you pray?' I felt there was no point in praying without understanding what was being said, so I abandoned this kind of prayer for several years.[13]

One day he told a missionary sister that he would very much like to know the way of Jesus, but he was not a student. The sister reassured him that Jesus had not come just for students but for everyone. Tondi began to follow instructions at the mission. He wanted to find God:

> My comrades did not want me to abandon them and said that I was only going to the religion of the whites for the sake of money and not because I was looking for God. But I knew the truth about myself. When they saw that I was not prepared to change, they stopped criticising me, although not completely . . .
>
> For me, it is a joy to be a Christian.

After being baptised, along with his wife, Felix continued his study of Christianity and he now has a diploma from a catechists' school.

LAOUALI BOULAMA

We hear again from Niger of a young man who is still preparing for baptism.[14]

Before, I was a Muslim and used to go every day to the mosque. I prayed five times every day. Sometimes I followed the readings from the Koran in a French translation. Everything was done in Arabic, and as I did not know a word of this language I lost interest. I heard from a fellow-pupil that catechism lessons were given at the mission. I started going there, I think in 1975. The Christian religion attracted me because Christians prayed in all languages. It was less difficult than Islam.

I am now in my fifth year of catechism and I follow it step by step. I am not sure whether I will continue because people today criticise Christians. I will have to see how things are when I grow up. And then science too is making people give up religion. I am waiting.

Laouali wonders if he will be able to resist temptations to doubt as he continues his studies:

Supposing you have been baptised and then, in the top class at school, you feel that you have been 'captured' by science, what then, when you have already promised?

If you begin with religion, you should continue with it, but you do it step by step until you are free to do what you think right, without being harassed either by your parents or by science. Even if you are not baptised, you still feel the love of Christ deep within you.

For Laouali the choice of Christianity signifies also freedom, a freedom from rites that he cannot understand, from mocking comrades, from parents who tell him what religion he must follow. But there is more to it than freedom. He also feels love for the person of Jesus Christ. It is on this that he relies as he faces a future which he still finds daunting.

HAWA NASAMOU

This Nigerian Muslim woman was born in 1957 and had been instructed in Islam from the age of three. The daughter of

Muslims, the wife of a Muslim, mother of four children, she is, surprisingly, preparing to become a Christian. The people around her do not discourage her but say, 'If we pray, we are all on the same road.'

> Sometimes my husband asks me how it came about that I have taken this path. I explain to him that the way of Christ is best for me. He answers that he can see that my heart is full of joy, and that if that is what I want, it is well.
>
> My Muslim female friends are also kind to me. For example, I had no radio and one of them brought me one, so that I could hear the Catholic broadcasts on Sundays. They too have asked me why I have taken the Christian way. I told them that the words of Jesus speak well of God and that I understood the gospel. They said that the two ways were the same, but one must know what one was doing.
>
> For me one of the differences between the two ways is that in the Muslim way you pray but do not really understand the words; in the Christian way I understand better and when people ask me questions, I can answer them.
>
> Prayer is very important for me. I ask God to guide me so that I can offer service until the end of my life. I ask God that we may help each other and exchange joy with each other. I ask him for a long life and for forgiveness for our sins.

Hawa is President of the Christian women of her village. She would like to be a nurse. For her, to understand means to take charge of her own life and destiny, while at the same time committing them to God. She looks back on her years as a Muslim as a time of fear and helplessness: 'Before, there were things that made me afraid. Sometimes at night I had terrifying dreams. I saw a camel-driver who wanted to kidnap me.[15] I cried out, but no one heard. There has been a change. I fear nothing.'

The fear in this dream was connected with Hawa's inability to make herself heard or understood. At the time when she could not express herself, she felt locked up into a fearful solitude. 'What I want today is to be baptised and to understand better the way of Christ.'[16]

Again she speaks of 'understanding'. Like her two compatriots, Felix and Laouali, Hawa too shows that when she understood her own prayer, she discovered who she was. It was in meeting God that she became herself.

In these cases, everything seems relatively simple. Leaving an Arabic-speaking Islam for a Christianity that spoke in their mother-tongue, these people felt at home in their new religion, although they met difficulties which they do not attempt to conceal.

IMPOSSIBLE TO PRAY IN PERSIAN?

A young Iranian, born in 1951, had a more difficult road to tread.[17]

> 'At school I followed the courses on the Koran, although I had little taste for them. Some of my relatives were devout Muslims, but my parents left me free and I never went to the mosque or recited the prayers.'

During his military service, he felt the pull of God, but not in the same way as those of his comrades who prayed in the Muslim fashion. Treated as a renegade by his officers and comrades, he did not abandon his quest for God. One of his friends on military service was a Christian, and this seems to have inclined him towards Christianity, although he took no steps in this direction.

> When I came back to my family, I met again my friends and neighbours. Among them were Christians, some Chaldeans, some Armenians. But I had never spoken with them about Jesus, any more than they, regarding me as a Muslim, asked me questions about my religion. This situation continued for a certain time.
>
> For some years I had been tempted by drugs. I wanted to stop but could not. I prayed to Jesus to help me and I managed to stop. This made me think that he could really come to my assistance.[18] From that moment I got into the habit of praying, very simply but from the heart. On the big Christian feast-days I would go to a church, but I stayed at the door, full of hesitations and conflicting desires. I met friends who invited me to go in, but I could understand nothing of what was being said. If only at that period a priest had spoken to me in Persian!

To understand this remark, one should know that even though Iranians speak Persian, they hardly make use of this language in their prayer-life. Islamic law obliges Iranian Muslims to pray in Arabic, while the majority of Christians belong to churches which have kept the ancient liturgical languages, like Chaldean and Armenian, which are hardly used any more in daily life.

A Muslim who becomes a Christian cannot therefore find a Persian-speaking Christian community. Our young Iranian thus found himself engaged in a solitary search. One may note that he experienced an interior call. He was not simply following his own whims but really trying to find out what was God's plan for him:

> Through the trials and difficulties, the call of which I was conscious was transformed into a search for Jesus Christ. I cannot say why, but I trusted him and relied on him. All I can say is that at this time Jesus was like a friend for me. But there was no way of really getting to know him. How then could I continue with my search?
>
> My difficulty was that I did not know that there was such a thing as a Gospel in Persian. I could not imagine a priest speaking Persian, which everyone regarded as a Muslim language.

We see here a situation only too common in the Near and Middle East, and indeed elsewhere, in which religious affiliation is determined by social, political or ethnic factors. Social and political conflicts thus take on a religious colouring, as was seen most clearly in Lebanon, not to mention Northern Ireland. Each religious community is entrenched behind cultural and linguistic barriers, and this is a major obstacle to any missionary activity, whether Christian or Muslim.

> Quite suddenly I decided to ask for baptism. You might wonder how I could possibly take such a step without ever having read the gospels or sought anyone's advice. How could I possibly know Jesus? How could I know the importance of baptism? The explanation is that I had seen a number of films on television about the life and teaching of Jesus. I had

also eagerly studied pamphlets on Christian prayer and other matters which Christian friends had given me.

However it came about, I had taken my decision and I then began to consider where I could find a country in which I might be baptised. So it was that, during the Christmas festivities, I left Iran for the first time in my life and went to Greece.

He stayed there for nine months, earning his living by washing up in a restaurant. He had to abandon his ambition of studying medicine. But the problem of language was still not solved. He prayed in solitude, as best he could. He was then finally told by a friend that it was possible to read the Bible without having to learn a foreign language.

This was a surprising piece of information, and I telephoned to a Christian friend in Iran to ask him to send me a Gospel in Persian. So it was in Greece that I read the Gospel for the first time. No doubt my reading was superficial, but it warmed my heart.

Later he was introduced to a group which prayed in Persian. He explains:

In comparison with the life I had known in previous years, this was really an illumination. I found other books written in Persian and made friends with other people who, like myself, were searching for Jesus Christ. We used to meet several times a week. In short, I entered a community in which we sought for Jesus together.

It was a novel and delightful experience for me to be surrounded by brothers, whether Chaldeans, Persians or others, with whom *I could talk to God*.

We studied the Bible in groups, and it was then that I realised how superficial had been my earlier reading of the gospel. We could freely speak about God and listen to each other. I felt like a man dying of thirst who is suddenly thrown into a pool . . .

I prefer not to speak about my own interior life. I had come to the end of a period of prolonged solitary research, of a life marked by interior debates and hesitations. It was also the beginning of a new search, the search for life in the Church, and of a new interior struggle, with the help of the Holy Spirit.

The young Iranian's happiness was short-lived. He is now baptised, and obliged, like so many others, to live in exile. His witness remains valuable as showing how Christians need others who are searching to reach beyond the borders of their particular cultural or linguistic group.

Conclusion

It was the thirst for prayer that drove these Muslims out onto the pilgrim road. They are now established Christians. What, we may ask, have they found which they could not have found elsewhere? Their reply is simple. They have found a personal God who is interested in everyone and who wishes to be known and loved in himself; a God who is Father, to whom one can speak like a son or daughter. They have found liberation and the rapture of finally being able to understand the words of their dialogue with God and to hope for a reply.

All had the same fundamental experience which puts them at the heart of the Christian tradition, reflected in the prayer which Jesus left to his own: 'When you pray, pray like this . . .' (Matthew 6:9).

Notes

1 For a fuller treatment of these events, consult: E. Renaud, 'Une tempête sur la presse égyptienne: Tawfîq al-Hakîm et son "dialogue avec Dieu" ', *Se Comprendre*, No.84/08, 28 September 1984. (*Se Comprendre*: 5 Rue d'Issy, 92170 Vauves.)

2 This phrase, with its negative stress, should help us understand that Islam tries to cleanse religion (*tanzîh al-tawhîd*) of excessive expressions. This is borne out in the 'creed' (*No* god but God), and in all theological writings. Nevertheless, this ideal can generate deep feelings of adoration and praise. See, for instance, Mohammed Talbi, 'A Muslim experience of prayer', *Encounter*, No.34, April 1977. (*Encounter*: Viale Trastevere 89 - 00153, Rome.)

3 K. Baker, 'Bridging Three Worlds: Lamin Sanneh's Journey of Faith', *Harvard Divinity Bulletin*, XII, No.4, April–May 1982, pp.12–14. For the personal witness of L. Sanneh read his 'Muhammad, Prophet of God, and Jesus Christ, Image of God: A personal testimony,

International Bulletin of Missionary Research, Vol.8, 1984, No.4, pp.169–174.

4 Of course, the young man is drifting away from the Islamic 'orthodoxy' as defined by Muslim scholars. Thus speaks one of them: 'You, Christians, speak of God willing and wanting to reveal himself to man. God does not reveal himself. He does not reveal himself to anyone in any way. God reveals only his will.' (I. al-Faruqi, *International Review of Mission*, No.260, October 1976, p.405.

5 This tradition is based on Koran 4:157 which states that the Jews 'did not kill (Jesus), they did not crucify him, but it has been made to look like it'. With incredible boldness, commentators began to invent stories where Peter, Judas or another character take Jesus' place on the cross. The number of these 'fictions' which all claim to be 'historical' shows how flimsy they really are.

6 A. Iba Zizen, *Le Testament d'un Berbère, Un itinéraire spirituel et politique* (Albatros: Paris, 1984).

7 *Ibid.*, pp.31–32.

8 *Ibid.*, p.77.

9 B. Sheikh, *I Dared to Call Him Father* (Word Books: Waco, Texas, 1978, 1980).

10 This practice is called *Istikhâra*, when it is used to know which decision one should take. Used in Islam, it has been known in Christianity as well. Francis of Assisi became aware of his call to absolute poverty in just that way. Beginners in the faith often resort to that practice in order to discern God's call in the turmoil of our daily lives.

11 B. Sheikh, *op. cit.*, pp.48–53.

12 The Bible uses this possessive vocabulary to express the intimacy and reciprocal love existing between God and humankind: 'You would call me "my Father" '(Jeremiah 3:19) 'You will be my people and I will be your God, (Jeremiah 30:22). Mystical circles in Islam have adopted the same approach to describe the intimate link between God and *his* servants.

13 R. Deniel, *Sur le Chemin Chrétien* (Vie Chrétienne, Supplement to No.274, Paris, 1984), pp.59–60.

14 R. Deniel, *Chemins de Chrétiens Africains* (Inades: Abidjan, Ivory Coast, 1982–1983), No.10, pp.21 ff.

15 In Hawa's subconscious mind, would this frightening figure be a symbol of Muhammad and Islam?

16 R. Deniel, *Chemins de Chrétiens Africains* (Inades: Abidjan, Ivory Coast, 1982–1983), No.10, pp.13–15.
17 Drawn from confidential documents. We have seen, in chapter 2, the beginning of his spiritual journey.
18 We have seen in chapter 2 how Jesus may manifest his power to save before allowing people to know him in person.

CHAPTER 9

A CALL FROM GOD?

Again the Lord called, 'Samuel!' And Samuel got up and went to Eli and said, 'Here I am; you called me.' 'My son,' Eli said, 'I did not call; go back and lie down.' Now Samuel did not yet know the Lord: The word of the Lord had not yet been revealed to him.

(1 Samuel 3:6–7)

In the last days, God says, I will pour out my Spirit on all people.
Your sons and daughters will prophesy,
your young men will see visions,
your old men will dream dreams,
Even on my servants, both men and women, I will pour out my Spirit in those days.

(Acts 2:17–18).

Changing religion is not to be regarded as a matter of social convenience. It makes sense solely as an act of obedience to the call of God. As converts say, it is a vocation.

What exactly do we mean by the word 'vocation'? Sometimes it is used to mean no more than a vague feeling of destiny, or perhaps a choice dictated by our own particular cluster of talents and tastes. Converts, however, use the word of a precise experience: they are convinced that they are guided by God, called by him, in the strict sense of the term. Vocation for them means a direct call from God. How can such a thing be possible?

What do we mean?

We may first note two currents in religious thinking. They are fairly common in our world and their struggle may be felt in the heart of each of us:

On the one hand, there is *certitude that God speaks to men*. Both the Bible and the Koran are called the 'Word of God'. Furthermore, within these books there are various accounts of how God spoke to certain men, like Abraham and Moses.

On the other hand, there remains *the feeling that God no longer speaks*. We have seen that Islam considers that nobody can claim any further direct communication with God, since Muhammad was the last of the prophets.[1] As for Christians, they believe that the Spirit of God speaks to the heart of everyone, but they are often very dubious about the possibility of God really speaking in their daily life.

An experience of God?

The orthodox Muslim believes that God speaks through the Koran alone. As a Muslim scholar once said, 'I would suggest that Christians wishing to enter into dialogue with Muslims eschew the "personal", "experiential" basis on which [they base] religious knowledge as epistemologically precarious. Any prejudice or hallucination can then masquerade as 'religion' and claim authority on that basis.'[2]

Some Christians would probably agree with this opinion. However, it cannot be accepted without undermining the very foundation of the Christian faith:

- Both the Old and New Testaments are the result of *personal experiences of God*.
- Our certitude concerning the resurrection of Christ is derived from *a personal experience of God*.
- Christian saints past and present owe their sense of personal vocation, their mystical experience, and their ideal of service to others, to *a personal experience of God*.
- Jesus speaks of *a personal experience of God* when he promises to send the Spirit, the consoler. He will lead to all truth and will speak

within the hearts of the faithful, manifesting to them the presence of the Father and of Jesus.[3]

- Finally, converts from Islam speak here of *a personal experience of God*.

It seems therefore that we must accept at least the possibility of a personal experience of God. In this way we achieve a great freedom and objectivity. We can be open to the facts.

We achieve freedom because we are no longer obliged, on some kind of principle, to dismiss all claims to experience of God as illusion.

We are able to be objective because we can look reality in the face, without prejudice one way or the other. We are certainly not obliged to regard as authentic all pretended religious experience. We know that God speaks and acts within the heart of every human being. We must, however, examine all these experiences to discover whether or not they find their source and origin in God.[4]

God beyond the senses

The first principle which we must bear in mind when attempting to 'discern' the reality of religious experience is that God is transcendent. It is a principle strongly affirmed by both the Bible and the Koran.

When Moses wanted to see the face of God, he received the reply, 'You cannot see my face, for no-one may see me and live' (Exodus 33:20). How could the finite human mind comprehend the God who made all things and who infinitely transcends all that is? Even our purest idea of God falls short of God's reality. He is the wholly other, the beyond. Our faculties cannot encompass him.

At the same time, in this same passage from the book of Exodus, God does not exclude the possibility that humankind can have a certain experience of him:

The Lord said, 'There is a place near me where you may stand on a rock. When my glory passes by, I will put you in a cleft in the rock and cover you with my hand until I have passed by. Then I will remove my hand and you will see my back; but my face must not be seen.' (Exodus 33:21-23)

These are images: the 'face' of God is 'God known directly', while the 'back' of God is God perceived otherwise, after the event, by his tracks as it were. The Bible continually asserts that humanity cannot meet God as he is in himself. He manifests himself indirectly: he shows his 'glory'; he sends his 'angel'; or puts forth his 'hand' or 'arm'. Even when he makes himself visible, he hides in a cloud.

God creator

There is however a further message running through the Bible. This is that God is the master, the sovereignly free creator, who needs no instruments to accomplish his designs.

'He said: and so it was.' Because he is God, he can act within our inmost being, in the secret depths of our personality. He has no need to force an entry: indeed he belongs there, he is at home there. To say that God no longer acts in the world but that he only operates indirectly amounts to saying that God is no longer God. It is to put him on the same level as creatures to imagine that his way of acting is on the level of ours, and a rival to ours.

Just as we may say that God does not need tongs to handle a burning coal, so we must affirm that he does not need an intermediary in order to speak to the hearts of his human creatures.

Certainly he can make use of instruments to teach us: the Bible, doctrine, liturgy, the sacraments. But, to be effective, all these means need in the heart an echo which he alone gives: 'I planted the seed, Apollos watered it, but God made it grow' (1 Corinthians 3:6). 'The Spirit himself testifies with our spirit that we are God's children' (Romans 8:16).

In another context, the Koran, like the Bible, teaches that God works in us without impediment, that he guides whom he chooses.

Dreams and visions

Muslim converts to Christianity often speak of their religious experiences in terms of visions, dreams, voices. Why is that so frequent?

There may be two explanations. First, God's call is being repressed and pushed back into the subconscious. As a result, it has to 'raise its voice' to make itself heard. Secondly, the cultural background of most converts is very similar to that of the Bible where such phenomena are considered normal.

A repressed call

The Christian vocation of these converts from Islam was often accompanied by anguish, as they contemplated the inevitable hostility and the probability of rejection, even by their own family.

Tranquil, disinterested reflection is very difficult in an atmosphere of polemics and contempt. It is not therefore surprising that many converts go through an interior struggle. Even before becoming aware of their own ideas, they are conscious that changes and decisions may be called for. Fear, the instinct for conformity, prejudices, social pressures: all these factors tend to drive God's call, and the attraction of Jesus, back into the subconscious.

All this is quite natural, and, if we are honest with ourselves, we may confess to often reacting in the same way. It is perfectly understandable that these secret debates in the depths of the spirit, these repressed appeals, finally burst out in the form of symbols, dreams, visions and other phenomena which are familiar to modern psychology, however disturbing they may be for our conscious and rational mind.

These phenomena occur so often[5] that we should pay great attention and respect to their significance as symbolic expressions of deep psychological realities.

The cultural factor

Post-enlightenment Western thought has tended to dismiss dreams and to be suspicious of visions and healings. Rationalism, even scientism, triumphed. More recently however the rise of the human sciences, and especially of psychology, has revealed that reasoning is not the only mode of thinking.[6]

We have already observed that early Christianity accepted the reality of those sorts of experiences and indeed treated them as normal. The texts about the conception and birth of Jesus, for example, find nothing strange in the fact that God talks to Joseph in dreams, and to Mary and Zechariah through a vision. The Bible is full of stories of people who came to recognise God's will through phenomena of this kind: Jacob's dream and Daniel's interpretation of dreams are two examples among many.

It is true that a number of these stories can be explained as a literary convention. Nevertheless, behind such a convention must lie a conviction that it is possible for God to communicate with people in these ways. The tradition of the Church has been mindful of this inheritance, and many spiritual authors, from the Fathers of the desert to Ignatius of Loyola[7] and beyond, have suggested rules for interpreting these phenomena.

In practically all Muslim cultures, people believe that dreams have a meaning which has to be deciphered. Whole volumes have been written on the subject, some of them available in Europe.[8] There is however a difference between the Islamic and the biblical traditions. In the latter, people are invited to listen to God as he speaks to them; in Islam, one only looks for a message either from a saint or from the Prophet himself.

As explained above, many converts from Islam go through a more or less long period in which they try to repress their doubts and their questions in order to avoid dramatic and painful confrontations with their own people. Sooner or later however their deepest being compels them to face up to the situation, and the dream may be the only way in which they can bring themselves to do so.

Furthermore, a dream experienced, a vision seen, or a word heard, allows the subjects to present their behaviour as an act of obedience to a divine call. They are not acting on some personal caprice, but on the authority of God himself. God has taken the initiative. In this way the subjects are relieved of responsibility for their actions. If people want to complain, they should address their complaints to God.

Psychologically therefore these phenomena are perfectly explicable. But we should not overlook the fact that the obscure mechanisms of the human psyche are also subject to divine action. God may use psychological phenomena too as vehicles of his call. He speaks to us in the kind of language we can understand, and it is not surprising if he uses dreams and visions and healings to speak to people who believe in them.

Some examples

This type of encounter with God will become clearer if we consider some examples, chosen from many.

STEVEN MASOOD

We have already met Steven Masood, inspired to set out in search of the truth by his perception of the divisions within Islam.[9] We noted how he suffered from family squabbles and how he tried to understand the teaching of his Ahmadiyya community. We may now turn to consider the spiritual ardour which accompanied his religious quest.

With a childish faith, he threw himself into the river, sure that God would enable him to walk on the water. This faith matured and maintained him in a constant dialogue with God. This dialogue developed with the years, but quite early on he had experiences which prefigured his ultimate Christian vocation, even though he did not understand them at the time.

For instance, when he tried his unfortunate dive into the river, people made fun of him and his parents scolded him. On the following night, he had a dream which he found so significant that he later placed it at the beginning of his book:

> I came to the crossroads, a lost and weeping boy. I asked the passers-by which road would lead to my home, but no one could tell me. Finally, I chose a road at random and walked on, desolate.
>
> I was hungry, and as I walked I saw a beautiful garden with laden

fruit trees. The garden had a high boundary wall and before me stood a big gate, closed. I tried repeatedly, but I could not open it.

I cried out, 'Please open the gate. I'm so hungry. I have to buy some fruit. I have money and I am hungry. Please open to me. In front of me the gate swung silently open.

In the garden some children were playing I went up to them. Seeing me, they stopped and I told them, 'I have forgotten my way home. If I get home late my parents will beat me.' As I watched, a child took a bite from his apple. I looked at him and repeated, 'I am very hungry.'

The children called out, 'Daddy, see who has come!' I turned, and there among the bushes I saw an old, old man, but healthy and strong, coming towards us. I had the strange feeling that he was my Daddy too! And yet, suddenly, I became afraid and turned to run away, but his voice stopped me 'My son! My child! I am not angry with you. You are my child like these others.'

His voice was not my father's voice, but I turned to him and then I was in his arms and he was holding me. The other children crowded round and kissed me. They gave me fruit from their baskets and told me about the old man, their Father, and how he loved. I begged them to let me live with them since I felt so unloved in my own home.

'Please let me live with you. I will go to school with you and I'm sure the teacher will not beat me as Muhammad Ismail does!'

Father smiled at me, 'Son, I have asked Muhammad Ismail not to beat you. I have told him that he is to take care of you for you are a good child.'

I clung to him and buried my face in his white garments.

'No, Daddy. I will live here with you.'

'Son,' he said to me gently, 'you are a good child and good children obey their Father. Go back to that school now and when you have finished your studies there, I will see that you are admitted to my school. Come on now. Let me take you to your home.'

The next day at school, Masood did not receive the cutting, public reprimand which he feared. Plucking up his courage, he said to the learned old man who taught them: 'Sir, last night I had a dream . . . .' The master looked at him thoughtfully and blurted out: 'A dream? You too?' When Masood recounted his dream, the master told him not to tell anyone. But in the child's heart the conviction grew that the dream was from God, that God was concerned about him and loved him. He replied when one called to him.

Some time later this conviction received confirmation. Masood's family was very poor. The father's income was insufficient to maintain all his wives and their children, each living in their own house. The boy did not even have the money to buy paper for his school exercises:

> I used to walk the mile to school each day and that day as I went I prayed, 'O God, I want to find a rupee on the way to school so I can buy two exercise books, a pencil and an eraser at the school bookstall.'
>
> My faith was strong and I checked the ground carefully, sure that I would find my heart's desire. About half-way to school, I decided that perhaps my expectations had been too great and prayed yet again, 'Well, God, if one rupee is too much then a fifty-paisa coin (half a rupee) will do!'
>
> The school gate came into view and I reduced my request to twenty-five paise, and then just ten paise for some pages to paste into my book. But the ground was bare of any coin: and, greatly discouraged, I walked on towards the gate and the bookstall that stood close by. Just then I heard a familiar voice say, 'Son, my child.' My heart leapt. I knew this voice. Instantly I turned and saw the white-robed old man of my dream. I began to tremble from surprise and fear. As if from a great distance I heard his voice again, 'Son, don't be a coward. Take this rupee. Buy your things and finish your homework. There is still time before the bell is rung.'
>
> The voice faded and as though in a trance I heard the bookstall owner say to me, 'Well now, what do you need?'
>
> I was utterly surprised and confused. I was standing at the bookstall and a rupee coin was in my hand. I managed to give my order to the man and sat down on a nearby bench to complete my homework. Just as I finished, the bell rang for class.

Masood was twelve years old when these events took place. He did not yet realise it, but his dream already revealed God to him, God as a Father—not a Father who replaced his own parents, for the 'old man' had sent him back to them, but still a Father even nearer and more present to him.

Even at this early date there was the hint of a change of community: 'I will see that you are admitted to my school.' This dream introduced the child to a new relationship with God, a relationship of trust and familiarity. He was already praying in a spontaneous, informal way which was unusual in his community. Finally, the incident of the rupee, mysteriously deposited in his hand, confirmed his intuition: this paternal figure was truly God himself, from whom he had asked for the rupee.

All this affected Masood's intellectual quest, marked by incessant questioning of the official answers given by his religious community. His sense of dissatisfaction was no longer simply a systematic doubt or a restlessness of spirit; he had had a positive experience of the paternal tenderness of God, and this did not figure in any teaching of the Ahmadiyya sect.

After his flight from this sect, Masood sought in orthodox Sunni Islam a reflection of the truth he had felt. But there too he found no encounter with the Father God.

Rational argument must not obscure this other level of Masood's search. In looking for truth, he was not looking simply for doctrine but for an encounter with the Father such as had already been granted to him.

NUREDDIN ISHRAQIYYAH

We already know this Lebanese teacher, hurt by his experiences in a madrasa (school) training future Muslim religious leaders.[10]

His whole religious milieu filled him with distaste, and he left home to teach in other Arab countries. He would never have felt the attraction of Christianity if it had not been for a *dream* whose meaning he did not at first understand. He dreamed that he was on a road, which he then left to take another, at the end of which was a church. He had this dream several times, at shorter and shorter intervals. Each time he saw a different church, but it was always a church.

Added to this dream was a sort of vision, as remarkable as its effects were unexpected. His general attitude was one of bitterness towards the past, anxiety for the future and discomfort in the present: 'This vision changed the bitterness into sweetness, anxiety into peace, despair into happiness and a feeling of fulfilment.'

The vision, which came to him with irresistible force, presented Jesus, whom he had previously regarded as no more than one prophet among many, in universal majesty and power. He saw Jesus on the cross: nailed, covered with blood and crowned with thorns, but whose presence seemed to fill the universe with compassion, love and forgiveness. As he says himself, this was not just a physical vision but also a spiritual illumination. Whereas previously he had rejected the crucifixion, not understanding its meaning, now, quite suddenly, he *grasped*, deep within his heart, the love, the saving power, the victory, which it signified.

At the same time he was possessed by the conviction that Jesus, the Christ, was entering his life, opening to him his arms and inviting him to give himself to him. A voice echoed within him like a gong: 'Come to Christ, he wants you, why are you hesitating? He forgives you, however heavy your sins. Why are you afraid? He loves you, he is waiting for you, he wants you, come.'

This experience was so powerful that at first he wanted to run away from it into the street. But how could one flee from such gentleness? The old dream of a road leading to a church became clearer, more urgent, more frequent. He even saw himself going into the church. He still did not understand the meaning of all these psychic experiences. Eleven years were to pass before he finally came to understand that he was feeling called to become a Christian.

The realisation came to him in Tripoli during a conversation with his fellow-teachers. One of them explained that he had felt obliged to leave Christianity because the cross seemed to him the symbol of weakness and defeat. After so many years of continual meditation on the theme of the cross as victory, Nureddin had the opposite feeling and he explained to his colleague that the cross meant love and forgiveness extended even to the enemy. He was thunderstruck when his friend responded: 'So you are a Christian?'

A Christian? Yes, perhaps. *Yes indeed.* The next day, a Sunday in 1967, he went to mass in the cathedral. Yes, he was at home.

He now knew that he was being called to become a Christian, but a few more months of struggle were needed before he finally *accepted* the offer which God was making to him.

Nureddin's pilgrimage thus began with a feeling of revulsion for the education he had received. This was followed, more decisively, by an experience of the meaning of the cross of Christ, an experience conveyed by a vision and accompanied by dreams. The persistence of these experiences over several years both reflected and strengthened his interior growth. The vision described here may be compared to the eruption of a volcano. The volcano was already in Nureddin's heart, but only when it erupted, by the power of God, did he come to see the meaning of the insights which had been growing there secretly all these years.

JAHANGIR B. KHAIR-ULLÂH KHÂN

This Shi'ite from Pakistan, of Afghan origin, provides us with a further example of how a vision can bring a repressed conviction to consciousness.[11] He was a strict Muslim, a cabinet-maker by profession, who started to read the Gospels and felt himself challenged by them: 'You, Jahangir, are a sinner and an enemy of God. There is no true peace through good works.'

Attentive reading first of the Gospels, then the rest of the New Testament disturbed him, but he could not think of leaving Islam in order to believe in Christ. He did what he could to accept the ideal presented by Jesus and saw his character change for the better. But he remained troubled. One night he heard a voice saying to him: 'The cure of a troubled spirit is faith, the faith that Jesus is the Messiah and the Son of God. If you want to join God's family, then call his Son Lord.'

Like many other converts, as the moment of decision arrived he returned to the sources of Islam to find a word which would justify him in taking this step. He found a tradition according to which the Prophet said that at the last day, all would pay homage to Jesus. 'I will do it now,' he thought. He remained a secret disciple of Jesus for months without revealing his convictions, but the feeling that he had to bear witness to Jesus grew stronger and stronger, and finally he let his conviction be known. But it was only later, in 1947, after many years of further search, that he finally sought baptism.

At the moment of his baptism, by triple immersion, he felt like a blossom just opening and coming into full bloom: 'On going under the water the second time I saw Christ's cross; I saw Christ himself taking me and uniting me with himself.'

KHADIJEH JAN-NESAR (1880–1957)

We now come to an Iranian lady, daughter of a bookbinder of Ispahan.[12] From childhood she had lived in the shadow of the mosque and the Koranic schools, for which her father worked. Married at eleven, she was a mother at sixteen, a widow shortly after, and then married for the second time to a strict and severe Muslim.

While visiting the doctor one day, she met two Armenian Christian women in the waiting-room. They talked, and the women gave her a picture of the Virgin Mary holding her child. She was then twenty-six. She loved the picture and carried it about with her in a little case which she made for it.

Some time later she had a *dream* which made an impression on her. She was in a mosque, full of people dressed in white, listening to a preacher. He spoke from a high pulpit, but his body was hidden in a bright, shining cloud, and his face did not appear. Below the pulpit was a woman, Mary, the Mother of Jesus. Khadijeh spoke to Mary: 'Where is my way home?' Mary signed to an assistant who took Khadijeh by the hand and, before leaving her, handed her a bunch of herbs: 'Saint Mary told me to give these to you.'

When Khadijeh told this dream to her father, who had a reputation as an interpreter of dreams, he told her that she would have a child who would be for her a source of joy. Then, weeping, he added: 'Alas, you will become a Christian.' This detail is important, for it reflects a classical Muslim interpretation of dreams in which Christian religious personalities appear.

Having made friends with Christian missionaries, Khadijeh began to read the Bible and to learn about Christianity. As she progressed in her knowledge of the essentials of the Christian faith, a series of dreams presented these to her in symbolic form. For instance, she once dreamed that she saw Christ, as if in a portrait. The being in the picture stood before her as a small child, and then he gradually went up and up, borne aloft by two hands. She had not yet accepted the Christian belief in the divinity of Christ but she felt its appeal. Meanwhile her family began to harass and threaten her, and a mullah was brought to instruct her. She was not allowed to eat with the rest of the family. But she herself began then to feel that she had to pursue her search to the end.

She then had another dream. It was judgement day, and she was in a field with a large crowd of people. Christ appeared in glory on his throne. A chain was let down and the cry went up, 'Who longs for salvation?' Khadijeh took hold of the chain and began to climb. She then noticed that her ring was getting in her way, but it did not prevent her from reaching the top, where a mystic sprinkled her three times with perfumed water. When she woke she could still smell the perfume. She considered the meaning of the ring and concluded that it referred to the affections which still had too great a hold on her heart.

The meaning of the symbols in this dream is fairly clear: the dreamer perceives more clearly the importance of Jesus, who has really become the Saviour, the supreme judge. She feels that the decision she takes concerning Jesus involves her eternal destiny. The dream shows too that she has already taken the decision. She is aware of the consequences: trouble and struggle. The family, represented by the ring, is perceived as an obstacle which she has to overcome.

The sequel showed the truth of these presentiments. Her family's opposition hardened. She was taken on pilgrimage to Kerbela, the Shi'ite sanctuary in Iraq, her books and her Bible were torn, she was cut off from all contact with her Christian friends. All was in vain. She was finally baptised, almost in secret.

She continued to live with her husband. Some years later her daughter, Maimanat, was also baptised. As so often happens to women in their situation, both mother and daughter were repudiated by their respective husbands, on grounds which had nothing to do with religion. They were now independent women and were able to live openly as Christians, earning their living by running a small photographic business.

THE STRANGE HISTORY OF A SUDANESE CLAN

It is more difficult to find a psychological explanation in the case of a group of seventy-two persons who recently became Christians after a series of visions.[13] It happened at Wad Medani, some one hundred and twenty miles south-east of Khartoum. The clan, of Arab ancestry, had come from elsewhere and settled in Wad Medani in 1960.

Shortly after their arrival, the leader of the clan had a strange encounter with a venerable old man with a long grey beard. This stranger spoke to him in a friendly but firm tone: 'You and your families must embrace the true religion. You must become Christians and live accordingly.'

The leader was impressed. For the moment, faced with the radical change in their way of life which such a decision would involve, he was content simply to think about his experience while doing nothing about it. Some months later, while he was making his way through the crowd on a station platform, he suddenly found himself face to face with the same old man who asked, 'What prevented you from doing what I advised you to do?' He vanished before the leader could answer him.

This second encounter led him to summon the family heads and weigh with them the pros and cons of the old man's proposal. Finally they contacted the priest of the local Catholic community. Not suprisingly, the priest was embarrassed and feared trouble with the Muslim majority in the area. He contented himself with giving the newcomer some Christian books and a Bible.

Without any further contact with the local church, the members of the clan began to study these books. At the end of some months, a delegation returned to the priest. They proved that they had absorbed the Christian teaching, and asked for baptism. The priest was still hesitant and referred the matter to the Bishop. The latter was also a prudent man, and he consulted the Governor. The latter, having satisfied himself that the request really came from the parties concerned and not from the clergy, declared that there was freedom of religion in the country and that these people could be baptised. It was done. This clan is now trying to integrate itself into the local Catholic community, something which can be done neither easily nor quickly.[14]

The meeting with the old man was the turning-point. It does not seem to have been preceded by any approach to Christianity. It is possible that a natural explanation can be found. Nevertheless, the striking fact is that the words of the old man found an echo in the hearts of the clan leaders. If one wishes to see the action of God in this story, it is there that one must look for it first. The prudence and delays of the leaders show that their ultimate response was no mere caprice or passing enthusiasm but a conscious commitment.

The history of the missionary Church is full of these strange encounters. One may think of the centurion Cornelius in the Acts of the Apostles (chapter 10). 'He clearly saw' an angel who gave him the order to summon Peter. He then became the first non-Jew to be baptised. In the same book, we hear of the Ethiopian eunuch. He saw, not an angel, but Philip, a messenger, says the account, specially sent by an inspiration of the Holy Spirit (8:26–40).

A God who speaks

It is hard not to believe that God is directly involved in some of the dreams and visions which converts report.

We may recall some details from the life of the 'freedom-fighter' *Ghulam Masih Naaman*.[15] Some of his experiences, like the light which enveloped the Christian family he was preparing to kill, were totally unexpected, but might be explained as a protest rising up from his own conscience, even though he had hardly begun to ask himself questions about the atrocities he was committing every day. But his hearing of the words, 'My grace is enough for you,' in the station waiting-room come from a book he had never read and in an idiom not his own. That, with the effect these words had on him—liberation, forgiveness, reconciliation, and even union with God—can only be explained as the action of God on the secret recesses of his heart. There is something here which transcends anything people can achieve by their own efforts.

It is difficult too to explain in purely psychological terms the healing of the young Pakistani paralytic, *Gulshan Esther*. In reply to her prayer, she hears a voice directing her towards the Koranic texts concerning Jesus, and then she has an apparition of Jesus surrounded by twelve persons (the Koran does not speak of twelve apostles). In the course of this apparition, she is cured of her paralysis and receives instruction from Jesus, including the words of the Our Father which became her daily prayer before she had met a single Christian.

As for *Bilquis Sheikh*, she shows a variety of ways in which one can perceive God's calls.

She speaks in the first place of the atmosphere of certain days when she felt in some indefinable way that her uneasiness, or her readings, had a richer meaning than usual.

She speaks of her dreams, in which she eats with Jesus, and then finds herself in the presence of one whose name she knows without having ever heard it: John the Baptist. 'What a strange name,' she thinks, and she adds: 'The Lord came and was my guest for two days. But now he is gone. Where is he? I must find him! Perhaps you, John the Baptist, will lead me to him?' The meaning is clear. Deep within her, beyond the conscious mind, Bilquis is looking for Jesus. But how can we explain the fact that she knows the role of John the Baptist, whom she had never heard of? Was it perhaps some forgotten memory of an earlier reading? Or should we speak of an interior revelation? No one can say.

We have described at length the series of decisive experiences during which she felt herself in the presence of the Father, of the Holy Spirit. These seem to have been encounters at a deeper level than any vision or imagination, and Bilquis heard a voice within her replying to her questions.

Finally she learns to live continually in the presence of God and to abandon to him the conduct of her life. If she tries to go against the will of God, she becomes acutely conscious of an inner solitude and desolation.

These last two modes of divine manifestation are familiar to a

Christian and particularly well known to disciples of Teresa of Avila and Ignatius of Loyola.

We may think also of *Asha Wadai*, a young leper woman from Harar in Ethiopia.[16] When she arrived at the leprosarium in 1939, at the age of fifteen, she was very anti-Christian. Out of curiosity she went one day to a church service. Suddenly she cried out, 'Look, what a pretty child!' She was the only one who saw in the host which the priest had exposed on the altar a child whose heart was bleeding. She however was convinced of what she had seen, and was so struck by it that she decided to follow instructions and ask for baptism. She became Anacleta Maria and lived in great fervour until her death from leprosy four years later. The priest who saw her die recounts: 'I went to give her a last blessing. Prostrate with suffering, when she saw me arriving she lifted herself up, joined her hands and looked earnestly at the crucifix I was carrying. Then she fell back and gave up her soul to God.'

Prophecy: a traditional experience

All these witnesses show how God can use psychological mechanisms as the vehicles of his call. Images, symbols and intuitions arise out of our deepest self as do our normal ideas and decisions. One may nevertheless sometimes observe words or ideas which it is hard to avoid calling 'revealed', although this is not the usual case.

It could be that we have here a rediscovery of prophecy as a permanent feature of the life of the Church. Moses had wished for it: 'I wish that all the Lord's people were prophets' (Numbers 11:29), and Paul had seen this wish fulfilled in the first Christian communities: 'You can all prophesy,' he told the Corinthians (1 Corinthians 14:31).

The Second Vatican Council did indeed remind all Catholics that they had inherited this gift and this ministry, but the word 'prophecy' has often been so devalued that it means no more than a particularly sharp or provocative word. In fact, 'prophecy' is a word received from God before it is uttered, and it is its origin in God which is the secret of its power.

God makes us capable of receiving his word. It is possible to perceive the call of God in the ordinary circumstances of daily life, according to the promise of Jesus that he would not leave us orphans (John 14:18). Apparently, these believers made precisely this discovery: they found a Father who speaks to them and guides them.

The call to the sacraments

The call felt by converts is not in the first place an invitation to change their religious community: they simply feel the attraction of a new way of relating to God and their neighbours.

At the same time, this encounter with God leads sooner or later, and often sooner, to a discovery of the personality of Jesus and of his role as Saviour.

If this were all, the call would not necessarily involve converts in any great difficulties. The fact is, however, that almost always the encounter with God and with Jesus involves a further call— a call to give expression, in visible and irrevocable acts, to what one has experienced. This invitation may go against all their inclinations.

The call can be an invitation to join a group of Christians, but it may also take the surprising form of an overwhelming desire for the sacraments, those ritual encounters in which Christians let Christ touch them at certain key moments of their existence.

The impossibility of dissimulation

Faith in Christ brings about tensions and separations in one's family life. If only one could avoid it! But in the Gospels, Jesus does not hide that this may be the cost of discipleship. The day inevitably comes when the convert has to make his or her choice between what is prudent and what is demanded by faith, between family demands and the call of God. The tension can build up until it becomes simply intolerable.

This was the case with *Joseph Sallam* (1877–1947), a young Egyptian from Alexandria who discovered truth in Christianity when he heard about the miracles of Lourdes.[17] Anxious not to break with his family, he tried to combine outward Islamic rituals with interior Christian prayer. His Christian educators knew his secret and tried to persuade him to keep it to himself. He simply could not. On one feast of Corpus Christi, he detached himself from a group of Muslim students as they watched the Christians passing in procession, and, in full view of everyone, threw himself on his knees before the consecrated bread.

Then there was *Paul Mehemet-Ali Mulla* (1881–1959), whose conversion developed under the influence of the philosopher Maurice Blondel.[18] Some months after his baptism in 1905, he went back home to his family in Crete to try and break the news to them, gradually, of what had happened to him. He stayed there for a year, living with his parents, a Christian in secret. He was able to speak with his father, brothers and brothers-in-law, but his mother and sisters remained closed and gave him no opportunity of taking them into his confidence.

He found this double life a heavy trial. The more he tried to live in harmony with his family, the more he experienced the need for spiritual nourishment. Finally he felt he could not go on living without the sacraments. He contacted a priest in a neighbouring parish and arranged to received Communion, at least from time to time, before dawn:

> He agreed to meet me on Friday at 5.30 am and give me Holy Communion. You will pray for this I know, and that gives me confidence. I have nothing to reproach myself for. With all this discretion and silence, this continual hiding of Jesus for the sake of Jesus, the least I can do is to offer him this little furtive moment. For me it is indispensable, for I count on him to bring unity and simplicity in my life, while I am all the time putting on a brave face, making concessions, taking part in the life of the family. The scene of the night of Thursday 30 November was my Vatican Council. Sulking, suspicious, scowling, until then, like the Church after the Reformation, now that I have made it clear that I mean what I say, I will perhaps be able to open myself more easily to affection and charity.[19]

The incident to which Paul Mehemet-Ali here refers was a joke of his father's which caused him to lose his temper. He could no longer put up with a situation in which his outward existence was out of step with his faith:

> Papa called me a madman who should be locked up and then changed the subject. It was only about 7.30 in the evening, but I retired to bed. I could not sleep. I was in a real spiritual agony. I needed strength from somewhere, and about 9.30 pm I was seized with an irresistible and pressing inspiration to go to the Catholic Church in Iraklion. I saw the Capuchin Superior, explained my situation and asked him when I could receive the help of Holy Communion. He told me that there was not the least difficulty and that I could come any day I liked at daybreak.

It seems that the strain of living this double life, in which he had to continually hide his convictions, brought Paul Mehemet-Ali to feel that he could not manage without the sacraments. It was this almost clandestine practice of his faith that gave him the strength to go on living with his Muslim family.

Along with this urgent need for the sacraments, he also discovered a priestly vocation. He knew that he was called to satisfy in his brethren the sacramental hunger he had himself experienced. Eventually, after a few years as priest, he was called by the Pope to teach in the Oriental Institute in Rome.

The need for the Eucharist

The attraction towards the Lord's Supper does not come from a desire for outward conformity. It is rather an interior and almost irresistible need. We once heard a convert weeping at the back of a church because his baptism had been put off indefinitely and he could not receive Communion.

Always and everywhere, Christian communities have gathered to share the Lord's Supper. The tradition goes back to the first disciples (1 Corinthians 11:23), and by a kind of instinct, which theologians would explain as the action of the Holy Spirit, Christians ever since have treated it as something essential. We find this same instinct among converts.

We already know *Dr Sa'eed* (1863–1942), who passed from

anti-Christian polemics to faith in Christ. What had attracted him more than anything else was the example of Yohanân, a pastor who stayed there for a few months. When the pastor left, Sa'eed was on his own.

In his heart, he knew that he was a Christian, but he was not attached to any Christian community. There was none where he lived and his situation was such that he could not go and live elsewhere in order to join a church.

For some considerable time, Sa'eed tried to hide his faith under a Muslim exterior. He accepted to be the imam, or leader, of his mosque. He issued the call to prayer from the minaret, but after each verse he added, 'O God forgive me.'[20] He was supposed to lead the prayer in the mosque, but he would deliberately delay coming down from the tower so that someone else would start. When among the faithful, he would prostrate himself like everyone else, but secretly he was reciting Christian prayers: the Our Father and the Creed. He even composed a private litany, consisting of thirty Our Father's and Credo's, in imitation of the devotions practised in the mystical confraternities.

In Sa'eed's case too, little by little this life of dissimulation became intolerable. He felt a hypocrite. Finally he confided in a friend, who reacted by trying to reconvert him to Islam. It was in these circumstances that Sa'eed discovered, one is tempted to say by instinct, the Eucharist—the Lord's Supper.

At a party with lively friends, yet feeling alone, he could bear it no longer. He took a piece of bread and went out into the countryside among the vines, meditating on the death of Christ. Then he broke the bread and drank some grape-juice in memory of Christ.[21]

Perhaps without even knowing it, he had discovered for himself the ancient central rite of Christianity, the Lord's meal. No one told him to do it; he was impelled by some inner force. His faith, in short, absolutely demanded exterior expression. The inevitable consequence was that family life became impossible for him and he fled to join a group of Christians.

We meet something of the same in *Victor Mamoudou Arouna*, a Nigerian born about 1950. At the age of fifteen he began to feel attracted to Christianity. His Muslim family strongly disapproved and he was not allowed to eat with the other members:

> 'When everyone else has finished, you can eat the scraps.' I said nothing and went away. When they had finished, I came back and ate the remains and then went into the village. My heart was very sad. But deeper than sadness I felt a joy which I could not at all explain.
>
> For a week I ate like this every evening, after everyone else had finished. One night, while I was in bed, I prayed and thought . . . 'I used to be with my friends and now I am alone, I used to eat with my family and now I eat by myself. How is it that I love the Christian religion and am not afraid of the difficulties I meet?' I could not answer my question.
>
> Next morning I got up. I had a few cents and I bought five fritters. But then I felt too sad to eat them and I gave three to some children. Suddenly I said: 'I know what I have to do. I must do what the Father does at Mass when he blesses the Eucharist and says, "Take this and eat it, this is my body."' Perhaps I would find some strength. I copied the Father, then I ate and was content.

When Mamoudou returned home his father called him and asked him what he saw in Christianity. When he heard the son's reply, the father gave him a blessing and said: 'If it is in your heart to follow your religion, you are free. I followed the religion which I wanted.'[22]

The need for baptism

Even more than the Eucharist, converts feel the need for baptism, often amounting to an irresistible compulsion. This leads them to feel agonising impatience with the, to them, incomprehensible hesitations of the Christians to whom they address their demand. 'I am weary of this law, this hierarchy, I have had enough of all this suffering,' rages *Sakina*, the young woman whose baptism was refused first because she was only fifteen, then because she was still in a religious institution, then because she was living with a young man whom she was unable to marry officially. She was torn between the emotional blackmail of her father on the one hand and the requirements of the Church on the other. She only got her way when she was twenty-four, after nine years of painful waiting.[23]

Khalil was the imam of a mosque in Niger, and he was converted to Christ after reading the prologue to St John's Gospel.[24] He was rejected by his community and by his family, and lived alone with his wife, working as a poor peasant. But he was still not baptised:

> Perhaps people are afraid that I would go back to my old ways once I have been baptised. And then I do not know the Bible properly. Perhaps I should wait until I know it better. I think that is why I still cannot obtain baptism, but now I have no strength because I have not been baptised. I cannot go on living without baptism in this milieu.

Could one say it better: 'I have no strength because I have not been baptised'? Khalil does not deny his insufficient preparation, but, like Paul Mehemet Ali Mulla, he knows that he cannot live in a social atmosphere hostile to his faith without the interior strength which Christians have always received in baptism.

It is striking to notice in these converts, amidst all the ups and downs of life, a need for baptism which corresponds both to traditional theological formulations and to the writings of the New Testament. Indeed, are not these writings the witness of the first converts and an account of their experience? Their insistence on the necessity of baptism is the fruit of their experience rather than of any theoretical theology.

The desire for baptism may not be automatic and immediate. The convert may have waited for a long time, measuring the risks and putting it off as long as possible. The moment comes however when delay becomes intolerable, when there is an irresistible feeling that the hour has struck.

The history of *Bilquis Sheikh* shows us how the call to baptism can become imperious. After a night of agony and interior struggle, she finally fell asleep. When she woke up, she began to pray:

> My Lord was still standing before me.
> 'It is time for you to be baptised in water, Bilquis,' he said.

Water baptism! I had heard the words distinctly, and I did not like what I heard . . . I knew that the significance of baptism is not lost on the Muslim world. A person can read the Bible without arousing too much hostility. But the sacrament of baptism is a different matter. To the Muslim this is the one unmistakable sign that a convert has renounced his Islamic faith to become a Christian. To the Muslim, baptism is apostasy.

So, here was a difficult testing point. The issue was clearly drawn. Would I yield to the fear of being treated as an outcast, or worse, as a traitor, or would I obey Jesus? First of all I had to be certain that I was really obeying the Lord, and not some illusion. For I was far too new at being a Christian to trust 'voices'. How could I test my impression better than through the Bible.

She went therefore to the Bible, to the Gospels, and found that baptism was indeed prescribed. She went to the missionaries and told them of the call she had received. They hesitated. She went back to the Bible, and found the passage where Philip baptised the Ethiopian eunuch immediately after his conversion. 'It was as if the Lord was telling me all over again, "Get your baptism and get it now!" I felt sure he meant that if I waited much longer, something or someone might prevent it.'

Faced with her insistence, the missionaries decided to send her to another locality where she could be baptised. But when she went home, the feeling that she had to obey without delay was so strong that she filled the bath and baptised herself:

What I proceeded to do may have some theological problems. But I wasn't thinking in theological terms. I was simply trying to be obedient to a strong urge which was backed up by Scripture. I was supposed to be baptised *now*, and with the impediments that I felt marshalling themselves, I had doubts about waiting even until the afternoon.

So, because I wanted more than anything else in the world to stay in the Lord's presence, and the way to do that was through obedience, I walked into the bathroom and stepped into the deep tub . . . I placed my hand on my own head and said loudly:

'Bilquis, I baptise you in the name of the Father and of the Son and of the Holy Ghost.'

I pressed my head down into the water so that my whole body was totally immersed. I arose from the water rejoicing, calling out, and praising God. 'Oh Father, thank you. I'm so fortunate.' I knew that my sins had been washed away and that I was acceptable in the sight of the Lord.

Some hours later she was baptised again, very discreetly, in the midst of Christian friends in another village.

The interior experience of conversion leads to a pressing need for the visible rite of baptism. Experience calls for sacrament and vice-versa. The same phenomenon recurs in the Acts of the Apostles: rite and experience are conjoined. The apostles intervene when the rite has not been preceded, or followed, by an interior experience of the Holy Spirit. They intervene again when inner experience is deprived of its full expression in the rite.[25]

The freedom of God

Certainly Bilquis or Khalil bring to light the distance between converts and the Christians from whom they ask for baptism or the Eucharist.

The convert is convinced that God is calling. The call may come through personal encounters, through teaching and reading, sometimes through dreams and visions. Why does God call this one and not that? Why does the call come today, and not yesterday or tomorrow? Why in this place and not in that? There is no answer to these questions. All that the convert knows is that when the call comes, he or she must obey.

The Christian community, on the other hand, hesitates when a convert comes knocking on their door, they stall for time and check before finally accepting the authenticity of the call. For 'cradle Christians', conversions such as those we have described serve to underline the sovereign liberty of the one who gives faith as and when he chooses. It is a sobering experience to find oneself before God's untamed freedom. He will not be restricted by our customs or theological frameworks.

Scepticism or discernment?

Conversion often takes forms that leave us baffled. The forms are secondary. The only important question is whether God is truly calling one through these various experiences which, suddenly or progressively, challenge a human conscience.

We have to avoid taking up fixed positions. It would be as unwise to see the hand of God everywhere as to see it nowhere.

The role of the Christian community is to help converts to decide whether or not God is truly the source of the call they feel or whether it is all an illusion. If the call is genuine, the Christian community can confirm converts in their conviction that God is calling them to take a decision.

Without such community endorsement, individuals can easily be deceived by their own subjective states. They need this external assistance to discern what really is happening to them.

Openness is essential if the community is to carry out its function with regard to converts. The decision cannot be made simply by invoking principles. Each person is unique, and likewise each experience of conversion. One must come down from the level of principles in order to meet the very real person who calls on us.

Notes

1 In popular Islam, people speak of dreams and apparitions of saints. Dreams where the Prophet appears deserve special attention as signs of God's will to a person. But orthodox Islam is suspicious of such phenomena.

2 I. al-Faruqi, Chambésy meeting (1976), *International Review of Mission*, No. 260, October 1976, p.385.

3 One could read all the Gospels, starting, in particular, with the following passages: John 14 and 16; Matthew 10:20; 11:27–28, etc.

4 On this question one could consult: A. Godin, *Psychological Dynamics of Religious Experience* (Religious Education Press: Birmingham, Alabama, 1985). From another perspective: D. Gelpi, *Experiencing God: A Theology of Human Emergence* (Paulist: New York, 1978); W. Conn, *Christian Conversion: a developmental interpretation* (Paulist: New York, 1986).

5 In about ten per cent of the cases studied here.

6 Even in the West, psychologists remind us of the importance of dreams in the discovery of our deepest self. Beyond and deeper still, the Christian can discern God's action on this level. One could read: J.A. Sanford, *Dreams, God's Forgotten Language* (Crossroad: New York, 1984), and *Dreams and Healing* (A succinct and lively interpretation of dreams) (Paulist: New York, 1978). The author is a Jungian analyst and an Episcopal priest.

7 One could consult St Ignatius of Loyola, *Spiritual Exercises*, Nos 313–336; or the well-known handbook of A.A. Tanquerey, *The Spiritual Life* (Newman Press: Westminster, Md., 1948).

8 For instance a new edition made in Beirut in 1982 of *Tafsir al-ahlâm al-kabîr* (the main handbook on interpreting dreams). This book has been falsely ascribed to a famous author, Abû Bakr Muhammad Ibn Sîrîn (654–728).

9 See chapter 3. All particulars are drawn from S. Masood, *Into the Light—A young Muslim's search for truth* (STL Books/Kingsway: Eastbourne, UK, 1986), pp.9–10, 22, 28.

10 These experiences are described in chapter 4. His testimony is given in a book: Nur-ed-Din Ishraqiyyah, *Al-Dâ'i` yagidu tarîqahu ilâ l-salîb* (Lost, he finds his way to the cross) (Centre for young adults: Basle, Switzerland), in particular pp.70–75.

11 R.W.F. Wootton, *Jesus More than a Prophet, Fifteen Muslims find forgiveness, release and new life* (Inter-Varsity Press, Leicester, UK, 1982), pp.23–25.

12 W.McE. Miller, *Ten Muslims Meet Christ* (Eerdmans: Grand Rapids, Mi., USA, 1969, 1980), pp.96–104.

13 Mgr A. Baroni, 'A small Muslim community becomes Catholic', *Amecea Documentation Service*, No.238, 29 March 1982, Nairobi, Kenya).

14 Under the present regime, in July 1994, the leaders of this clan have been arrested by the local police and beaten up before being released on orders from Khartoum. Cf. *Vigilance Soudan* (BP 184, 75665 Paris Cedex 14), Nos 22–23, August–September 1994, p.12.

15 Ghulam-Masih Naaman and V. Toon, *The Unexpected Enemy, A Muslim Freedom-Fighter Encounters Christ* (Marshalls: Basingstoke, UK, 1985).

16 E. Foucher, 'La merveilleuse conversion d'une jeune lépreuse musulmane, *Missions Messages*, No.346, 9 October 1984, pp.14–15.

17 See chapter 6: God's Community: the Discovery.

18 See chapter 3: Thirst for Truth.

19 C. Molette, *'la VERITE où je la trouve' MULLA ZADE, Une con-science d'homme dans la lumière de Maurice Blondel* (Téqui: Paris, 1988), pp.176–177.

20 *Astaghfiru 'llâh.*

21 J.M. Rasooli and C.H. Allen, *Dr Sa'eed of Iran, Kurdish Physician to Princes and Peasants, Nobles and Nomads* (W. Carey Library: Pasadena, Ca., USA, 1957, 1983), p.43.

22 R. Deniel, *Sur le Chemin Chrétien* (Vie Chrétienne, Supplement to No.274, Paris, 1984), pp.60–61.

23 Sakina's case is described by A. Salles, 'De l'Islam au Christian-isme, (2) L'intégration difficile', *La Croix*, 5 March 1987, p.14, See as well the explanations of the priest who advised her in *La Croix* 10 September 1987, p.12.

24 R. Deniel, *Sur le Chemin Chrétien* (Vie Chrétienne, Supplement to No.274, Paris, 1984), pp.28–36; and R. Deniel, *Chemins de Chré-tiens Africains* (Inades: Abidjan, Ivory Coast, 1982–1983), No.2, pp.25–34.

25 One may read, in particular Acts 2 (Pentecost), Acts 8 (the Samari-tans), Acts 9:18 (Paul's conversion), Acts 10 (Cornelius' conver-sion), and Acts 19 (the Ephesians). All these texts show a refusal to dissociate the rite of baptism from the conversion experience and vice-versa.

CHAPTER 10

ALONE AND REJECTED

'You believe at last!' Jesus anwered. 'But a time is coming, and has come when you will be scattered, each to his own home. You will leave me all alone. Yet I am not alone, for my Father is with me. I have told you these things, so that in me you may have peace. In this world you will have trouble. But take heart! I have overcome the world.'

John 16:31–33

Thus spoke Jesus on the eve of his passion, betraying on the one hand his sense that he would be abandoned by his friends, and on the other a deeper sense of the presence of his Father.

We hear an echo of these words in the reaction of a young Pakistani woman driven from her home by her family because of her conversion to Christianity.

'Where can I go, Father?'

I stood alone by the side of the Samanabad Road, trying to fight back the tears of shock and pain at the scene I had just experienced, and looking up and down for some clue as to what to do next . . .

I saw that I, Gulshan Esther, poor and hated by those who should care for me, and turned away from their door, was now free of encumbrances. The veil of inherited religion, which had once separated me from a God whom no one could know, had been torn away, revealing him in the face of Jesus Christ, my Lord. Now the path of discipleship was marked out, and, whether pleasant or painful, I must walk it in obedience. But I was not alone. There was one with me who was strong and who would provide for all my needs.[1]

The solitude of the rejected one

Gulshan Esther's testimony articulates the suffering of the Muslim who changes religion.

The passage quoted above refers to the time when her brothers, after threatening to kill her, finally drove her out of the house. She had no longer any right to an inheritance, she was literally on the streets. It was the final episode in a series of several similar painful treatments she had had to endure.

Her sister had given her the address of a good woman well known for her generosity and connections, and Gulshan plucked up courage and went to see her and ask for work. After receiving her politely and advising her to return to Islam, this good woman asked Gulshan to come with her and proceeded to take her . . . to prison and leave her there. Her husband, a civil servant, had given orders for her to be put in prison. She remained there for several weeks, without any charges being levelled.

Some time later she succeeded in finding work as a journalist. One day the editor of the newspaper called her and told her to choose between returning to Islam and the sack. She lost the job.

Such is the fate of the rejected one.

Interior solitude

However, not all feelings of solitude are caused by one's circumstances or neighbourhood. Most, perhaps all, converts have only been able to question the beliefs and practices in which they have been brought up because they have in themselves the ability to question received ideas.

You have to think for yourself before you realise that other ideas are possible. There has to be a certain independence of spirit, a certain non-conformity, before one can begin to ask questions about the official thinking which most people simply take for granted. And this means a certain *inner alone-ness*.

When we contemplate these stories and testimonies, however, we are struck by the fact that there may be, at the same time, many people who feel lonely in their search and yet follow the same road, thus forming a much wider hidden current in their society where people—and particularly the young—express the same questions and are engaged in a similar religious pursuit.

In fact the reaction of the Muslim community betrays its deep insecurity. It feels itself threatened, not so much by the single defector, as by the wider trend which he or she represents.

Self-defence, communitarian as well as individual, is instinctive. Every family, every clan, every nation, has an awareness of its essentially precarious situation. Xenophobia, hatred of the stranger, seems to be at bottom a fear of losing or diluting the group identity, and it is a phenomenon by no means confined to Muslim countries. The threat of death hangs over communities as well as over individuals.

In Europe, at the present time, the foreigner is often considered a threat to national identity or employment.

All communities, including religious communities, therefore develop defence-mechanisms to protect their integrity against the menace of 'foreign' influences and defection. 'Deserters' affect the morale of the group and depress statistics. We have only to think of the grievous weight borne in Christian history by words like 'apostasy', 'heresy' and 'schism'.[2]

Apostasy in early Islam

From the outset, the Islamic community suffered political convulsions which threatened its unity and faith. After the death of the Prophet, a number of tribes refused to recognise his successors and queried various points of the Islamic faith. The consequence was what is known as the 'War of Apostasy' in which the dissidents were eliminated. Further conflicts left the community divided into political clans which evolved into separate sects like Sunnites and Shi'ites.

Later theologians attempted to justify the decisions taken by the religious leaders during this troubled early period. Their books usually include a special chapter about 'apostasy' and its suppression.

The modern world has brought about changes of mentality in all traditional societies. One consequence has been that, of late, the notion of apostasy and heresy has been used more frequently.[3]

In recent years, some Muslim thinkers have come to believe that the old concepts need revising, and a real debate is in progress in the Muslim world on the issue.

Apostasy in question

Without going into all the details of a highly complex discussion, one could distinguish three schools of thought.

The classical position

The classical position is that the bloody repression of dissidents, such as was carried out by the first successor of Muhammad, is normal and legitimate. It claims the authority of the Koran for this view.[4] In fact however the Koran speaks only of punishments in the next world.[5] Appeal is therefore also made to a saying of Muhammad, of doubtful authenticity: 'If someone changes religion, kill him.'

The scriptural basis of this school of thought is, to say the least, uncertain. Nevertheless down the ages it has become the most widespread and popular. There is no question here of asking why people leave Islam. The sole emphasis is on the necessity of protecting the unity of the community and of forestalling any harm which might be inflicted on it by a deserter.

Freedom of belief

A number of modern authors recognise that there is little scriptural support for the classical view. They believe that the death penalty for apostasy was in fact instituted in a specific historical context and basically for political reasons, and they recommend religious freedom today.

They see a wave of de-islamisation spreading in the Muslim world. These authors believe that it is best countered by accepting freedom of belief (which naturally implies the freedom not to believe or to stop believing). This attitude would reflect the essential message of the Koran as a call from God which respects human freedom.[6] God himself gives us the example in respecting humanity's decision. Repression only encourages religious indifference beneath an outward show of conformity. A freer atmosphere would allow Islam to recover its authenticity and its original fervour.

Militant Islamism

A third trend, more vocal in its expression, is that of the radicals. They believe that it is above all lack of political power that is bringing modern Islam into crisis. What is needed is the re-islamisation of the state, the constitution, the judiciary.

The problem and its solution are placed on a political level. As a result, pluralism is denounced as an offence to the ideal Islamic society. Re-islamisation may need 'violence and blood'.[7] Out of this segment of the Muslim community come the terrorists and the rigorists who demand exemplary punishments on those who give comfort to the enemy by abandoning Islam.[8]

An ancient history

The classical position then was that anyone who left Islam for another religion was to be put to death. Any person who had helped or advised the 'apostate' was also subject to the death penalty.

In a context where religious communities entertained a deep hatred for one another, intervention by the political authority was rarely needed to enforce this law: popular opinion was sufficient either to prevent desertion or to punish it after the event. The family itself would often take the responsibility for killing one of its members who had, in leaving Islam, brought dishonour on the clan.

In Muslim lands, Jews and Christians did not seek to make

converts among Muslims, preferring to remain passively defensive, although the consequence of such an attitude was that they lost thousands of members in every generation. Strangely enough, Muslim public opinion continued, notwithstanding, to regard them as a threat to the faith of Muslims. In 855, when Christians were becoming Muslims in large numbers, the great writer Jâhiz still felt obliged to sound the alarm:

> Moreover, our nation has not been afflicted by the Jews, Magians, or Sabians as much as by the Christians . . .
>
> Indeed, for all our grief over the seduction of our youth and unintelligent we have primarily the Christians to blame. And when one hears their notions about forgiveness, and wanderings in quest of God . . . abstinence . . .
>
> they have filled the earth and exceeded all others in numbers and fecundity. Alas! This circumstance has increased our misfortunes, and made our trials stupendous! Another cause for the growth and expansion of Christianity is the fact that the Christians draw converts from other religions and give none in return.[9]

Down the centuries we hear the same cry repeated by Muslim writers: Christians and Jews are a menace because they tempt Muslims to adopt their customs.[10]

There was of course a similar attitude in medieval Christendom. The Christian majority regarded non-Christians, especially Jews, with the same mixture of tolerance and exclusion, and there too the apostate was liable to the death penalty. Only with the Enlightenment did a more flexible attitude finally prevail.

In Muslim countries, things changed little at popular level. Even if official laws have changed, popular opinion remains implacably hostile towards 'apostates' from Islam and indeed towards dissidents of every sort.[11]

The convert becomes a 'non-person'. They may be refused identity papers, and their marriage declared invalid. Their children may be taken away and entrusted to Muslim members of the family, and they lose their rights in the family inheritance. Any applications they may address to officialdom to obtain their legal rights meet with mysterious delays.[12]

Some recent facts

Popular resentment and the arbitrary exercise of local power combine to put pressure on the convert to reverse his decision. Some recent examples may be briefly considered.

In 1986, ten Egyptian converts were put in prison for several months simply because they had changed their religion.[13]

Some years earlier, the fiancée of an imprisoned convert was found dead in a canal after she had refused to break off her engagement to the 'apostate'.[14]

Esther John was called *Qamar Zea* when she left her family in southern India to go to Pakistan to be baptised. Brought up as a Muslim, she had been touched by chapter 53 of the book of Isaiah, in which the passion of Christ seems to be described in great detail centuries before the event. She suddenly acquired the conviction that Jesus was living now, never to die again, and that he was a Saviour whose power could change her heart. After several years of preparation, during which she worked as a nurse, she was baptised in 1954. Five years later she was still working for the Christian mission.

One day she received an ultimatum from her family, but she refused to return home unless she received a guarantee that her religious convictions would be respected. In the last days of 1959 she was found murdered in her room. The police never discovered a motive for the crime.[15]

Even if the convert is not always threatened with physical death, it is often made clear to them that they are 'legally' dead. When Jean-Mohammed Abd-el-Jalil, a young Moroccan from Fez, became a Christian, his family conducted a symbolic funeral service for him.

We will now hear from a person whose identity we must conceal as his story has never been published. We shall call him 'J'. He belonged originally to the Muslim Brotherhood of Egypt, a militant, fundamentalist group, and was converted to Christianity.

> I finally left the Muslim Brothers in 1951 because they did not accept the basic principles of love and charity. How can people be compelled to believe?. . .

I became friendly with a Christian called W ... He was always talking about the life of Christ, his miracles, his love, his redemption of humanity. On one occasion he said Christ was the Son of God. I could not control myself and struck him in the face. He replied: 'May God forgive you and bless you.' I felt at that moment the pettiness of my own soul. I was disgusted with myself and asked his pardon.

This incident stimulated J to compare the teachings of the Bible and the Koran. Little by little he became more and more convinced that Jesus was the Saviour of humankind. One evening, in a prayer meeting, he gave his life to Christ.

I began to pray in the morning. About seven o'clock, my sister and a cousin came and asked me, 'Is it true that you have become a Christian?' I said it was true. They beat me viciously, saying, 'You have dishonoured us.'

I began to pray and read the Bible and to talk to the workmen about the love of Jesus for humanity. One day some strangers came and attacked me. They wanted to kill me. My employer contacted a mosque sheikh. He wanted to make me return to Islam. Otherwise he would authorise my death officially. Then he beat me violently with his stick. I endured the pain with joy. My employer dragged him away from me ...

In my work, I found there were people who had taken an oath to kill me. One of them came up to me with a knife and swore that he would kill me if I did not renounce Christianity and return to Islam. I said: 'I am ready to die, with the grace of God.' I knelt down and asked God to forgive my attackers and to give me the strength to endure the pain unto my last breath.

My friend W witnessed this scene and was afraid for me and for himself, but the one who had sworn to kill me went away. The others however attacked me with sticks and injured me so severely that my neck is not right to this day. I had to leave the job.

The document proceeds in the same vein. J names some of the persons who had begun by insulting and beating him but who were then touched by his insistent forgiveness. Many of them in fact became Christians as a result:

By the grace of God, I explained to all who attacked me why I had converted. One of them struck me three times. I prayed to Jesus and asked him to appear to this man and bring him to faith. One day I had a book called: *What is the Meaning of the Expression, Christ, Son of God?* I pretended to run away from this man, but dropped the book so that he might pick it up. He did in fact pick it up and read it, with the help of a Christian friend. He ended up by being baptised, with his wife and their son and daughter . . .

One day a friend came to see me and he dined with us. All we had was a loaf and a little salt. While we were asking God to bless this bread, some policemen came in, armed with sticks. They then beat us cruelly, me, my mother and my friend. Then they dragged us into the street and gathered a crowd of people who continued to beat us, shouting: 'Let the one who loves the Prophet beat the renegades.' Then, covered in blood and with our clothes in tatters, we were taken to the police station before Officer F.

The story continues, but we need not pursue it further. Such cases are common in all countries. Nearly all the converts speak of the violence and threats of violence of which they have been the target.

Family dramas

Physical violence combines with bitter rejection by relatives. Muslim families very often feel dishonoured when one of their members converts to Christianity.

Shame and disgrace

This feeling is understandable when one realises the image which people have of 'renegades'.

- They are thought to be in bad faith. Islam being self-evident, how could anyone in good faith possibly abandon it?
- It is thought that renegades have abandoned everything positive in their faith, including God. They are rejected as godless, atheists, free-thinkers.
- They are often suspected of having evil designs on their community and country. They are traitors to their religion and therefore traitors

also to their country. People whisper that they are probably in the pay of the imperialists, or the CIA.

- Most probably, people say, they have been bought. It is commonly believed that the task of missionaries is to buy adherents by exploiting their greed and weakness. Sometimes converts may be asked how much they have been paid. . .
- The best construction of the event is that the convert is mentally deranged. How otherwise could anyone believe that it is possible to adore three gods, while saying they are also one? Popular Islam abounds in such sarcastic caricatures of Christian faith.

A letter from a distressed father

One can then understand why Muslim families react as they do. Physical violence is by no means rare.

Sometimes however families are content simply to drive out the convert. This can be a very serious matter in a society based on family and clan connections. Here is a letter from a father who had just heard that his son had become a Christian while studying abroad. It is from Syria and dated 1966.

In the name of God, the merciful and compassionate.

My son,

Salvation be on our lord Muhammad, the most noble of the prophets and the best of the messengers of God.

God said: Honour your parents, always speak to them respectfully! I hear you have disobeyed God and his messenger.

God said: Anyone who follows a religion other than Islam cannot be pleasing to God. Do you not realise—may God bring you back to the right path!—that you have become an infidel, a renegade, one of those whose repentance cannot be accepted and for whom all intercession is useless? Do you not know that in becoming a Christian you have left Islam, that you are far from the truth and from the right way? It is a thing I cannot approve and which I wish did not exist. I will never be able to accept it. Do not draw down upon yourself and upon all your actions the anger of God. If you have really decided to do this, you are no longer my son and I am no longer your father. I shall never again be able to recognise you. This I swear before God.

I cannot erase from my memory the moment when you told me you were seeing a priest at B. How did you ever come to that point? What reason can you possibly have? Do you not understand, do you not realise? Where is the faith which used to light up your face?. . . What of the prayers you recited so often?. . . and your extra fasts?. . . Where are the lessons you learned from your wise teachers in Hama and Damascus? Have you forgotten your guide, Sheikh A?

My son,

do not abandon the commandments of God to follow the devil's wiles. It is I who warn you: do not leave in my heart a wound whose pain I shall feel as long as I live. Have I not worry enough in caring for your little brothers? Do not let my heart suffer and burn with pain. Do not be the cause which makes me bow my head before God. What pains I have already suffered for the sake of yourself and your brothers! And you pay me back by an offence, worse, a shame, which will attach to me and to the whole family for ever. Become again what I hoped for you, according to the education you have received. Do not make me a laughing-stock among the people.

If you have no care for the sufferings you are causing to others, think at least of yourself. Return to God and do not cut yourself off from him.

If you are not touched by what I say to you and persist in your design, never appear before me again and never send me your news. You will have shown that you prefer misery to happiness, and hell to paradise.

If you abandon this project, let me know at once so that I can bring you back here. Then you will have abandoned the path of the devil and of those who wish to deceive you and will be on the right path again. Do not wander about. A man of sense and intelligence must walk straight. All this is a deceit of the devil. You know how to distinguish truth from error, faith from infidelity, light from darkness. How can you read the books of men and abandon the book of truth?

PS. If you persist with this project, do not even try to write to me again. Your father.

This letter has been reproduced in its entirety because it helps us to understand the drama both of the converts themselves and of their families. The misunderstanding between father and son is total. For the father, as for the Muslim community in general, the young man is deliberately abandoning truth and embracing error. This corresponds to the definition of the complete renegade—if such a person can ever exist! Or has ever existed!

In fact of course the converts are not choosing error but a truth which seems to them more solid, or more universal, than that which they have received from their community of origin. We have already seen that it is Islam itself which gives the taste for truth which may lead converts to Christianity. For others, it is the sense of God which Islam gives that helps people to encounter God in Christian prayer.

It is of course the same with people who convert to Islam. They are not rejecting their original faith, but are discovering in Islam a facet of the truth which appeals to them.

Families and communities can only see the negative aspect: for them the convert is abandoning their group and their faith.

Anguished converts

How then do the converts react in this situation? Very often they feel heart-broken. They need time to weigh the pros and cons. Sometimes there may be a kind of irritation, as in the case of *Sakina* whose father went on hunger-strike when he discovered that she was going out with a Christian.[16]

Said Hireche (1903–1932) was a young Kabyl from a family of marabouts. He became interested in Christianity while in France, but it was only when he returned home and was seriously ill with tuberculosis that he asked for baptism. He opened his mind to his father, Si Arezki, who replied:

> My son, think again ... Keep your convictions, but do not declare yourself a Christian. It would be my ruin and my death ... No one would dare to approach a marabout whose son had become a Christian. If you persist and are baptised, I will deny you and disinherit you. You shall no longer even bear my name.

After the departure of his father, Hireche wrote to a priest in these terms:

> I am greatly in need of your encouragement to strengthen my faith, especially now when, I must frankly admit, a diabolical wave has been released against me ...

As you know, my father visited me last Tuesday. He left me with three problems. He is stubbornly opposed to my becoming a Christian. If I persist, he will disinherit me and deprive me of everything, even of my name. What shall I do to arrive at my goal of baptism? This is how I see the situation:

1) I can revise my catechism and the instructions required for baptism and then have myself baptised in one of your houses, without telling my father. Then I can practise my faith as far as I can without letting it be seen. Is this right to do so? For myself, I must say that it looks rather like stealing my salvation.

2) I can simply oppose my father's will and become openly a Christian. Then, with head held high, I can work for the glory of God. That, Father, is my dream. What could be more beautiful or more pure than to work for such a cause in a place where one is hated! This dream however seems to be unrealisable, at least for the present. My recovery is still uncertain,[17] but even if I do get better, I would be unable to undertake manual work and I am unqualified for anything else. How could I, doing nothing but rest from morning till night, provide for my wife and especially for myself?

3) My last position is this: to wait in prayer and patience until God sees fit to sound the hour . . . My faith is unshakable: I believe in spite of all. I end by the cry: Long live Jesus![18]

After this painful meeting, Si Arezki waited for another month before returning to the hospital to visit his son. They had a further conversation:

'Well, son, have you thought about it?'

'Father, I have. My will is made up. I shall become a Christian.'

'Well then, hear me. You are a man. The will is not to be broken. You wish to be a Christian. So be it! Be a Christian. But at one condition: . . . You shall be a Christian like Optat.[19] On this condition you shall return home, you shall remain my son. But if you become a Christian like X (a Christian who had returned to Islam), then I shall not recognise you, I shall deny you.'

Sorrowfully he added, with head bowed, 'What will they say of me when they know that my son has become a Christian?'

Hireche was baptised some weeks later and took the name Augustine. His father, true to his word, came and witnessed his son's step. Three months later Hireche died of tuberculosis.

The attitude of Si Arezki was a combination of loyalty to his own principles and respect for the decision of his son, provided this was respectable. More and more often, one finds a similar attitude in the families of other converts. Then there are those who begin by rejecting the convert, but later realise that their decision was an act of faith in God which they can respect and they do not sever their links with them.

So *Victor Mamoudou Arouna*, from Niger, received his father's blessing: 'If you have it in your heart to follow your religion, you are free. I followed the religion of my choice.'[20]

Antoine Douramane discovered Christ while serving in the French army. We have already described how that man, also a native of Niger, returned to his country and became a catechist to his people, without any regular link with the Church. He explained to his father that he had found someone to lead him on God's road, someone who 'took to God all the sacrifices of the ancestors by offering himself as a sacrifice'. His father replied: 'If you have found a guide to the road of God, follow it.'[21]

The Muslim who is on the point of converting to another religion often feels the need for a word of approval from his family, his community of origin, or Islam. Some receive it from their father, others from a religious leader, like this marabout from Niger:

The marabout whom I served was called Modi Sadi. He was a Peul from Dire. I spoke to him about Jesus. He told me that the religion of Jesus was good, but too difficult for black people. I was pleased that he said this religion was good. Then I gave him a pair of shorts and two shirts as a sign of friendship and farewell. I never saw him again.'[22]

Others turn to the Koran or to the books of Islamic prophetic traditions. There, they find quotations which could be understood as a confirmation or an approval of their decision, but they may still experience a great loneliness which will remain for a long time.

Our times provide ever more numerous examples of how a spirit of openness and respect can overcome the first reaction of rejection and violence. The latter however remains by far the most common reaction.

The solitude of the catacombs

It is evident that the path of a Muslim who feels called to become a Christian is marked by fear. Some manage to overcome it, others escape to a foreign country, while others again live in continual anguish.

Forced exile

We have heard at length the story of *Bilquis Sheikh*, the Pakistani lady who dared to call God 'Father'. This is what happened after her baptism:

> Not one relative, friend or acquaintance turned off the Grand Trunk Road any more toward my house; never did the phone ring.
>
> Then at 3.00 one morning my white bedside phone did clamour. I reached toward the instrument, my heart pounding. No one would call at this hour unless there had been a death in the family. I picked up the phone and at first heard only heavy breathing. Then three words were thrown at me like stones:
>
> 'Infidel, Infidel, Infidel.'
>
> The phone went dead. I lay back on my bed. Who was it? One of the fanatics my uncles constantly warned me about? What might they do?
>
> 'Oh Lord, You know that I don't mind dying. But I'm an awful coward . . . Oh, I pray that I will be able to bear pain if it comes . . .'
>
> What did come next was a threatening, anonymous letter, 'Let's be clear. There is only one word to describe you. Traitor.' Then there was another letter and shortly still another. They all contained warnings, I was a turncoat and I would be treated as such. Late one afternoon in the early summer of 1967, about six months after my conversion, I stood in my garden with the crumpled remains of one such letter in

my fist. It was particularly vitriolic, calling me worse than an infidel, a seducer of the faithful. True believers, the letter said, had to burn me out like gangrene was burned out of a healthy limb.

Burn me out? Was this more than just a figure?[23]

Other warnings arrived at intervals, reminding Bilquis that a group of militants from the neighbouring town were planning to make an example of her. After four years there was a change of government and the friends who had formerly been able to exercise their influence in her favour lost their positions. 'It was not too long before I began sensing a growing hostility. I saw it in the eyes of men as I walked in Wah.'

In 1971, her house was set on fire. Had it not been noticed immediately, everything would have been destroyed. That evening Bilquis took her Bible, and a text from Genesis struck her: 'Make haste, escape there; for I can do nothing until you arrive there' (19:22). She then realised that she would have to resign herself to leaving her country.

Hidden Christianity

In some countries where the atmosphere is particularly stifling, a movement like 'Jews for Jesus' develops. Jews for Jesus are Jews who have discovered in Jesus the Messiah of Israel, the Saviour, but are not attached to any Christian church. Similarly there are Muslims who have discovered Jesus as Lord and Saviour but who find it impossible to disclose it to their family, partly because of the reaction that it would provoke in the neighbourhood, and partly because of the risks to themselves in their own country.

They have therefore no choice but to behave like the early Christians in the catacombs. Far from any official church, these little groups live out their faith in great secrecy. So does religious history repeat itself. These modern Christians are living not only like the early Christians in the catacombs, but also like those of Japan lived for centuries, and those in Eastern Europe under communism. One must include also in this category the persecuted Muslims of Renaissance Spain.

One may wonder whether the current debates in Islam on tolerance and human rights will allow these secret Christians to come out into the daylight. It is possible. Will fundamentalism, on the contrary, incline people towards the type of society that rejects and persecutes its dissidents?

Time alone will tell.

Notes

1 Gulshan, E. and Sangster, T. *The Torn Veil, Christ's healing power breaks through to a Muslim girl* (Marshalls: Basingstoke, UK, 1984), pp.127–130.

2 A short definition of these terms is not out of place here: *apostasy* is used for a person who rejects globally all the teachings of his or her religion; *heresy* applies when a person only rejects part of these teachings; finally, *schism* describes a group that breaks up into two 'denominations', one section breaking away from the parent group.

3 Some groups taxed the Shah of Iran and President Sadat of Egypt with apostasy before overthrowing the first and murdering the other.

4 The Koran speaks of apostasy in terms of *unbelief (kufr)*: 2:217; 47:25–27. It speaks of *turning back (ridda)*: 16:106–109; 2:108; 3:86–90, 177; 4:137; 9:66, 74.

5 Koran 9:74 warns of a punishment in this life and in the next, but apparently God will inflict this punishment when and as he decides.

6 As an example of this opinion, one could read: M. Talbi, 'Religious liberty: A Muslim perspective', *Islamochristiana*, 11, 1985, pp.99–113; or, by the same author, 'Islam and the West: Beyond confrontations, ambiguities and complexes', *Encounter*, No.108, October 1984. (Both publications available at PISAI, Viale Trastevere 89, 00153 Rome.)

7 Expression used by the *Jihâd* group in Egypt.

8 For a short presentation of these various trends, one may read: Hmîda Ennayfar, 'De la Ridda (apostasie) à la foi, ou de la conscience du paradoxe', *Conscience et Liberté*, No.35, (1988), or *Se Comprendre*, No.88/05, 5 May 1988.

9 Drawn from Al-Jâhiz's Refutation of the Christians (*Radd `alâ 'l-Nasârâ*), translated by J. Finkel, 'A Risâla of al-Jâhiz', *Journal of American Oriental Society* (New Haven, 1927), pp.311–334.

10 This was the position of Ibn Taymiyya (1263–1328), an author often quoted by present-day radicals. Consult, for instance, M.U. Memon, *Ibn Taymiyya's Struggle against Popular Religion* (Mouton, 1976).

11 One may remember the fate of many communist sympathisers in various countries, or the case of Mahmûd Taha, this Muslim leader hanged on the grounds of heresy in the Sudan on 18 January 1985.

12 For a study of the juridical angle, see S. A. Aldeeb Abu-Sahlieh, 'Liberté religieuse et Apostasie dans l'Islam', *Praxis Juridique et Religion*, 3, 1986, pp.43–76.

13 *Le Monde*, 11 July 1986, p.4. Their release was announced in *Le Monde*, 22 October 1986.

14 This happened in Egypt. Drawn from confidential documents.

15 R.W.F. Wootton, *Jesus More than a Prophet, Fifteen Muslims find forgiveness, release and new life* (Inter-Varsity Press, Leicester, UK, 1982), pp.47–51.

16 A. Salles, 'De l'Islam au Christianisme, (2) L'intégration difficile', *La Croix*, 5 March 1987, p.14.

17 At the time, he was in hospital where he died of tuberculosis less than six months later.

18 Unpublished source.

19 Optat was a Christian of the Ouadhias, in Kabylia, whose integrity made him the admiration of all. When he died, his Muslim friends asked if they might have the privilege of carrying his coffin.

20 R. Deniel, *Sur le Chemin Chrétien* (Vie Chrétienne, Supplement to No.274, Paris, 1984), pp.60–61.

21 J.M. Ducroz, *Les Actes des Premiers Chrétiens du Gorouol* (Nouvelle Cité: Paris, 1977), p.18.

22 *Ibid.*, pp.38–39.

23 B. Sheikh, *I Dared to Call Him Father* (Word Books: Waco, Texas, 1978, 1980), pp.96–97.

CHAPTER 11

BETWEEN WELCOME AND REJECTION

People were also bringing babies to Jesus to have him touch them.
When the disciples saw it, they rebuked them. But Jesus called the
children to him and said, 'Let the little children come to me, and do
not hinder them. For the kingdom of God belongs to such as these.'
(Luke 18:15)

Then Peter said, 'Can anyone keep these people from being baptised
with water? They have received the Holy Spirit just as we have.'
(Acts 10:47)

One is struck in nearly all of the testimonies we have heard by the loneliness of the subjects. Whether at the beginning of the conversion process or at the end, Muslims called to become Christians find themselves on their own.

If they are immigrants, far from their family, they will already be acquainted with loneliness, but their conversion may remain unknown to their own people. If they are at home, however, they may have to hide what is going on within them, even from their own family; otherwise they may find themselves rejected and perhaps persecuted.

We may now ask whether the converts' requests to be accepted into the Christian community finally puts an end to their solitude. Do they find another community to take the place of the one they have left? And what is the attitude of the Church?

Welcomed by Christians?

Contrary to what one might imagine, Christian communities in general are far from welcoming to new converts.

When someone, and particularly a Westerner, becomes a Muslim, he or she is received with open arms by the Muslim community which celebrates the event as a victory. The fact of that conversion is widely publicised, especially if the convert is a well-known person, like the Emperor Bokassa or Roger Garaudy.

Reluctant communities

When a Muslim becomes a Christian however, and perhaps especially a Catholic, the silence is positively deafening. One can understand that a certain degree of discretion is desirable for the sake of other people whose lives might be put in danger by too much publicity. But is this really the whole story?

IN MUSLIM COUNTRIES

For centuries Christians in Muslim countries have been exposed to a tremendous amount of social pressure exercised on them by a triumphant majority. They were forbidden to spread their faith, to occupy important positions, to build new churches, especially in the vicinity of mosques. They were condemned to the status of a perpetual despised minority.

This centuries-long experience may have something to do with the way in which these communities receive converts coming to them from Islam.

First, there is *fear* of the repercussions which the news of a conversion might have on the Christian community. Dr Sa'eed's conversion was blocked for a long time by such fear. After leaving his native Kurdistan to escape death, he lived as a refugee among Armenian Christians, living and dressing like them. Very soon the Armenians took fright and he had to return to his Muslim dress.[1] He was compelled to adopt an attitude of dissimulation, behaving as a Christian when among the Christians and as a Muslim when among the Muslims. This nearly stopped his conversion altogether: his faith grew weak and his fervour diminished. Fortunately he came across a hymn attributed to St Francis Xavier and this aroused him anew and strengthened his faith. Shortly afterwards this same community took fright again when Sa'eed took a Christian fiancée. He was obliged to leave the town and go to Tehran, where he would be less visible. Only there could he be finally baptised and married.

Secondly, the long history of *antipathy* between the Christian and Muslim communities has left traces. The Muslim who calls for information or even asks for baptism is still regarded as belonging to the enemy group. In countries like Pakistan, the majority of the Christians come from non-Muslim minorities, like Hindus. Muslims who seek to join them are thus doubly outsiders. Their language, their name, their customs: all mark them out as different from other Christians. Their eventual conversion may not completely obliterate these differences. When *Ghulam Masih Naaman*, the converted Kashmiri 'freedom-fighter', went to ask a missionary what he should do in order to become a Christian, the missionary was away and Ghulam had to wait for three days. When the missionary returned, none of the Christians living at the mission station had given any food to the visitor.[2]

Thirdly there is *mistrust*. The sight of a Muslim engaged in a religious quest and asking questions about truth is so novel for Christians that their first reaction is to wonder what he or she really wants. During his enforced fast, Ghulam Masih heard the Christians talking about him: 'One said that I wanted to become a Christian simply because I wanted to find a young girl to marry. Another said that I was looking for employment as a mission servant. Yet another said that I merely wanted money. I heard it all but said nothing.' There is also fear of the police. It is believed, not without reason, that spies sometimes infiltrate groups of converts in order to obtain information on 'dissidents'. These may then be imprisoned, along with those who helped them to become Christians.

IN OTHER COUNTRIES

Even in a different context, similar attitudes can be found.

There is *suspicion* of motives. Would the 'convert' be looking, in fact, for a residence permit, or for the regularisation of a marriage?[3] Moreover, it is known that Muslim countries send agents to spy on their citizens living abroad, and there too they may infiltrate convert circles. All these suspicions are connected with the myth that Muslims are 'unconvertible', and that the only real Islam is the radical wing implacably and eternally hostile to Christianity. Then again, Muslims looking for truth outside their community are often considered unstable and abnormal, or perhaps swindlers who regard all Christians as easy prey. Naturally, people entertaining these ideas do not want to have anything to do with them.

General *antipathy* to foreigners may also play a part and this is particularly true in certain countries.

Low level of genuine faith leads some Christians to regard their religion above all as a burden, they cannot comprehend the fervour and enthusiasm of the convert who says that he has been liberated by his Christian faith. They too start looking for hidden motives.

Rejection

As a result, a Muslim who asks for baptism may meet with a lot of difficulties.

Contrary to the popular notion, then, it is by no means easy for a newcomer to find acceptance in the Church.

'WE ARE NOT INTERESTED'

This is the response experienced by *Lamine Sanneh*, a young Gambian. We described how his spiritual journey led him from the idea of God's transcendence to the discovery of his presence in the world through Jesus.[4]

Sanneh describes his faith as threefold: first, as assured personal faith in God; second, as the assurance of Jesus' role as mediator; and finally, Sanneh came to realise that Jesus' death on the cross was not only a cosmic event, but a personal one. With the third realisation, Sanneh said his first impromptu and personal prayer to God.

Sanneh soon realised that he needed to join a Christian community. 'I had discovered that my Christian experience was incomplete without membership of a Christian church,' he explains. 'This was a very hard lesson to learn.

The Christian Church for me had always been a symbol of religious failure, of religious hypocrisy, and it was more than galling to have to pitch camp in the midst of these people.' Sanneh also realised that he had been right to criticise the Church. 'My church was weak,' he points out, 'and it had many problems.' For this very reason, however, Sanneh saw that he had to join the Church: 'It was as if God was saying to me, precisely because you know what is wrong with the Church, precisely because you know its weaknesses, I want you to join it!'

Sanneh sees the weakness of the Church as reflecting his own weakness. Just as God accepts human beings, so human beings must accept each other through the Church . . . Despite our imperfection we are loved.

Sanneh went to a Protestant missionary church where he introduced himself, explaining that he wanted to join a Christian church. The church leaders were wary of accepting him and suggested that perhaps he really did not want to be a Christian. He returned after a year, stating that he was sure he wanted to enter the Church. He was then sent to a Catholic church, which showed no more interest than the Protestant one. He eventually decided to join the Protestant church 'as there appeared to be no better choice, apart from not joining a church at all'.[5]

One might imagine that the cold reception accorded to Sanneh was an exception, but unfortunately it was nothing of the kind. Many converts have had similar experiences.

Banine, who died recently, was an old lady of eighty-two, a native of Azerbaijan who had lived in France since 1924. She felt called to the faith in the 1950s, when she was living in total despair:

'I spent hours walking the streets of Paris alone. One day I pushed open the door of the chapel in Rue Cortambert. I may note in passing that I might equally well have pushed at the door of the Protestant church which was just opposite! But I entered there. I was transfixed by what I saw in the chapel. Several sisters were kneeling on their prie-Dieu and I knelt down too, praying with all my heart to this hidden God, this God-problem, this enormous and secret God, this God-nothing perhaps.'

'Did you come back to this church?'

'Often. But now I began to feel a growing desire to share in the sacraments, to be part of the Catholic Church, to communicate. And so to be baptised. But my problem was that I could not find priests prepared to take an interest in me. In other times the Church would burn those who refused to be converted; but now, in the mid-twentieth century, no one was at all interested in converts.'

'Really?'

'Yes, the three or four priests whom I met simply ignored me. The one who took most interest in me, and did in fact eventually baptise me, had little confidence in the genuineness of my desire and kept on saying: "During the ceremony of baptism, I shall ask you if you believe in the divinity of Christ. I fear you are the sort of person who might reply, 'Perhaps'!" Quite simply, he did not trust me, and only the support of no less a person than the celebrated Father Daniélou finally convinced him that he could baptise me.'[6]

Is this suspicion or indifference? Some feel that it looks more like racism.

IT CANNOT BE DONE

The adventures of Günther Wallraff are well known. This German journalist spent a year disguised as a Turk in order to find out what it was like to be an immigrant in the Federal Republic of Germany. He pursued his enquiry into the religious sphere, presenting himself as a Turk who had been converted and wanted to be baptised in the Catholic Church.[7]

There was certainly more than a touch of anti-clericalism in his make-up, and this may have been partly responsible for the resistance he encountered from priests. His experiences however correspond to those of so many genuine converts that they deserve to be taken seriously.

He made no less than seven applications for baptism. None was successful. Here is the first.

'I'm a Turk, I used to be with Muhammad, but now I want to be baptised. It is better with Christ! I want it quickly because . . .'

He looked at me with great round eyes. You would have thought I was asking him to circumcise me rather than just baptise me. He pushed the door to, leaving only a crack. 'Just a minute, my friend, it is not as simple as that. There are all sorts of conditions.' Then, with a contemptuous glance at my ragged clothes, 'We do not accept just anyone in our parish.'

I refused to be put off and insisted that my request was urgent. I was liable to be deported at any moment. This made not the slightest impression on him. 'Gently, my friend, gently! I must first talk to the Parish Council. But above all you must first bring me a proper residence card.'

I objected: 'Christ, he had no place, no roof.' He probably regarded this remark as blasphemous, for he slammed the door in my face without more ado.

Some of the priests whom Wallraff contacted were less brutal, but even those who were more polite also gave a downright refusal. On his last attempt, the priest refused to take the request for baptism seriously, regarding it as no more than a trick to obtain a residence permit. He offered to give the applicant a false baptismal certificate.

Some allowances should no doubt be made for the deliberately provocative attitude of this anti-clerical journalist-turned-Turk. Nevertheless the fact remains that not one of the priests he met made any attempt to discuss the spiritual dimension of his request for baptism.

IF YOU TRY LONG ENOUGH!

Augustin Iba Zizen tells us of the difficulty he had in finding a priest willing to take his conversion seriously. He speaks of his interview with the priest who eventually baptised him:

I made no progress in my attempt to be admitted to a baptistry of the diocese. At the beginning I was sure that interest would be taken in my case. I would never have imagined that, in the midst of Catholic Paris, her own home, my godmother would meet with so many obstacles. Several priests, and even a well-known prelate, did not hide their astonishment at seeing this badly-dressed old woman, whom they no doubt classified as some sort of religious crank, taking an interest in the baptism of a young Algerian who, after all, gave no guarantee of sincerity.

Such lack of understanding and such indifference affected her deeply and filled her with shame on my account. This state of affairs continued for several months. To us it was a sad disillusionment and it seemed more like a century.

Finally a priest agreed to receive Iba Zizen and examine his case. The other priests had not even gone as far as this.

The canon received me in his house with a degree of reserve, but cordially enough to make me feel relatively at ease. He got me to recount my history. He seemed very attentive when I explained that in my Muslim upbringing I had come to know certain essential truths which are common to the Bible and the Koran. I proceeded to explain how some Christian truths had been revealed to me in extraordinary circumstances. They had made a great impression on me and I had become irrevocably committed to them.

He looked at me with sharp eyes, like a man wishing to convey that he can see through any insincerity or trickery. He asked several questions to test my religious knowledge. They were very elementary and I realised that he was only asking them out of duty, for he knew perfectly well that I would not have come if I had not already possessed the elements of the faith. In truth he was testing me in other ways, and as the interview progressed I felt that I was truly being sifted and tried and weighed in the balance, that none of my secrets would remain hidden. Up till then his expression had been serious and attentive. Suddenly his face relaxed, and he said, without transition, in a firm voice:

'Under whose patronage do you wish to receive the sacrament?' I had already decided on Augustine, the great fourth-century Berber saint. It was now the beginning of August.

'Very well, that will do nicely. 28 August is the feast-day of your patron. I shall baptise you on that day. Prepare yourself. You will come the day before for confession and you will make your first Communion on the following day, 29 August, at the eight o'clock mass.'

It was cordial and authoritative. I thought I was hearing again one of my former colonels shouting, 'Dismiss!' But this time my heart had a special reason for beating fast: with joy. At the end of our interview, the priest was so far won over as to embrace me. He left me with a resounding, 'May God bless you, my child!' I found myself in the street stunned by this brusque end to my troubles.'[8]

WHO WILL BE MY GUIDE?

When we leave Europe and go to India, we find the same general scenario. We shall now hear the rebuffs endured by a young Indian Muslim who read the Gospels and became convinced that he was called to become a Christian. He knew no Christians, and did not know who to turn to. He looked around to find a pastor or a priest.

We are in Calcutta, in the year 1910. This young convert will later become a Methodist bishop called *John Abdus Subhan*.

Picture him, then, as day by day he walked the streets of that great city waiting expectantly, hoping that some one would turn up to whom he might open his heart. Was it, for instance, this apparently well-known European, garbed in cassock and girdle, whom grown men followed and children hailed with delight? But no, as it turned out later in an interview, the padre knew no Urdu and Subhan's attempts at English proved incomprehensible. Once he ventured into a Roman Catholic Church while a service was in progress, but his too great curiosity in what he heard and saw was frowned on by the worshippers and he soon left. On another occasion he felt more hopeful on hearing an Indian Christian preacher addressing a crowd in Hindustani at a street corner. The man was urging his hearers to accept Christ as the only Saviour from sin. At the close Subhan made known his desire and was invited by the preacher to his home. That was the first of several visits and the talks they had proved helpful, but he found his friend's tendency to dwell on the one theme of how to meet Muslim objections to Christianity not only boring, but quite unsuited to his need; so he discontinued his visits.

Finally he found a pastor who guided him in reading the Bible and taught him how to pray:

He was a man much given to prayer, and Subhan was never allowed to leave his presence without a period spent on their knees before God.

Hitherto, prayer for him had been mostly a matter of ritual, but when this man prayed he seemed to be looking on things unseen and to be speaking heart to heart with God. These new contacts and experiences only increased the lad's longing to become a Christian, but he was told that his baptism could not be considered yet because he was under age.[9]

Many conversions take place between the ages of sixteen and thirty: at that period of life, a person can take personal decisions and remain open to self-evaluation and radical appeals.

RESPECT FOR FREEDOM

Some converts are very young, and many clergy are afraid of taking advantage of their generosity and enthusiasm. They recommend patience. We may think again of *Sakina*, who was only fifteen when she asked for baptism:

> It would be better to wait until she was of age so that everyone would recognise that she was acting of her own free will. Sakina was patient and started working in a parish.
> When she was eighteen, she asked again. The obstacle this time was that she was still in a religious school. It would be better to wait until she had left, to avoid all suspicion of pressure. The Church in fact has often been accused of applying such pressure. But for Sakina it was a bitter pill to swallow: 'They took away the carrot they had been dangling before me for three years.'

It is of course wholly necessary, both for the sake of the convert and for the Christian community, that sufficient time is taken to make sure of the authenticity of the prospective convert's call. The local church and the convert him or herself have to be sure that this desire for baptism is unshakeable, and not some passing youthful caprice. It is important for the convert to feel free, financially independent of the Church they are proposing to join if they are not later on to experience doubts about their own motivation. Any suggestion of 'interested' motives would then only poison their relations with the Christian community.

Nevertheless a balance has to be struck. People have to be protected against self-deception, but they may not be deprived of their freedom. They have the right to convert, as well as the right not to convert. Too many delays often give the convert the impression that their freedom is not being recognised.

Some reflections

After these various examples, chosen from among many similar cases, we may now try to explain the negative reaction of priests when a Muslim seeks baptism.

There may of course be simple antipathy to foreigners, especially when hatred has accumulated through centuries of bitter fighting between Europeans and those 'Turks' or 'Saracens'. And of course the antipathy is heartily reciprocated.

We are however interested in more respectable reasons for clerical resistance to conversions from Islam. Perfectly sound pastoral principles can have unfortunate effects if they are not balanced by other, equally necessary, considerations.

WHAT KIND OF PRUDENCE?

It is clear that the convert must make an adult decision. If we consider carefully the case of Sakina, we can see that there is a gap between the disposition of the person concerned and the general rules of prudence. Those who were advising Sakina had one eye on her and the other on public opinion: 'everyone would recognise that she was acting of her own free will ... The Church has often been accused of applying undue pressure.'

In the law, as in medicine, the client's or patient's interests must always be paramount, and the law in general recognises the privileged character of exchanges between professional and client. The same principle must apply in spiritual counselling.

As the cases we have cited clearly show, the situation is seriously distorted when other considerations are allowed to obscure the essential priority of the client's interests. We might consider Sakina as a special case, but it may happen that some clergy adopt a kind of diplomatic prudence. Indeed the writer of the article about Sakina admitted: 'There must be no question of upsetting the Muslim authorities. They do not like seeing Catholics carrying out any kind of proselytism, and such conduct is an obstacle to the Islamo-Christian dialogue.'[10]

We saw this prudence in action in the case of the seventy-two clan members in the Sudan.[11] The clergy sought permission from the governor of the province before they were prepared to administer the baptisms. What would have happened, one wonders, if the governor had refused his 'permission'? Would the local church have had the courage to respect basic human rights, including the right to conversion, by going ahead and acceding to the request for baptism?

Could it be that all this prudence is not always as supernatural as one would expect? Which of us could give a clear-cut answer to this question? A prudence which is at the service of the encounter between God and the person he is calling is wholly in order. But it becomes illegitimate when it is no more than the instinct of self-preservation.

Fear of Proselytism

The article about Sakina talks of 'proselytism'. In our world of openness and tolerance, this has become a dreaded word, calculated to strike fear into the heart of any priest.

The term is frequently used in Muslim circles, as well as in the media and among many Christians. Public opinion fears, or pretends to fear, that the Church, its priests and missionaries are engaged in a permanent publicity campaign to gain more and more recruits.

No doubt proselytism has existed down the ages, among both Christians and Muslims, and it may still exist here and there. But it seems that the accusation of proselytism today is more often a reflection of how people conceive human relations, in politics as well as in religion, that is, as a battle in which the stronger must always get the better of the weaker or less numerous. Many political and advertising campaigns which are regarded as harmless and legitimate do in fact constitute proselytism in the worst sense of the term. Can one really approve for example of persistent and aggressive attempts to persuade people that one brand of soap is superior to another? Or one party better than another?

The truth is that, as far as the Church is concerned, in Europe and everywhere else, the clergy are so burdened by the multiplicity of their ordinary tasks that they are reluctant to take on more. Most missionaries to whom we have spoken about their contacts with Muslims say that they have more than enough to do in coping with their own congregations to have time for others. The cases we have studied clearly show that conversions arise, not from any action on the part of the Church, but from the spiritual needs of the convert when these cannot be satisfied in their community of origin.

Yet the accusation persists, and it is not without effect on those who are its target. They begin to fear, not only proselytism, but even the appearance of proselytism.

Proselytism in the proper sense is the 'attitude of he who calls on his interlocutor to meet him on his own ground without being concerned about the other's true vocation'.[12] Proselytism begins when one stops being attentive to the personal vocation and calling of those one meets.

To invite a Muslim to become a Christian without any consideration of their own interior call is to be guilty of proselytism. But to welcome a Muslim because they have felt called to become a Christian is no more than a proper respect for human freedom.

It is not clear that the media, society in general, and Muslim society in particular, define proselytism in this way. In some countries, merely to welcome a convert is considered proselytism. This was the case in Islamic medieval societies,[13] and it is still the case in a number of Muslim countries in which the passage from Islam to another religion is punishable by law.[14]

One fears that merely accepting converts will *seem to* justify accusations of proselytism. What will people say? Won't the Muslim community be offended? Some priests are so obsessed by the fear of being accused of proselytism that they paralyse themselves and each other.

An example will help to clarify the point. We have seen how liberating the discovery of Christ and forgiveness can be. We have read letters of prisoners who have been so overwhelmed by this discovery that they have asked for baptism.

But we have also met priests who, instead of rejoicing over these conversions, complain that we are using people's misfor-

tunes to bring them to the gospel. And yet we have before us written evidence that one had simply been responding to insistent
demands coming from the prisoners themselves. Here is a complaint against a prison chaplain from a prisoner who was transferred from one prison to another:

> Christmas here in X[15] is not like Christmas in Y. There hundreds of
> people would come together to celebrate the birth of Christ and there
> was an atmosphere of communal joy which made us forget our soli-
> tude, our suffering, our misfortunes. Here, there may have been some
> manifestation in the prison chapel, but no invitation was sent out by
> the chaplain who, unhappily, is not like the chaplain of Y. He is only
> interested in those who are registered as Christians on their cards. His
> objective seems to be to reduce the number of faithful. If you are not
> written down as Christian, even if your heart is Christian, you have no
> right to help or humanity. It is really horrible. But happily God exists,
> and chaplains like the one at Y do what others do not.

He adds a note for Z, the chaplain of Y: 'Carry on doing good and
giving joy to those who are looking for God and God will give
you blessing, grace and light.'

These accusations may be unjust, but unfortunately one cannot
be sure. Respect for the other is so often expressed in negative
terms as a refusal to 'touch' the other for fear of influencing him
or her that one is not surprised if priests with this mentality
restrict their attention to the members of their own community
and refuse all contact with anyone else.

THE BURDEN OF CHRISTIANITY?

It is clear that, among Christians themselves, Christianity is
often regarded as a burden which one should not seek to impose
on others.

Yet the various testimonies from African converts do not
speak of a burden but of *new strength*. What they discover in
Christianity is the power of Christ who changes us by loving us
as we are.

Let us remember the number of times we heard converts speaking of the joy and liberation they experienced when they welcomed Christ into their life:

> I saw that I was no longer myself, that the Lord had started to change me. I was filled with a new life ... soon afterwards I was liberated from cigarettes ...
>
> Since I accepted Jesus as my personal Lord and Saviour my life has completely changed. I have become more affable with people and this has greatly astonished them. I have started to hate lying and sin of every kind ... I have therefore received Jesus into my heart because of what he has done for me. He is not a 'religion' but a living person.
>
> I knew that the words of Jesus were the truth because, whereas previously I was so anxious, he has given me rest, joy and peace ...
>
> He has broken my sadness.

When you listen to Christian preaching, you may often receive the impression that faith means doing things, being committed, accepting obligations. Where is the power, the joy, the liberation of which these converts speak?

No doubt joy is not absent from this sort of spirituality, but often it seems to be a human-made joy, the result of effort and commitment. Converts speak in quite the opposite way. They have first received joy and liberation, and this has impelled them into commitments.

Which is it: commitment leading to joy, or joy leading to commitment?

There is continual misunderstanding between those who see in Christianity the long sought-for treasure, and Christians who find it such a burden that they are unwilling to impose it on others.

THE KINGDOM OF GOD, NOT OF THE CHURCH
There can be a further cause of misunderstanding between converts and the clergy to whom they present themselves.

The renewed theology of the Second Vatican Council has helped many priests to realise that they were at the service of God and his kingdom before they were called to serve the interests of the Christian community. They set about defending the values of the kingdom of God with renewed zeal, seeking to spread love, peace, justice, fraternity, forgiveness. They discovered that these values could bring together, not only Christians, but all persons of good will. All could respond to the one human vocation to form a single family under the love and care of God.

In a more provocative mood, some priests have occasionally found it fitting to speak of defending the kingdom of God against ... Christians, particularly against those church-going Christians whose lives are really governed by egotism and the lust for power.

This ministry of preaching and living the values of the Gospel seems to have a special appeal to priests living in Muslim countries, for they recognise in it the ideal by which they have long lived. Sometimes without a Christian community, and without any hope of founding one, they have consecrated their lives to spreading the values of the kingdom of God.

This attitude of maximum openness to the will of God for others, and a refusal to 'convert' others, is found everywhere, but especially among those, in Europe and elsewhere, who work among Muslims.

Given this general attitude, it is not surprising that a request for baptism tends to catch these priests, and sisters, off their guard. Unused to such a situation, they would incline to refuse, and this can cause tension between the convert and the priest.

The half-open door

The picture we have painted is sombre. It should be said that in some places the situation is better; but also that in some it is even worse! Recent experience suggests that priests are becoming more open, but have not lost their reserve.

We are not however interested in distributing good or bad marks to priests. The crucial point is to recognise the terrible isolation of these supplicants for baptism. A cold reception from Christians can make them feel that they have been abandoned by everyone.

It is not a matter simply of replacing refusal with acceptance.

To agree immediately to baptise a convert is no better than refusing it indefinitely.

Sometimes baptism may be administered too quickly, not out of any proselytising zeal, but rather because one has no time. One deals with the *administrative* or intellectual requirements without taking the time needed to help the applicant engage in spiritual discernment of his or her personal vocation.

Over and above this professional haste comes the general *indifference* of a Christian community which is not prepared for an influx of Christians from 'outside'. All this gives the convert the sense that they have never been truly recognised as a person whom Christ has called by name in order that they may play a role within the people of God.

However, there are places in Western European countries where every attention is given to the convert, most notably catechumenate groups which cater for people from all religions and none.

There are also various groups of Christians who carry out public 'evangelisation' in the streets or elsewhere. A priest who leads one such group says that we should not describe their activity as 'proselytism', for whereas the proselytiser seeks to convince, evangelisation is concerned only with proclamation.

These groups are becoming more and more numerous. At the same time, the number of adults seeking baptism is also increasing. All the churches feel the need for structures to receive and guide people who are seeking entry. Such structures enable a true dialogue to be initiated between the Christian community and the converts. It becomes possible to listen to their needs and offer them the right kind of help in discerning their vocation.

What kind of welcome do they need?

The reception accorded to the converts is to be determined by their personal spiritual needs before and above the interests of the group. The offence in proselytism, as in rejection, is that the persons are not considered in themselves.

Respect and counselling

The candidates for baptism must be given the opportunity of explaining themselves. We have seen from the experience of the disguised Günther Wallraff that this doesn't always happen.

On the other hand, one may be too quick in responding to the request for baptism. This was the case with the Indian policeman, *Ali Bakhsh*. He discovered the person of Christ in 1887 after reading the Bible, and immediately decided to ask for baptism. He was sent to a catechist who made him learn the Ten Commandments, the Our Father and the creed by heart. He was then baptised.

There is no doubt that his conversion was sincere and solid. He showed considerable spirit in resisting his family's attempts to make him change his mind. But no one had taken the time to answer his questions:

After baptism I wanted to learn further of the new faith, but none cared to teach me, or to remove my doubts and objections. I was rather shamed to ask such things after baptism.

I took up work with the police, mixed with Christians, longed to learn more, but was disappointed and discouraged in every way. The result was that I grew colder and colder, and thought perhaps I had made a mistake in my choice. The lives and dealings of Christians were not in conformity with their Scriptures, and they could not explain their faith to others, and did not care to teach new converts.

But the Lord who guided me so far did not leave me. At that time there was a Hindu fair in a village near Kangra. I went there on duty, and saw a crowd of people gathered round some Europeans. I stood in the crowd, and found out that a missionary was preaching the gospel.

He did not know me, so I put some questions to him, and expressed some of my doubts concerning certain doctrines. He laboured for more than an hour, heard me patiently and answered me reasonably. Meanwhile another elderly missionary came who knew me. When he saw the missionary talking to me, he asked him why he was explaining the teachings to one already a Christian. On being asked why I had not said I was a Christian at first, I replied that I knew from my past experience that if he knew me to be a Christian he would not have given me so much time. He loved me and took me in his arms and began to take an interest in me.[16]

From that day he received the help he needed, as he explains in his ingenuous way:

> Up to that time I did not know of the atonement, nor the Trinity, nor the new birth. I knew only that if I followed Jesus Christ, he would intercede for me with God in the last day, and that my sins should be forgiven and that I should enter paradise.

One must consent to walk in step with the persons engaged in that spiritual journey. This means respecting the stages of their spiritual growth, answering the questions raised at each period by their dialogue with God. This is what the catechumenate groups seek to provide.

Some criteria

When this period of 'spiritual counselling' is over, the person concerned should be able to see clearly whether God is calling them to be a Christian or perhaps to take some other route.

A PRINCIPLE

A basic principle which must guide all parties at this stage is that *one does not choose one's religion*, as if it were an article picked off a shelf in a supermarket.

We do not choose, *we are chosen*: our part is to respond to the choice. This is clear from a number of the testimonies we have presented, including that of Ali Bakhsh: 'But the Lord who guided me so far. . . .'

There has to be instruction. We have seen how much Ali Bakhsh was anxious for it. But more important than the instruction itself is the echo which it finds in the heart of the one who is truly called, a sort of reverberation through which the Holy Spirit confirms and calls to faith. One might think of the echoing effect felt by Bilquis Sheikh when the sister suggested that she should speak to God as a father.

IS THERE A TRUE CONVERSION?

There has to be some kind of assurance that one is dealing with a genuine religious experience and not with an illusion. Strong religious feelings may simply be an emotional 'high'. It is possible to 'try out' religion, as one might experiment with drugs.

We might think of advertisements for a perfume, or for a particular brand of cheese. We are shown a woman with closed eyes, totally absorbed in her sensations. Spiritual states can constitute a similar kind of infantile regression to the purely sensible. Is that particular person locked in his or her own 'states', indulging religious emotion for its own sake?

True conversion is an encounter:

with the all other: God who calls us . . . his word;

with the other: our neighbourhood, the world around us.

An encounter with God implies a certain fidelity to remain in his presence, for his sake, even when the sensible experience has faded.

An encounter with the other always finds expression in an effort to serve the real needs of the neighbour.

In this way, one makes sure that the convert is genuinely in touch with his world and open to the presence of others, although this should not be misunderstood as meaning that one must be on excellent terms with everyone, nor even be involved in some specific 'good work'. This differentiates a genuine religious experience from a dream with a religious content:

> When I think of the Christian faith and try to live within it, I have a feeling that I am near to people, particularly to the poor and abandoned. I feel nearer to them, I understand them . . .
>
> When I think of Jesus, I make myself little, I tell myself that I am like the others. Unfortunately, most of the time I forget, I become 'a superior person', I become odious. These meetings help to strengthen me and to make me poorer, humbler, nearer to others.

Another important consideration is the *atmosphere* in which the religious experience takes place. God is not a nervous, frantic type. No doubt, he addresses himself to people who may be very anxious, excited, frantic. But his call, in the long run, always produces *peace*, joy, love, self-control in the measure that it is listened to; when it is resisted, the result is anxiety and discomfort.

There must then be a real encounter with God and a real openness to the world. These may be regarded as signs that the call is authentic. But clearly they cannot be regarded as sufficient in themselves to prove that one is called specifically to become a Christian. Perhaps one is being called to Islam, or to some other religion.

IS IT A CONVERSION TO CHRISTIANITY?

There are therefore further signs which may be taken as decisive. They indicate that one is progressively guided towards Christianity.

One is *attraction to the person of Jesus Christ*. We have met this so often in the conversion stories we have heard. One can be truly touched by his presence, even though one hardly glimpses his mystery:

> I discovered another world: Christian faith, Jesus. I had never really imagined that Muhammad existed, that he was in any sense alive for me. But when I speak of Jesus, or when someone else speaks of the faith, I always have the odd impression that an extra person is present. There is a man there listening to us. He might say nothing, but his presence is a great help. When I speak with Muslims, I do not feel that I am being in some way penetrated, I am not touched. But when I speak of Jesus I feel light, I feel unburdened.

A second sign concerns Christian truth.[17] It can happen, as we have seen especially in chapter 3, that converts find themselves in mysterious, spontaneous agreement with Christian teaching. We are not speaking of theological knowledge in any theoretical sense but of a profound agreement, a firm trust, sometimes beyond all reason. The convert simply does not know why they feel in harmony with the teaching they hear. This was the experience of Banine, the old lady from Azerbaijan who believed everything while harbouring incessant rational objections to the divinity of Christ. She only found peace when she came to understand that she had put all her trust in the person of Christ as he presented himself, divinity included. But her reason continued to run free.

A third sign that the call to become a Christian may be genuine is *attachment to the Church*. We have seen how often it is through the Church that converts come to Christ. This does not mean a material or financial dependence on the Christian community, but a quiet certainty that God is calling one to live and pray in this community of faith. This 'instinct for the Church' has of course to be directed and perhaps purified by later instruction, which will show the convert that the role of the Church is solely to lead people to God. But a permanent feeling, however confused, that the Church is *the way* willed by God may be taken as a sign that we are not dealing with some passing fancy but with a substantial call.

One may think in this connection of the testimony of a young Muslim, one of those 'catacomb Christians' we have mentioned. Without having originally any idea of changing his religion, he took part in a Christian discussion group simply with the idea of deepening his sense of God:

> Am I at the moment a Muslim? Or am I a Christian? It is a matter of no importance, it belongs to another dimension. This Christian faith allows me to be frank and not to mislead others whatever people may think. I respect Muslims, but I do not feel at home among them.
>
> At first I hoped that I would recover my faith through these meetings and that would strengthen me; but the fact is that I did not recover my Muslim faith.
>
> I discovered a certain freedom within myself: not complete, but there has been progress. Most important:
>
> I have met a small group;
> I feel involved with it;
> I have found my way;
> I have found my faith;
> it has brought me to love Jesus.
>
> For me the essential thing is that I have found love in this small group. I have fallen in with a group which has made me love Jesus. I do not think that I am in error. I believe that I am on the way.

These criteria may make it possible for the Christian community to welcome converts and help them to verify the authenticity of their call.

Integration

Once the authenticity of the call has been established, and it has become clear that the candidate is really being called by God to become a Christian, the Church has no right to refuse baptism.

The role of the Church is purely instrumental. If Peter baptises, it is Jesus who baptises. The Church is not the mistress of baptism. Nor is it an association which co-opts its own members. It is God who chooses, as a modern theologian affirms:

> Baptism is an act of the risen Christ. It introduces a person into the community of the Church, but it is not simply an act of the community, an initiation ceremony. Baptism is not a co-option rite performed by the Church. A Christian has no right to choose who will be his brethren in Jesus Christ. The Church is not the mistress of this act which is baptism, although it is of vital concern to the Church.[18]

At the same time, integration into the Christian community involves more than baptism. As we have heard from the anonymous 'catacomb Christian', it is important for converts to escape from their solitude and find a community where they can be at home.

ACTIVE PARTICIPATION

New converts need to be invited *to participate in functions* where their new religious identity is recognised, approved and strengthened, allowed to mature through action. This can be done in the liturgy, various groups, catechesis, parish organisations. Most converts are quite eager to help.

One can understand Sakina's distress when the priest of the parish where she worked learned that she was not baptised and refused thenceforth to entrust her with responsibilities within the parish community. She was both uncomprehending and indignant: 'I was refused responsibility in the Church because

I was not baptised, when the only thing I wanted was to be baptised.'

FRIENDSHIP

Like every human being, converts need natural human friendship and hospitality. This is particularly the case with those who come from societies in which hospitality is the traditional expression of family and social bonds. It is therefore very desirable that converts find a group within the Church which is trying to live some kind of community ideal.

Catacomb Christians, living anonymously in Muslim countries, spontaneously form communities without either joining the official Church or breaking with it. Their difficulty often is that they cannot openly practise their faith in the official Church without giving themselves away, and anyway they may not find there the welcome they need:

> People almost run away the minute the mass is over. They have done it and then they disappear, without using the opportunity to meet each other.
>
> I love the Christians I know outside the Church rather than inside. Outside, they are alive, and I feel closer to them than inside.
>
> Our little group is a real church community, even though we do not have the mass. What is more important is what we say to each other, what we bring to each other. Even if we do not make any prayers together, I receive a great sense of peace, and that leads me to reflect. What we discuss today is a sort of beacon which lights my way for tomorrow. Tomorrow I shall reflect. It may be only a moment, but it helps me to find my way.
>
> For me, this is the real community. It is us. It is small, but what matters is not size, but what is lived.
>
> When a community has the same faith in Jesus, this means for me a sharing, in good and evil fortune; it means compassion, a love. A community should share everything. Jesus did not need a temple. He did everything outside the Temple. You can pray anywhere. I cannot go to mass every Sunday,[19] but on the occasions when I do go I have not felt a spirit of solidarity in the church. People are there, they pray, one has the impression of praying, but I think people's minds are

elsewhere—I don't mean everyone, but this is the impression I have. One is not in communion with Jesus.

I meet the Christian outside, in the street.

It is very good that groups like the one referred to here are becoming more and more numerous, even in Europe. These are the charismatic communities, the local groups, the parish councils, various movements, new communities. Some converts find them and feel at home in them. It is a cause for rejoicing.

However, some of these groups adopt an attitude of systematic criticism of other Church organisations, and this can be a source of scandal to the newcomer who is not accustomed to a confrontational faith. On the contrary, in leaving Islam they hope to leave behind the atmosphere of anti-Christian controversy and to find beneath the stereotypes the true face of the Church.

We may observe finally that conversion to Christianity does not necessarily imply integration into the social fabric of European Christian believers. Some, as we have seen, feel called to preserve their original culture and to remain members of the community in which they were born. Unless they are able to form their own Christian group in such a situation, however, they run the risk of being seriously isolated.

Interior dialogue between two religions

New Christians who have come from other religious cultures are bound to look on the Church with high aspirations. Their very presence constitutes a challenge summoning long-established Christians to rediscover the fullness of their faith-commitment.

Those who come from Islam will be aware of certain deficiencies in Christians' prayer life and social life. At the same time, they help us to discover unique features in the Christian faith which we may have overlooked.

Converts from Islam are thus precious instruments of dialogue between the two religions, a dialogue made of common and contrasting values, taking place within the converts themselves, and constitutive of their personality. More than anybody else they know by experience the positive and negative dimensions of this encounter.

NEGATIVE ELEMENTS

We have seen how conversion is often preceded by a long period of religious dissatisfaction and frustration. Future converts feel summoned to live an experience which they cannot find within the framework of the religion in which they were brought up.

Rightly or wrongly, they cast a critical eye on the religious teaching and practice of their native community. Even before their actual conversion, their aspirations will often have aroused the mistrust and even the hostility of their co-religionists. They may have been the target of harassment, mockery and ill-treatment, all in the name of God or Islam.

It is natural therefore for Christian converts from Islam to be at first highly critical of their former religion. It contradicts the particular dimension of the Christian faith which they regard as their most precious discovery: Jesus, undeserved salvation, the Church, Christian prayer.

They still have in their head all the arguments and insults against Christianity which were drummed into them in their youth. It can be very useful at this stage for them to read books of Christian apologetic theology in which these arguments are answered in the light of Christian faith. In this way their new faith will become both stronger and more tranquil. Their way of life will change and they will no longer feel obliged to stand aggressively against their cultural inheritance.

POSITIVE VALUES

After this first, negative phase, young Christians will come little by little, perhaps only after several years, to appreciate the positive elements in their Islamic education. Once they have recovered peace of soul, and the family and social ruptures have been healed, God's call becomes clearer as a positive invitation and they can see how God was active in their life before their conversion, or before their discovery of Christianity. They see how their Islamic apprenticeship in faith, in the sense of God, in prayer, in community commitment, were all preparing them for their Christian vocation.

Conversion is no doubt in part a break with the past, but it can also be seen as a fulfilment of the converts' previous religious life in Islam. They may also come to see that there are areas of life in which Christians have much to learn from Islam.

As they move through these various stages, negative and positive, converts have the right to the respect and support of the Christian community. Maturation is very often a slow process, and it is unwise to try and hasten it. Each stage is necessary and each offers its own opportunity for growth which must be seized as it occurs.

THE INITIATIVE RESTS WITH GOD

Wherever converts come from, be it Islam or elsewhere, when they come knocking on the Church's door and demanding admittance, they are a potent reminder to us, Christians, that we do not own the Church, it is not our property, we are not masters but merely stewards of a treasure which belongs by right to everyone. When converts claim their share, they are reminding us that we have no right to show ourselves inhospitable to our brothers and sisters. The Lord has called them from afar in order to give them to us.

We cannot resist concluding by reproducing a letter written by a convert from Niger, Khalil, a former mosque imam. He is writing to a group of priests who were hesitating to baptise him:

> I greet all Christians. I am happy to be with you. Pray for me that a friend may join me and that we may together follow the way of Jesus. He can stand witness for me so that I can receive baptism with him.
>
> For three years I have belonged to Jesus Christ with all my strength. Everywhere in the country I am known as a Christian. In the village, everywhere, everyone knows that I am a Christian and nothing else. Have no hesitations about me. I have given my faith to Jesus, Jesus is the Son of God. Don't mistrust me because I come from the Muslim religion. And do not say either that I shall be unable to enter the religion of Jesus. For me, I have seen that Jesus is the Saviour of the

world. I am not going to refuse the way of truth . . . I do not accept to leave the light to enter the darkness.

I salute his Lordship and all the Christians. I am happy in this Catholic Church. For three years I have given my faith to God and to Jesus the Christ. I have become the witness of Jesus, I am not afraid. Nor am I ashamed. Do not hesitate about me. Truly, truly, I believe that Jesus is the Son of God.[20]

Let the witnesses speak

This touching message from one of these witnesses, living alone in his African village, a Christian coming from Islam, is a fitting conclusion to our study. What kind of a reception do we give to a word like this?

We should be clear on one point. This type of witness is bound to become more frequent. Sooner or later we shall all have to deal with it. People today are travelling a great deal; but there are also the intellectual, ideological and religious journeys, leading people from one intellectual system to another, from one religion to another.

There are Christians coming from Islam, and there are Muslims of Western origin; there are Buddhists asking for baptism, Jews for Jesus, Christians who have rediscovered Judaism. The days of closed, homogeneous, unchanging societies are rapidly disappearing and they will not come back.

Mass culture is spreading all over the globe, thanks to modern means of communication. Yet, despite all this, people feel more and more alone as they face the great choices of existence, and more and more helpless before the trials of our human condition. Social conformity will no longer suffice to deal with the great questions of life and death, of suffering and illness.

The media and publicity, family and school education, churches and mosques: in the end, all these instruments and institutions can do no more than propose values and suggest choices. In the end, in moments of crisis, every human being has to make his or her own choice by himself or herself. What has changed however is that for the first time in the history of the race, people find themselves truly embarrassed by the number of choices available. There is no longer one single solution, no one foolproof system, no religion with all the answers. Whatever exclusivist claims may be made in certain quarters, the individual can always hear other voices in the background, other views, other revelations, other scriptures.

Modern men and women are sceptical about systems, ideologies and dogmas. But they are eager for testimonies, memoirs, confidences, for anything which explains how some public personage, for example, sees his or her life and makes their choices.

For the great religions, as for all other institutions, teaching must become testimony or it will have no impact.

What gives to the testimonies of converts their unique importance is that they are totally independent of any current fashion. With one voice they tell us that they have not themselves chosen but have been chosen by another, they have heard an appeal coming from outside themselves, from God, they say. They are witnesses only because they echo another witness whom, they say, everyone can hear, if one will only shut one's ears to the general tumult.

We men and women of today value independence and efficiency, but we are full of doubts when it comes to choosing. These witnesses tell us that we are not Christian or Muslim by personal, arbitrary choice, but by vocation. We are called only to listen to the voice of God which comes to every human being. In receiving these testimonies, we are also opening ourselves to the call which the same God is addressing to each of us personally today.

Notes

1 Traditionally, in the Islamic city, each religious community had to dress differently from the Muslims. This legal disposition has been copied later in the Christian countries of Europe where Jews were required to wear a distinctive sign on their clothes.

2 Ghulam-Masih Naaman and V. Toon, *The Unexpected Enemy, A Muslim Freedom Fighter Encounters Christ* (Marshalls: Basingstoke, UK, 1985), p.92.

3 Many seem to think that the main reason why a Muslim wants to convert to Christianity is his desire to marry a Christian woman. Hence their distrust. Of course, this case can happen, but it is very rare, especially at the present time since a Muslim (or any man) in Western European countries needs no baptism to contract a legal marriage or to live maritally with a woman.

   It is more frequent for a Christian man to become a Muslim in order to marry a Muslim woman because the woman's family requires it.

4 See chapter 8.

5 K. Baker, 'Bridging Three Worlds: Lamin Sanneh's Journey of Faith', *Harvard Divinity Bulletin*, XII, No.4, April-May 1982, pp.12–14.

6 C. Goure 'Conversation avec Banine—une vie', *Panorama*, No.232, December 1988, pp.48–53. Banine has written her testimony in a book: *J'ai Choisi l'opium* (Stock: Paris, 1959).

7 Günter Wallraff, *Tête de Turc* (La Découverte: Paris, 1986), pp.54–81: 'La conversion ou "têtes à couper sans bénédiction"'.

8 A. Iba Zizen, *Le Testament d'un Berbère, Un itinéraire spirituel et politique* (Albatros: Paris, 1984), pp.46–48.

9 L. Bevan-Jones, *From Islam to Christ—How a Sufi Found His Lord, life of Bishop J. Subhan* (FFM: Brighton, 1982).

10 A. Salles, 'De l'Islam au Christianisme, (2) L'intégration difficile', *La Croix*, 5 March 1987, p.14.

11 Mgr A. Baroni, 'A small Muslim community becomes Catholic', *Amecea Documentation Service*, No.238, 29 March 1982, Nairobi, Kenya.

12 This definition of proselytism was given by the Roman Catholic bishops of North Africa in a pastoral letter of 1979. *Encounter*, Nos73–74, March–April 1981, p. 22.

13 In Muslim Spain of the ninth century, the elect Bishop of Cordoba Eulogius, was beheaded for simply receiving a handful of converts.

14 This is the case, for instance, in Mauritania or Malaysia (on the latter, see *Eglises d'Asie*, No.51 or *Missi*, No.505, November 1988, p.332.

15 X is the prison where he is now detained; Y is the prison where he had lived before and where he had converted; Z is the chaplain who welcomed him (and other prisoners) in his spiritual growth. This witness is drawn from a thick file of personal testimonies. We chose to keep secret the names of persons and places.

16 J. Ali Bakhsh, 'The Story of my Conversion', *Muslim World*, 16, 1926, pp.79–84.

17 The word 'truth' should not receive any specific, restrictive label. Let the reader understand the meaning of this expression.

18 Paul Aubin, *Le Baptême* (Coll. Croire aujourd'hui, DDB/Bellarmin, 1980), p.30. See, as well, p.46.

19 We should remember that these reflections originate from underground Christians living in a Muslim country and deprived of the possibility to practise their faith in public.

20 R. Deniel, *Chemins de Chrétiens Africains* (Inades, Abidjan, Ivory Coast, 1982–1983), No.2, p.33.

BIBLIOGRAPHY

1. The converts

1 **Abdul-Haqq** *How I came to Jesus Christ* (Chandigarh, India, 1960).

2 **Abd-El-Jalil J. Md.** 'La conversion et les conversions', *Cordée*, No.45, December 1960, Paris.

3 **Abd-El-Jalil J. Md.(Fr Testis)** 'Les Musulmans sont-ils inconvertissables?', *Missions Franciscaines*, May–June 1935, pp.73–75.

4 `**Abd-Al-Masih F. (Metouali N.)** *Liqâ'î ma`a l-Masîh* (American, Australian and Canadian Coptic Associations, PO Box 9119, Jersey City, New Jersey 07304, USA, 1992).

5 **Abd-El-Masih M.** 'The testimony of Pastor Marcus Abd-el-Masih', *Muslim World*, 1945, pp. 211–215.

6 **Alavi K.K.** *In Search of Assurance* (Gospel Literature Service: Bombay, India, 1977).

7 **Ambrie H.** *God Has Chosen Me for Everlasting Life* (The Good Way: Rikon, Switzerland).

8 **Amrouche Fadhma A.M.** *Histoire de Ma Vie* (F. Maspero: Paris, 1968).

9 **WF Archives (Rome)** *Notices Nécrologiques*:
P. Roch Sghaïr Ben Halima (1860–1909)

P. Michel Larbi (1852–1911)
P. Barthélémy Ben Mira (1856–1931)
P. Joseph Sallam (1877–1947)
Fr Maurice Djelloul (1858–1878)
Fr Léon Mohammed (1850–1879)
Fr Clément Hassin (1856–1879)
Fr Valentin Mohand Ramdan n'aït Saâdi (1882–1909)
Fr Roch Mohammed ben Mansûr (1888–1933)
Fr Louis Hamoun (1919–1936)
Fr Géronymo J.B. Ahmed Foul (1890–1980)

10 **Assouline P.** *Les Nouveaux Convertis, Enquête sur des chrétiens, des juifs et des musulmans pas comme les autres* (Albin Michel: Paris, 1982).

11 **Anonymous** *Al-Maghrib yusabbihu l-rabb (Morocco praises The Lord)*, (The Good Way: Rikon, Switzerland).

12 **Anonymous** 'The first Moslem Convert to Christianity, 620 AD', *Muslim World*, 3, 1913, pp. 328–329.

13 **Anonymous (Syria)** *Al-Bâkûrat al-Shahiyya (Sweet first fruits)*, (Light of Life: Villach, Austria).

14 **Baker K.** 'Bridging Three Worlds: Lamin Sanneh's Journey of Faith', *Harvard Divinity Bulletin*, XII, No.4, April–May 1982, pp.12–14.

15 **Baker K.** 'Pont entre trois mondes: le cheminement spirituel de Lamin Sanneh', *Telema*, No.2/84, April–June 1984, pp.5–10.

16 **Bakhsh J. Ali** 'The Story of My Conversion', *Muslim World*, 16, 1926, pp.79–84.

17 **Banine** *J'ai Choisi l'opium* (Stock: Paris, 1959).

18 **Barakat Ullah** *From Karbala to Calvary* (Concordia Press: Vaniyambadi, India).

19 **Barine A.** 'Mémoires d'une princesse arabe', *Revue des Deux Mondes*, February 1889, pp.817–851.

20 **Baroni Mgr A.** 'A small Muslim community becomes Catholic', *Amecea Documentation Service*, No.238, 29 March 1982, Nairobi, Kenya.

21 **Barton J.L.** 'A Mohammedan Imam's Discovery of Christ', *Muslim World*, 6, 1916, pp.389–393.

22 **Ben Mira B.** *Mon Voyage sur Terre* (Inédit; Archives PB: Rome).
Autobiographie (Inédit, Archives PB: Rome).

23 **Bennassar B. and L.** *Les Chrétiens d'Allah—L'Histoire extraordinaire des renégats—XVI–XVII siècles* (Perrin: Paris, 1989).

24 **Bevan-Jones L.** *From Islam to Christ—How a Sufi Found his Lord, life of Bishop J. Subhan* (FFM: Brighton, 1982).

25 **Boudaoud A.** *Renaître, J'ai vaincu mon alcoolisme* (Salvator: Mulhouse, France, 1985).

26 **Bousselma A.** 'Réflexions sur le dialogue avec les musulmans', *Centre Evangélique de Témoignage et de Dialogue Islamo-chrétien* (G. Tartar, 1987).

27 **Bretault Mgr J.** 'Difficultés et générosité des musulmans convertis', *Le Christ au Monde*, 1964, No.3, pp.255–257.

28 **Butcher M.** *C'est par la foi . . .* (Carnets de *Croire et Servir*, supplement to Nos51–52, Paris, 1976).

29 **Castries (de) H.** 'Trois Princes Marocains Convertis au Christianisme', *Mémorial H. Basset*, pp.141–158.

30 **Chaudari Inayat Ullah** 'My conversion from Islam', *Muslim World*, 32, 1942, pp.69–75.

31 **Dehqani-Tafti H.B.** *Design of My World, Pilgrimage to Christianity* (Seabury Press: New York, 1982).

32 **Deniel R.** *Chemins de Chrétiens Africains* (Inades: Abidjan, Ivory Coast, 1982–1983).

33 **Deniel R.** *Sur le Chemin Chrétien* (Vie Chrétienne, Supplement to No.274, Paris, 1984).

34 **Deshmukh I.O.** *In Quest of Truth* (FFM: Toronto).

35 **Dewani I.** *Dhûqû wa-nzurû mâ atyaba al-rabb, hayâtî fî khidmati l-rabbi* (Taste and see that the Lord is good, my life at His service), (Markaz al-Shabiba: Beyrouth).

36 **Diallo G.** *La Nuit du Destin* (Salvator: Mulhouse, France, 1969).

37 **Ducroz J.M.** *Les Actes des premiers chrétiens du Gorouol* (Nouvelle Cité: Paris, 1977).

38 **Forest P.** 'Sénégal: Le Musulman et l'accueil de l'Evangile', *Annales de ND du Sacré-Coeur d'Issoudun*, June 1968, pp.106–114.

39 **Foucher E.** 'La merveilleuse conversion d'une jeune lépreuse musulmane', *Missions Messages*, No.346, 9 October 1984, pp.14–15.

40 **Gairdner W.H.T.** 'The Christian Church as a Home for Christ's Converts from Islam', *Muslim World*, 14, 1924, pp. 235–246.

41 **Garaudy R.** *Mon tour du siècle en solitaire—Mémoires* (R. Laffont: Paris, 1989).

42 **Gaudeul J.M.** *Appelés par le Christ—Ils Viennent de l'Islam* (Cerf: Paris, 1991).

43 **Goure C.** 'Conversation avec Banine—une vie', *Panorama*, No.232, December 1988, pp.48–53.

44 **Gulshan E. and Sangster T.** *The Torn Veil, Christ's healing power breaks through to a Muslim girl* (Marshalls: Basingstoke, UK, 1984).

45 **Gulshan E. and Sangster T.** *Dieu Était si Loin* (L'Eau Vive: Geneva, 1986).

46 **Hanna M.** *The True Path, Seven Muslims make their greatest discovery* (International Doorways Publ.: Colorado Springs, USA, 1975).

47 **Heinrich J.C.** 'Shell-shocked converts', *Muslim World*, 18, 1928, pp. 246–249.

48 **Hirji-Walji H. and Strong J.** *Escape from Islam*, (Kingsway: Eastbourne, UK, 1981).

49 **Iba Zizen A.** *Le Testament d'un Berbère, Un itinéraire spirituel et politique* (Albatros: Paris, 1984).

50 **Ilaim** *What Is That in Your Hand?*, (International Missions Inc.: Wayne, NJ, USA, 1979).

51 **Imad-Ud-Din L.** *The Life of the Rev. Mawlawi Dr Imad-Ud-Din Lahiz*, (Henry Martyn Institute: Hyderabad, India, 1978).

52 **Jadid I.** *Fî Sabîli l-Haqq (On the True Path)*, (The Good Way: Rikon, Switzerland).

53 **Linton J.H.** 'The Cost of Victory to a Moslem Convert', *Muslim World*, 15, 1925, pp.156–163.

54 **Lotfi N.** *Iranian Christian* (Word: Waco, Texas, 1980).

55 **Louis-Charles P.** 'Comment un Sultan du Maroc se convertit et se fait jésuite', *En Terre d'Islam*, May 1930, pp.188–191.

56 **Marsh C.** *Impossible à Dieu?* (Editions Farel: Fontenay-s/Bois, France, 1974).

57 **Masood S.** *Into the Light—A young Muslim's search for truth* (STL Books/Kingsway: Eastbourne, 1986).

58 **Miller W. McE.** *A Christian Response to Islam* (Presbyterian and Reformed Publ.: Nutley, NJ, USA, 1976).

59 **Miller W. McE.** *Ten Muslims Meet Christ*, (Eerdmans: Grand Rapids, USA, 1969, 1980).

60 **Missionary (in Near East)** 'Dynamic Converts', *Muslim World*, 31, 1941, pp.140–144.

61 **McMurray M.E.** 'Juramentados and a Moro Convert', *Muslim World*, 32, 1942, pp.324–328.

62 **Molette C.** *'la VERITE où je la trouve' MULLA ZADE, Une conscience d'homme dans la lumière de Maurice Blondel* (Téqui: Paris, 1988).

63 **Naaman Ghulam-Masih and Toon V.** *The Unexpected Enemy, A Muslim Freedom Fighter encounters Christ* (Marshalls: Basingstoke, UK, 1985).

64 **Nur-Ed-Din Ishraqiyya** *Al-Dâ'i' yagidu tarîqahu ilâ l-salîb (Lost, he finds his way to the cross)*, (Centre for young adults: Basle, Switzerland).

65 **Phillips H.E.** 'Should Moslem Converts unite with the Church?', *Muslim World*, 26, 1936, pp.119–126.

66 **Rabhi P.** *Du Sahara aux Cévennes ou la reconquête du Songe* (Ed. de Candide: Lavilledieu, France, 1983).

67 **Rajaiah D.P.** *Lights in the World, Life sketches of Maulvi Safdar Ali and the Rev. Janni Alli* (Lucknow Publ. House: Lucknow, India, 1969).

68 **Rasooli J.M. and Allen C.H.** *Dr Sa'eed of Iran, Kurdish Physician to Princes and Peasants, Nobles and Nomads* (W. Carey Library: Pasadena, Ca., USA, 1957, 1983).

69 **Riggs H. H.** 'Shall we try unbeaten paths in working for Moslems?', *Muslim World*, 31, 1941, pp.116–126.

70 **Sallam J.** *Autobiographie* (Archives PB: Rome).

71 **Salles A.** 'De l'Islam au Christianisme, (1) La foi et les racines', *La Croix*, 4 March 1987, p.15 and (2) 'L'intégration difficile', *La Croix*, 5 March 1987, p.14.

72 **Sanneh L.** 'Muhammad, Prophet of God, and Jesus Christ, Image of God: A personal testimony', *International Bulletin of Missionary Research*, Vol.8, 1984, No.4, pp.169–174.

73 **Seve A.** 'Zohra, Musulmane Chrétienne', *La Croix*, 1–2 January 1988, pp.8,13.

74 **Sheikh B.** *Dieu, j'ai osé l'appeler Père* (L'Eau Vive: Geneva, 1981).

75 **Sheikh B.** *I Dared to Call Him Father* (Word: Waco,Texas, 1978, 1980).

76 **Sultan Md. P.** *Why I Became a Christian* (Gospel Literature Service: Bombay, 1978).

77 **Syrjanen S.** *In Search of Meaning and Identity, Conversion to Christianity in Pakistani Muslim Culture* (Annals of the Finnish Society for Missiology and Ecumenics, No.45, Vammala, 1984).

78 **Tamur Jan** *Ex Muslims for Christ* (The Crossbearers: PO Box 230, Birmingham B11 1LR, UK, 1980).

79 **Wardan H.** *La Gloire de Peter Pan ou le récit du Moine Beur* (Nouvelle Cité: Paris, 1986).

80 **Willis A.T. Jr** *Indonesian Revival, Why two million came to Christ* (W. Carey Library: Pasadena, Ca., USA, 1977).

81 **Wilson J.C.** 'Moslem Converts', *Muslim World*, 1944, pp.171–184.

82 **Wilson J.C.** 'Public conversion and the Church', *Muslim World*, 31, 1941, pp.127–139.

83 **Wilson J.C.** 'Love must win Persian Converts (an Interesting Survey)', *Muslim World*, 16, 1926, pp.25–36.

84 **Wootton R.W.F.** *Jesus More than a Prophet, Fifteen Muslims find forgiveness, release and new life*, (Inter-Varsity Press, Leicester, UK, 1982).

85 **Wysham W.N.** 'From Islam to Christ' (the spiritual experience of a Persian Convert), *Muslim World*, 18, 1928, pp. 49–60.

86 **X** 'A letter from the Near East', *Muslim World*, 32, 1942, pp.76–80.

87 **X** *La lumière de la foi (Nûr al-îmân),* (In Arabic and French) (The Living Word: PO Box 65, Worthing, W. Sussex, BN11 1AX, UK).

2. Conversion

1 **Aldeeb Abu-Sahlieh S.A.** 'Liberté religieuse et Apostasie dans l'Islam', *Praxis Juridique et Religion*, 3, 1986, pp.43–76.

2 **Allard P.** Art. 'Martyre', *Dictionnaire d'Apologétique de la Foi Catholique* (Beauchesne: Paris, 1916), Vol.3.

3 **Allier R.** *La Psychologie de la Conversion, chez les peuples non-civilisés* (Payot: Paris, 1925), 2 Vols.

4 **Anderson J.D.C.** 'The missionary approach to Islam: Christian or Cultic', *Missiology*, IV/3, July 1976, pp.285–300.

5 **Aubin P.** *Le Problème de la Conversion* (Beauchesne: Paris, 1963, Coll. Théologie Historique).

6 **Bardy M.G.** *La Conversion au Christianisme durant les Premiers Siècles* (Aubier: Paris, 1949, Coll. Théologie).

7 **Billette A.** *Conversion and Consonance* (National Opinion Research Center, Dept. of Sociology, University of Chicago, 1965).

8 **Billette A.** *Récits et Réalités d'une Conversion* (Presses de l'Université de Montréal, 1975).

9 **Blomjous Mgr** 'Mission-Liberté-Conversion', *Mission et Liberté Religieuse* (37th Semaine de Missiologie de Louvain, 1967, DDB), pp.113–135.

10 **Bulliet R.W.** *Conversion to Islam in the Medieval Period* (Harvard University Press, Cambridge, Mass., 1979).

11 **Burton J.W.** 'Christians, Colonists, and Conversion: a view from the Nilotic Sudan', *The Journal of Modern African Studies* (Cambridge University Press), 23(2), 1985, pp.349–369.

12 **Claverie P.** 'Conversion et conversions . . .', *Le Lien*, No.143, May 1986 (Bulletin diocésain d'Oran, Algérie), pp.1–2; and No.144, June–July. 1986, pp.1–2.

13 **Collective** *L'Accueil et le Refus du Christianisme, Historiographie de la Conversion* (CREDIC, Actes du Colloque de Stuttgart, 1985, University of Lyon III, 1986).

14 **Collective** *L'Expérience de Dieu et le Saint-Esprit, Immédiateté et médiations* (Coll. Le point Théologique, No.44, Beauchesne: Paris, 1985).

15 **Collective** Special issue 'Christian Conversion', *Lumen Vitae*, English Edition, Vol. 42m, 1987, No.4.

16 **Collective** 'Panel de discussion', *Chemins de la Conversion* (45th Semaine de Missiologie de Louvain, 1975, DDB), pp.119–152.

17 **Collective** *Lausanne Occasional Papers*, No.13: 'Thailand Report: Christian Witness to Muslims' (Lausanne Committee for World Evangelisation: Wheaton, Ill, USA, 1980).

18 **Collective** *International Review of Mission* (Geneva), 72, July 1983, No.287: Special issue on Conversion.

19 **Congar Y.** 'The Idea of Conversion', *Thought*, 33, March 1958, pp. 5–20.

20 **Congar Y.** 'La conversion, étude théologique et psychologique', *Parole et Mission*, No.11, October 1960, pp.493–523.

21 **Conn H.M.** 'The Muslim convert and his culture', D.M. McCurry, ed., *The Gospel and Islam* (MARC: Monrovia, Ca., USA, 1979), pp.97–113.

22 **Conn W.** *Christian Conversion: a Developmental Interpretation* (Paulist: New York, 1986).

23 **Conn W.** *Conscience: Development and Self-transcendence* (Religious Education Press: Birmingham, Alabama, 1981).

24 **Conn W.** *Conversion: Perspectives on Personal and Social Transformation* (Alba House: New York, 1978).

25 **Cronin B.** 'Religion and Christian Conversion in an African Context', *African Christian Studies*, Vol. 3, No.2, 1987.

26 **Danielou J.** 'Se convertir n'est rien renier', *Bulletin du Cercle St Jean-Baptiste*, 24, June–July 1963; and *Comprendre*, Bleu 37, 1 January 1964.

27 **Doran R.** *Psychic Conversion and Theological Foundations: Towards a Reorientation of the Human Sciences* (Scholars Press: Chico, Ca., USA, 1981).

28 **Doran R.** *Subject and Psyche: Ricoeur, Jung, and the Search for Foundations* (University Press of America: Washington DC, 1977).

29 **Fesquet H.** 'Etre musulman et catholique ou juif et chrétien— La double appartenance religieuse ouvre-t-elle une nouvelle voie à l'oecuménisme', *Le Monde*, 29 July 1981.

30 **Fisher H.J.** *'Dreams and conversion in Black Africa',* N. Levtzion, ed., *Conversion to Islam* (Holmes and Meier, New York–London, 1979), pp.217–235.

31 **Fisher H.J.** 'Conversion reconsidered: some historical aspects of religious conversion in Black Africa', *Africa*, Vol.43(1), 1973, pp. 27–40.

32 **Fisher H.J.** 'The juggernaut's apologia: Conversion to Islam in Black Africa', *Africa*, Vol.55(2), 1985, pp.153–173.

33 **Fowler J.W.** *Stages of Faith: The Psychology of Human Development and the Quest for Meaning* (Harper and Row: San Francisco, 1981).

34 **Fraser D.A.** 'An Engel scale for Muslim work?' D.M. McCurry, ed., *The Gospel and Islam* (MARC: Monrovia, Ca., USA, 1979), pp.164–181.

35 **Frossard A.** *God Exists* (Collins: London, 1970).

36 **Gelpi D.** 'The Converting Jesuit', *Studies in the Spirituality of Jesuits*, Vol. XVIII, No.1, (January 1986).

37 **Gelpi D.** *Charism and Sacrament: A Theology of Christian Conversion* (Paulist: New York, 1976).

38 **Gelpi D.** *Experiencing God: A Theology of Human Emergence* (Paulist: New York, 1978).

39 **Glasser A.F.** 'Power encounter in conversion from Islam', D.M. McCurry, *The Gospel and Islam* (MARC: Monrovia, Ca., USA, 1979) pp.129–142.

40 **Godin A.** *Psychological Dynamics of Religious Experience* (Religious Education Press: Birmingham, Alabama, 1985).

41 **Goffi T.** 'Conversion', *Dictionnaire de la Vie Spirituelle* (Cerf: Paris, 1983), pp.197–201.

42 **Hadot P.** 'Conversion', *Encyclopaedia Universalis* (Paris, 1969), Vol.4, pp.979–981.

43 **Harms E.** 'Ethical and Psychological Implications of Religious Conversion', *Review of Religious Research*, Vol. 3, No.3, 1962, pp. 122–131.

44 **Hefner R.W. (ed.)** *Conversion to Christianity: historical and anthropological perspectives* (University of California Press, 1993).

45 **Hood R.W.** 'Conversion', B. Spilka, R.W. Hood and R.L. Gorsuch, *The Psychology of Religion* (Prentice Hall: Eaglewoods Cliffs, NJ, 1985).

46 **Horton R.** 'African conversion', *Africa* (Journal of the International African Institute), Vol.41, 1971(2), pp. 85–108.

47 **Horton R.** 'On the rationality of conversion', Part I, in *Africa*, Vol.45(3), 1975, pp.219–235. Part II, in *Africa*, Vol.45(4), 1975, pp.373–399.

48 **Ikenga-Metuh E.** 'The Shattered Microcosm: A Critical Survey of Explanations of Conversion in Africa', *Nouv. Revue de Science Missionnaire*, 41, 1985, pp.241–254.

49 **Johnson C.B. and Malony H.N.** *Christian Conversion: Biblical and Psychological Perspectives* (Zondervan: Grand Rapids, Mi., 1982).

50 **Loffler P.** 'Biblical Concept of Conversion', Anderson G.H. and Stransky T.F., eds, *Mission Trends No.2: Evangelisation* (Paulist: New York, 1975).

51 **Kedar B.Z.** 'Muslim Conversion in Canon Law', S. Kuttner and K. Pennington, eds, *Proceedings of the 6th International Congress of Medieval Canon Law, 1980* (Monum. Juris Canonici, Ser. C,Vol.7,Vatican,1985), 321–332.

52 **Khair-Ullah F.S.** 'Linguistic hang-ups in communicating with Muslims', *Missiology*, IV/3, July 1976, pp.301–316.

53 **Khair-Ullah F.S.** 'The role of local churches in God's redemptive plan for the Muslim World', D.M. McCurry, ed., *The Gospel and Islam* (MARC: Monrovia, Ca., USA, 1979) pp.566–580.

54 **Kraft C.H.** 'Dynamic equivalence Churches in Muslim Society', D.M. McCurry, ed., *The Gospel and Islam* (MARC: Monrovia, Ca., USA, 1979), pp.114–128.

55 **Levtzion N., ed.** *Conversion to Islam* (Holmes and Meier Publishers: New York, 1979).

56 **Loffler M.P.** 'Le précepte de la conversion et la liberté individuelle', *Mission et liberté religieuse* (37th Semaine de Missiologie de Louvain, 1967, DDB), pp.149–167.

57 **Marchant P.** 'Dossier: Islam, les convertis français', *L'Actualité Religieuse*, No.5, October 1983, pp.35–42; see letters from readers, *L'Actualité Religieuse*, No.6, November 1983, p.45, and No.8, January 1984, p.44.

58 **Maslow A.** *Religions, Values and Peak-Experiences* (State University Press, Columbus, Ohio, 1964).

59 **Masson J.** 'Diversité des conversions', *Chemins de la con-

version (45th Semaine de Missiologie de Louvain, 1975, DDB), pp.7–17.

60 **McCurry D.M.** 'Cross-cultural models for Muslim Evangelism', *Missiology*, IV/3, July 1976, pp.267–283.

61 **McCurry D.M.** 'Resistance/Response Analysis of Muslim Peoples', D.M. McCurry, ed., *The Gospel and Islam* (MARC: Monrovia, Ca., USA, 1979), pp.182–195.

62 **Michiels R.** 'La conception lucanienne de la conversion', *Ephemerides Theologicae Lovanienses*, T.41, 1965, pp.42–78.

63 **Mooneyham W.S.** 'Keynote Address to the 1978 North American Conference on Muslim Evangelisation', D.M. McCurry, ed., *The Gospel and Islam* (MARC: Monrovia, Ca., USA,1979), pp.22–37.

64 **Pinard de la Boullaye H.** 'Conversion', *Dictionnaire de Spiritualité* (Beauchesne: Paris, 1953), Vol.2.

65 **Rahner K.** 'Conversion', *Sacramentum Mundi*, K. Rahner et al., eds, (Herder and Herder: New York, 1968), 6 vols, Vol.2, pp. 4–8.

66 **Reinhard P.** 'Parole de Dieu et conversion, Reflexions sur un témoignage', *Parole et Mission*, 25, April 1964, pp.278–291.

67 **Rocher L. and Cherqaoui F.** *D'une foi l'autre, les conversions à l'islam en Occident* (Seuil: Paris,1986).

68 **Sagne J.C.** *Conflit, Changement, Conversion* (Coll. Cogitatio Fidei, Cerf-Desclée: Paris, 1974).

69 **Six J.F.** 'Sur le livre d'André Frossard: Dieu existe, je l'ai rencontré', *Informations Catholiques Internationales*, No.346, (15 October 1969), p.23. (See letters from readers, No.348, p.2 and No.351, pp.2–3).

70 **Stanley G.** 'Personality and Attitude Correlates of Religious Conversion', *Journal for the Scientific Study of Religion*, Vol. IV, No.1, Autumn 1964, pp.60–84.

71 **Talbi M.** 'Religious Liberty: A Muslim Perspective', *Islamochristiana*, 11, 1985, pp. 99–113.

72 **Teissier H.** 'Le temps de la conversion réciproque', *Chemins de la Conversion*, (45th Semaine de Missiologie de Louvain, 1975, DDB), pp.102–116.

73 **Vatican** *Attitude de l'Eglise Catholique devant les croyants*

des autres religions, Réflexions et Orientations concernant le dialogue et la mission (Secrétariat pour les Non-Chrétiens: Rome, 1984).

74 **Villanyi A.** 'L'évangélisation des bédouins nomades', *Nouvelle Revue de Science Missionnaire*, 1961, pp.303–310.

75 **Volkoff V.** *Le Retournement* (roman), (Julliard/L'Age d'Homme: Paris, 1979).

76 **Witherup R.D.** *Conversion in the New Testament* (Liturgical Press: Collegeville, MN, 1994).

77 **Wright, Jr T.P.** 'The movement to convert Harijans to Islam in South India', *Muslim World*, 1982, pp.239–245.

78 **Zafar Ismail.** 'The Muslim convert and the Church', *International Review of Mission*, Vol.72, No.287, July 1983, pp.386–392.

INDEX OF NAMES

The UNSEEN FACE OF ISLAM

This book is about weary and burdened human beings,' writes Dr Musk. The masses of Muslims live today at two levels. Beneath a veneer of conformity to a major world faith, ordinary Muslims express deep needs in their daily living.

'I hope that the readership will extend far beyond the specialists'.
Thousands of Christians in these islands alone live cheek by jowl
with Muslims. This book will help the Christian to understand
them.' – Lord Coggan, *former Archbishop of Canterbury*

'Carefully documented, sensitively written and patiently
comprehensive.' – Bishop Kenneth Cragg, author of *The Call of the Minaret.*

About the Author

The Rev Dr BILL MUSK studied history at Oxford and theology in London, Bristol, Los Angeles and Pretoria. He has worked with Operation Mobilisation, Living Bibles International, Middle East Media, Interserve, the Church Missionary Society and the Episcopal Church in Egypt. He and his wife Hilary have four children, and live in Maghull, Liverpool. He is author of *The Unseen Face of Islam* and *Passionate Believing* (both published by MARC).

The UNSEEN FACE OF ISLAM
Bill Musk
ISBN 1 85424 018 8   £8.99

Available from your local Christian Bookshop.
In case of difficulty contact Monarch Books,
Concorde House, Grenville Place, Mill Hill, London NW7 3SA

MONARCH
B O O K S

Touching the Soul of Islam

This book explores the many areas in which the worldview of Muslims differs from that of Westeners. It is only as we begin to understand how our Muslim neighbour thinks that we can present the Gospel in a way that will allow him or her to react to our message — and not just the messenger.

This lively and fascinating book will help Western Christians to:

- **Understand the way Muslims think and feel**
- **Express their own faith without offending**
- **Read the Bible with new eyes**
- **Discern the strengths and tensions in Muslim cultures**

About the Author

The Rev Dr BILL MUSK studied history at Oxford and theology in London, Bristol, Los Angeles and Pretoria. He has worked with Operation Mobilisation, Living Bibles International, Middle East Media, Interserve, the Church Missionary Society and the Episcopal Church in Egypt. He and his wife Hilary have four children, and live in Maghull, Liverpool. He is author of *The Unseen Face of Islam* and *Passionate Believing* (both published by MARC).

Touching the Soul of Islam
Bill A. Musk
ISBN 1 85424 317 9   £8.99

Available from your local Christian Bookshop.
In case of difficulty contact Monarch Books,
Concorde House, Grenville Place, Mill Hill, London NW7 3SA

MONARCH
B O O K S

ISHMAEL My Brother

This book tries to dispel some of the barriers and prejudices that hinder personal relationships between Muslims and Christians.

This is a study book. Each section has activities, points for reflection and guidance for further reading. The main section headings are: Christians and other faiths; Islamic beliefs and practices; cultural, historical and political development; and Islam at the end of the twentieth century.

'An excellent introduction to Islam and all its aspects... This book is suffused with the courtesy it recommends.' – Evangelism Today

'Urgent and welcome. The tone of the book is sensitive and compelling.' – Floodtide

About the Author

The Rev Dr BILL MUSK studied history at Oxford and theology in London, Bristol, Los Angeles and Pretoria. He has worked with Operation Mobilisation, Living Bibles International, Middle East Media, Interserve, the Church Missionary Society and the Episcopal Church in Egypt. He and his wife Hilary have four children, and live in Maghull, Liverpool. He is author of *The Unseen Face of Islam* and *Passionate Believing* (both published by MARC).

ISHMAEL My Brother
Compiled by Anne Cooper
ISBN 1 85424 233 4   £8.99

Available from your local Christian Bookshop.
In case of difficulty contact Monarch Books,
Concorde House, Grenville Place, Mill Hill, London NW7 3SA

MONARCH
BOOKS